# The Courage to Imagine

**Bloomsbury Perspectives on Children's Literature**

Bloomsbury Perspectives on Children's Literature seeks to expand the range and quality of research in children's literature through publishing innovative monographs by leading and rising scholars in the field. With an emphasis on cross and inter-disciplinary studies, this series takes literary approaches as a starting point, drawing on the particular capacity for children's literature to open out into other disciplines.

### Series Editor:

Dr Lisa Sainsbury, Director of the National Centre for Research in Children's Literature, Roehampton University, UK.

### Editorial Board:

Professor M. O. Grenby (Newcastle University, UK),
Dr Marah Gubar (University of Pittsburgh, USA),
Dr Vanessa Joosen (Tilburg University, The Netherlands).

### Titles in the Series:

*The Courage to Imagine: The Child Hero in Children's Literature*, Roni Natov
*From Tongue to Text: A New Reading of Children's Poetry*, Debbie Pullinger
*Ethics in British Children's Literature: Unexamined Life*, Lisa Sainsbury

### Forthcoming Titles:

*Literature's Children: The Critical Child and the Art of Idealisation*, Louise Joy
*The Alice Look: The Emergence of Lewis Carroll's Fashion Icon*, Kiera Vaclavik
*Rereading Childhood Books: A Poetics*, Alison Waller
*Adulthood in Children's Literature*, Vanessa Joosen
*The Styles of Children's Literature: A Century of Change*, Peter Hunt

# The Courage to Imagine

## The Child Hero in Children's Literature

Roni Natov

BLOOMSBURY ACADEMIC
LONDON • NEW YORK • OXFORD • NEW DELHI • SYDNEY

BLOOMSBURY ACADEMIC
Bloomsbury Publishing Plc
50 Bedford Square, London, WC1B 3DP, UK
1385 Broadway, New York, NY 10018, USA

BLOOMSBURY, BLOOMSBURY ACADEMIC and the Diana logo
are trademarks of Bloomsbury Publishing Plc

First published 2018
Paperback edition first published 2019

Cover design: Eleanor Rose
Cover image © 2002. From *Madlenka's dog* by Peter Sis.
Reprinted by permission of Farrar, Straus, and Giroux, a division of
Macmillian's Children's Publishing Group.
All Rights Reserved.

A catalogue record for this book is available from the British Library.

Library of Congress Cataloging-in-Publication Data
Names: Natov, Roni.
Title: The courage to imagine : the child hero in children's literature / Roni Natov.
Description: London ; New York : Bloomsbury Academic, 2018. |
Series: Bloomsbury perspectives on children's literature ; 5 |
Includes bibliographical references and index.
Identifiers: LCCN 2017019197 | ISBN 9781474221221 (hb) |
ISBN 9781474221238 (epub)
Subjects: LCSH: Children's literature–Themes, motives. |
Heroes in literature. | Children in literature. | Children–Books and reading.
Classification: LCC PN1009.5.H47 N39 2018 | DDC 809/.89282–dc23
LC record available at https://lccn.loc.gov/2017019197

ISBN: HB: 978-1-4742-2122-1
PB: 978-1-3501-1175-2
ePDF: 978-1-4742-2124-5
ePub: 978-1-4742-2123-8

Series: Bloomsbury Perspectives of Children's Literature

Typeset by Newgen KnowledgeWorks Pvt. Ltd., Chennai, India

To find out more about our authors and books visit
www.bloomsbury.com and sign up for our newsletters.

*To Lexi and Max,*
*and to Steve*
*In memory of George Wolfgang, Eddie Forman, Bart Meyers,*
*and Bernie Wagner—cherished and missed*

# Contents

# Acknowledgments

I believe that everyone I have loved in my life has inspired me, in one way or another, to write this book.

My husband, Steve, has stood by me, encouraged me, listened to me, and thoughtfully counseled me as the project unfolded. My sister, Melanie Kaye/Kantrowitz, with her brilliance has been with me as my witness and a source of inspiration throughout my life. Geri DeLuca, my writing partner for the past forty years, ever since we began *The Lion and the Unicorn*, has always been there for me. I don't believe I have published a single word that she has not read and, when needed, enhanced. Laura Atkins has informed my thinking about this project with her broad knowledge and her striking insights.

Cassandra Tan (a.k.a. Cat Bowen), my research assistant, has done a remarkable job with her amazing knowledge of how the publishing world works and her precision and speed. Peter Sis has been so generous and thoughtful throughout. And Lisa Sainsbury, my editor, has painstakingly worked on this book; even when I resisted, her words were sharp and helpful. I also appreciate the patience and encouragement of David Avital of Bloomsbury. In terms of their efforts for permissions, many thanks to Matthew Burgess and Brian Selznick and to Cat Tan and Neil Gaiman.

Always, there were my dear friends, each in her and his own way, who have inspired me: Judy Meiselman and Nancy Keness, Nancy and Steve Abrams, Corrine Ferstad, Deborah Rinzler, Amy Lubelski, Jane and Vicki Sufian, Paul Stevens, Ada Bieber, Mary Sheerin, Bob Atkins, Geoff Minter, Ellen Tremper, Wendy Fairey, Lee Quinby, Karel Rose, Joan Larkin, Susan Perlstein, Wendy Sachs, Kate Fincke, Alice Radosh, Lolly McIver—and Linda Meyers, Amy Lerner, and Barbara Wagner—my family who has always believed in me. I am grateful.

To my students, the many with whom I have shared Children's Literature courses in which we explored the topics and perspectives that helped shaped my thinking, this book would not have happened without you.

Finally, to my luminous grandchildren, Lexi and Max, and my wonderful son and daughter-in-law, Jonathan and Samantha, and Brian and Chris, my awesome step-son and daughter-in-law—you remain an endless source of creativity and love.

*The Courage to Imagine* contains a sampling of articles I published previously. I am grateful to those who kindly granted me permission to reprint parts of my original publications.

Chapter 4 contains parts of "Representing the Cultural 'Other' in Young Adult Fiction," *Interjuly: Internationale Kinder-und Jugend-literaturforschung* (February 2011): 89–100, as well as parts of "Childhood and Difference in Contemporary Autobiographical Picture Books," *To See the Wizard: Politics and the Literature of Childhood*, Cambridge Scholars Publishing, 2007, 2–40. Chapter 5 contains parts of "Death and the Monster: The Graveyard and the Dream," *Breac: A Digital Journal of Irish Studies* (2016), as well as parts of "Pastoral and Healing: The Image in the Imagination," *Deep into Nature: Ecology, Environment and Children's Literature*, edited by Jennifer Hardig et al., Pied Piper, 2009, 53–63. Chapter 6 contains part of "Pippi and Ronia, Astrid Lindgren's Light and Dark Pastoral," *The Liberated Child: Childhood in the Works of Astrid Lindgren. Barnbroken: Journal of Children's Literature Research*, Astrid Lindgren Centennial Conference, vol. 30, nos. 1–2 (2007): 92–100. Chapter 7 contains a good part of "Reaching Across Cultural Fault Lines: Empathy in Kate DiCamillo's *The Tale of Despereaqux* and *The Miraculous Journey of Edward Tulane*," *Relevant across Cultures in Modern Fantasy for Young Readers*, edited by Justyna Deszcz-Tryhubczak et al., Wroclaw, Poland: Oficyna Wydawnicza ATUT, 2009, 107–18.

# Introduction: What I Believe

The child does not need courage to imagine. She imagines freely, and in broad strokes. "It was thisssss big," she says, arms extended as far as her reach. Like a searchlight tracing an arc over the horizon, the child's imagination is naturally, inherently wide. And if encouraged, mirrored, held, smiled on, a child will remember, will have access to those sweeps of light. As he develops, his imagination will begin to explore the heroes and the monsters of the imagination, the complexity of those early poles of fairy-tale beauty and horror. When little Jonathan, at three, looks up at my son, also named Jonathan, and says, "Big Jonathan, if you add infinity to infinity, you still get infinity, right?" I am aware of a specially gifted child, of his awe as he imagines what for me is unimaginable. But this gift appears in different forms and to different degrees as the birthright of us all.

The child who has not been encouraged, or has even been traumatized, the child whose spirit has been damaged in one way or another, may need courage to explore the imagination that may contain emptiness or darkness as well as the potential for survival. Something, perhaps some unrecognized source, may inspire the child to imagine an alternative. This kernel of trust may be retained in the imagination until, hopefully, the powerless child moves from an imagined realm into the world—with agency. Whatever encourages that movement, whatever serves as a conduit to the child's imagination, whatever helps her not to retreat from potential richness—that is what I am looking for in great literature for children. I am seeking a literature of encouragement, a philosophy embedded in children's books that inspires children to imagine. Children need encouragement to develop their own courage.

As Albert Einstein has said, "Imagination is more important than knowledge ... [because] it embraces the entire world."[1] It helps to bridge gaps between who you are and who the "other" is, and to internalize otherness. That is what I want to look at in the children's books I have selected here. And because psychologists, philosophers, and those who study the imagination in its various forms agree that there is enormous difficulty in defining it, I assume that here we are reaching beyond one common definition of "image making." I am looking at the creative imagination and how it is depicted in children's literature.

One of the most noteworthy thoughts about creativity came from John Keats who urged, in his concept of "negative capability," the importance of learning how to tolerate ambiguity, to dwell in that area of not knowing. In his letters he wrote, "Let us not therefore go hurrying about and collecting honey-bee like, buzzing here and there impatiently from a knowledge of what is to be arrived at: but let us open our leaves like a flower and be passive and receptive" (L 1:232). His predisposition toward receptive intuition stresses the ability to be "in uncertainties, Mysteries, doubts, without any irritable reaching after fact & reason" (L 1:193). As Maxine Hong Kingston states, in *The Woman Warrior*, "I learned to make my mind large, as the universe is large, so that there is room for contradictions" (p. 35). Embracing contradiction and complexity engages the imagination. If we—and here I include along with child readers, teachers, parents, writers and illustrators of children's books, even children's literature scholars—if we have to "know" in advance of questioning and exploring, how can we discover? How can we invent or imagine? This is at the heart of creativity and needs to be encouraged in children.

Dealing with complexity, however, is a lifelong process, and while children tend to the black and white of things, reality, of course, does not fall into polar camps. Children need to understand, at whatever level, the complexity of their own natures. They need to feel that they are acceptable—with their ambivalent feelings toward parents, siblings, teachers, friends, and themselves, that they are still lovable with their imperfections, loved imperfectly by imperfect parents and siblings. Children who have had little of that acceptance need special help in this area. And the imagination can provide a safe childhood space in which to explore such ambivalences.

When I write of the courage to imagine here, I am, obviously, including both the child reader and the adult creator of the book. I want to raise the question of what the book offers in terms of a new way of seeing, an alternative to conventional perspectives, heroes, or story lines. I am interested in the ways in which books for children transgress boundaries and established norms, and the ways in which the author/illustrator imagines the vulnerability of children. It often takes courage to be vulnerable, and books have the potential to provide strength in the face of fear. Further, they can envision what it means to be a virtuous human being with ways of seeing the world that promote honesty, strength, and a fundamental kindness.

How is that imagined? I am aware of how personal, subjective, and highly idiosyncratic this process is, this active capturing of the child's imagination. Why and how does something previously unimagined or resisted become accessible? Books with unconventional stories, characters, narratives, and ways of telling stories can provide an opening for the imagination. Let that interior space be expansive, a large palette from which the child draws. Let books for children feature diversity and examine concepts of otherness. Let the portrayals of minorities make space for the unheard voices of children. Not only is it imperative for children to find themselves represented, but also portraits of minorities can refresh the artistic vision of the children's book author and illustrator.

According to psychologists David Cohen and Stephen MacKeith, "to be creative you have to dare to be different ... Being creative requires self-trust [and] receptivity" (17–18). And according to Scott Barry Kauffman, Director of the Imagination Institute, creativity and the imagination depend on being "open to experience ... engagement with perception, fantasy, aesthetics, and emotions."[2] I am interested in how a book supports this ability. One way to encourage children to be different and self-reliant is to imagine child characters who embody those traits. I have selected here for discussion mostly contemporary books that move in new directions to reflect the changing times; they exhibit a willingness to challenge notions of girlhood and boyhood, family, race, and issues of justice, fairness, and inclusivity. Change depends on imagining; the imagination, then, can be a place of hope. I am interested in looking at what encourages this hope with honesty, and here I mean honesty metaphorically as well as literally—including symbolic ways of reading. For example, consider the portrayal of death in E. B. White's *Charlotte's Web*, in which a spider-hero dies; it is sad but honestly reflects the natural cycle of life as Charlotte's babies emerge; Charlotte and Fern, the girl hero at the opening of the story, rescue Wilbur, the runt of the piglet litter, from an early death that would not have been "natural." Consider the fairy tales where death can be reversed or reimagined in some fantastic way that depicts the issue without confronting it realistically, like the way in which Hansel and Gretel get to "kill" the stepmother by shoving her magical replacement, the witch, in the oven, and return home to find the stepmother, their initial source of family rupture, gone. The imagination and creative expression can help children process impulses and strong feelings; it serves as a rehearsal for difficult emotions, offers a place to try them out and also to store them. It provides a way of making sense of what may feel overwhelming. It can incorporate what Jung termed the "shadow," which appears to children as a witch, a cruel sibling, or an ogre or other demon that can be relentless in its persistence. It can appear more safely in the child's imagination than the fear that it may be lurking in corners or behind furniture or under a bed at night.

Further, in this global and digital era it is particularly important that books include child heroes from a variety of backgrounds, cultures, and sensibilities. From Astrid Lindgren's Pippi (*Pippi Longstocking* series, 1945–48, and 1969–75) to David Almond's Mina (*My Name Is Mina*, 1999) and Louise Erdrich's Omakayas (*The Birchbark House* series, 1999–2012), these heroes all risk being different and learn to rely on themselves, sometimes with only a minimum of support from their elders and peers. They are reflective, imaginative, and challenge conventional ways of being in the world. And although they are extraordinary in some ways, their heroism suggests ways for "ordinary" children to gain courage and confidence. Although Harry Potter, for example, bears a scar that marks him as different, extraordinary, he is also an ordinary boy, less clever, less self-possessed than his peers, and just as vulnerable, so that he can figure as an Everychild. I believe that therein lies a major part of his popularity.

Throughout this book I try to encourage adults to offer children serious literature, psychologically challenging and issue-centered, as well as lighter work that also conveys subtle values and messages, and sometimes those messages can be pernicious. We have come to recognize that there is no such thing as a purely objective, apolitical stance; the conventional and the normative also have political implications.

I also want to look at books that challenge the concept of a single child hero who stands out above the group. Such books feature heroic groups or communities, new ways of looking at heroism, like Julius Lester's *People Who Could Fly* (1992), based on an African American folktale, or *Brothers in Hope: The Story of the Lost Boys of Sudan* (2005). They imagine acts of heroism that encompass community, a way of being heroic that positions the child with power through grouping together with others, rather than having to be beyond the powerful adults or older and stronger children. I have never been comfortable with Janie, in Madeleine L'Engle's *A Wrinkle in Time*, depicted as the hero responsible for saving her father, her brother, the planet, etc., or even Lois Lowry's *The Giver*, as the hero, isolated, must make the responsible choice in the face of world powers. Granted these are among children's most beloved books and I do not in any way suggest depriving children of the pleasures they offer. However, I want to provide alternative ways of thinking about heroic action.

The imagination and its images, how they appear to us, and the ways in which they are offered to and affect children remain for me somewhat mysterious. But my understanding that children are the least powerful group in our world[3] and my belief that every child deserves such exploration lead me to investigate this mystery. And that's what this book is, an exploration of the mystery of the imagination and its power in the literature of childhood. The literature of childhood provides a community. It articulates and represents the courage of children to imagine as well as those adult writers and illustrators who invoke stories to inspire children—to inspire all of us who may also need them.

1

# Landscapes of Childhood

## Pastoral: Forest, sky, river

At the heart of the imagination of childhood is the idea of pastoral, a shel-tered space where freshness and truth can be preserved. Pastoral is the natural world, the green world that functions to provide a resource for adults as well, as it engages the instinctual, the intuitive, and the creative parts of the self. It allows for courage to be different and to feel free from conventional social restraints. The dark pastoral, the other side of the green world, is as natural in its shadows as the light and sun of the pastoral.[1] The power to survive and to create is layered into both worlds. Nature itself, as well as human nature, con-tains the wildness necessary for creativity and is a natural part of childhood and of our darker feelings, like fear and anger. David Almond wrote in his article "The Necessary Wilderness" about writing as "a kind of exploration … of the wilderness outside, and an exploration of the wilderness inside."[2] And although traditional pastoral entails a retreat from and return to the urban/worldly/civilized world, darkness hovers on the outskirts. In the promise of "gather ye rosebuds while we may" there is a warning. We know that quotidian/chronological time will return and that death hides in the wings.

Pastoral time is subjective, rather than chronological; it is a timelessness associated with childhood where the knowledge of time passing, of death and endings, is withheld. The dark pastoral is also a retreat from the worldly world. It is the darkness and wildness of the primal forest of "Hansel and Gretel," full of dangers like the devouring witch. But it is also the place that must be entered to get to the jewels that will solve the problem of poverty and will enable the children to return home, safely, to the good though weak father.[3] Their return provides the new generation of boy and girl, or, as Carl

Jung suggested with the anima and animus, two sides of the self, working together. This doubleness, the light and the dark, and the dappledness of each, therefore, imagines the dark and light as complex and multilayered. Pastoral is a landscape that can suggest the states of mind most basic to the literature of childhood. The forest, the sky, and the river of folktale and myth represent the untamed and unrestricted. Each is wild and free. The forest, as Joseph Heuscher wrote (*A Psychiatric Study of Myths and Fairy Tales*, 1974), is represented according to developmental levels of childhood. In "Hansel and Gretel," the witch with her red eyes, her keen sense of smell, and her capacious desire for human flesh represents childhood's earliest fears and imaginings, where desire is focused on getting fed—told as a kind of eat or be eaten story. The children are starving; Hansel is fattened up to be eaten by the witch, but freed by Gretel as the witch burns in the oven. The children glean the jewels—so they will never go hungry again, and return to their father who could not protect them from the cruel stepmother, the more realistic double of the devouring witch-mother.

When we turn to the forest in "Little Red Riding Hood," no matter which variant of the tale, it always appears as dangerous, but, unlike the dense and dark forest of "Hansel and Gretel," it is marked by paths. Little Red is older, between child and nurturer; her journey is from her mother to caring for her sick grandmother. There is a sexual threat along the way and she must learn to protect herself. In the earliest-known version she escapes, in childlike brilliance, by asserting that she has to go outside to relieve herself.[4] She ties the rope that the wolf (a werewolf in this early variant) has wound around her to a tree and runs home. In Charles Perrault's variant, she is eaten, and in Jacob and Wilhelm Grimm's version, it takes a hunter/woodsman to save her. However, in all versions, the path through the forest indicates some light, some consciousness in this middle state of child development. Here is a relatively unknown version of child resilience and power. In each of the many forests of childhood literature, children need to be resourceful.

In the adolescent tales, in "Snow White," for example, the forest is filled with kind animals and the friendly dwarves, and although the source of danger, the jealous queen, finds her way into the forest, threats exist along with protection and warnings. In other wilder tales, like "Thousand Furs," where the girl is besieged by her father the king, the forest is still permeated with light and shadow; nature is reflected in the bright sun and in the beauty of the night sky in the dresses created to protect her. The forest, then, offers escape from uncivilized civilization. In most tales of adolescence, the threat to the life of the burgeoning young adult is not found in the natural world but in what is unnatural in the kingdom.

The landscape of the sky, that location without borders or boundaries, appears in "Jack and the Beanstalk" as a different kind of escape from the endless poverty of everyday life into the imagination where anything is possible. The magic beans, the magic of the ordinary, actually propel Jack into the sky where he escapes with the golden egg–laying hen, which will continue to provide for him and his mother. Obeying his mother and selling the cow would have delayed, not ended, their poverty. Jack was not satisfied with this, however. He wanted the golden lyre—the musical instrument that would provide a life beyond basic nourishment, a life of the spirit. The sky offers an aesthetic of light and beauty.

A few years ago, I was invited to speak at a conference on Astrid Lindgren in Sweden. Wandering through a gift shop, I discovered a poster of a haunting painting of a child flying on the back of a goose over beautiful mountains and water. The eyes of the goose were fixed and steady and the journey in the sky was so free, so boundaryless, that it brought me close to my dreams of flying—my favorite dreams where I scope the mostly pastoral landscapes with little effort, safe above the world, free to move in and out without restrictions. I found out that the illustration was by Lars Klinting, the cover of Selma Lagerlöf's book *The Wonderful Adventures of Nils*, published in 1906 and 1907 in two volumes. Lagerlöf was commissioned to write a geography text for the Swedish public schools, and researched folklore and legends, as well as natural bird and animal life, for three years before writing. It is also the story of Nils, a mischievous, indulgent boy who enjoys hurting animals on his family farm. One day he is turned into an elf and becomes tiny and powerless to torture the animals, whom he now has to placate. His adventures, flying all over Sweden on the neck of a wild goose, inspire him to become a better person. The image of his flight into the air and the freedom of the skies stirred in me a celestial pastoral state of imagining.

The third archetypal landscape often depicted in children's literature is the river as the source of life that also flows without boundaries. It is neither of one side of the land nor of the other. In the fairy tales, it is what must be crossed over from fantasy to the real world. It is the symbol of transformation. Hansel and Gretel's tale does not end with the jewels. The last part of their quest is to get home; they must cross the river and actually figure out how to do this. The journey of Huckleberry Finn and Jim takes place on a raft traveling down the river; the freedom of the river, belonging as it does to no society, provides the intimacy that develops between Huck and Jim.

These are the recurring imaginative landscapes of childhood. They inspire in children and in adults reading and writing about children a whole range of imaginings. With the aesthetics of light and the dark depths of the unconscious, tales of childhood unfold with the intensity and variety of the many stages between innocence and experience. As is clear from the forest of the fairy tales, the darkness can be a source of light within the dark, which affirms aspects of the journey. If we consider William Blake's state of innocence depicted in *Songs of Innocence and of Experience* (1789), we find embedded within innocence the beginnings of experience, and, of course, experience contains the possibility of goodness in wisdom—Blake's higher innocence.

## Interior landscapes: Private spaces

In *Secret Spaces of Childhood*, Elizabeth Goodenough collected pieces from a number of writers about the places where they as children felt safe, safe enough to imagine, where the child self could create. Often children found the space to read, which, as Mark Jonathan Harris, an Academy Award–winning filmmaker, writes, "helped assuage the loneliness I felt growing up, reassured me that I was not as strange or bad a person as I secretly feared ... Books were ... a private retreat, a hideaway I could visit whenever I needed, where I could respond more freely and openly than I often did with other people" (32–3).

Many writers found a small space, "a corner to build a world apart [without which] they [could not] plant 'the small crop of self'" (Ackerman, 2). D. W. Winnicott calls "transitional spaces" those corners where children feel empowered (3). Goodenough explores in her book the "enchanted language of interiority, as it is experienced from place to place." She writes that because it is "detached from the ongoing, intimate relation with siblings, parents, or other adults … [no matter how] humble the container, this site endures in memory as a receptacle of the growing imagination, which needs to feel protected as it expands within safe boundaries" (3). She asserts that children need to break "expectations … to get closer to something inside themselves," to write "transgressive" narratives, or at least those that feel "transgressive" (15). Frederick Buechner, memoirist, wrote that he felt safe as a child, outside, where he sat in a deck chair during the rain under a blanket that made him feel safe. Also at night in bed he experienced "both the wildness, wetness, windiness of things, and at the same time [his] utter protection from it" (29). As a child I felt safe and unsafe often in the same space. As an adult I wrote about this ambiguity:

> The Mother Story
> I am digging in the dirt
> in my red plaid pants
> on my grandmother's lawn
> under the red maple tree.
> It is autumn
> and the late afternoon sun is a low blanket.
> A red glow spreads across my face and arms.
> It lights up the maple
> and my red plaid pants.
> My mother is inside with my grandmother
> and I am safely near them
> and safe from them.

There are even children who feel safe when in public, safe from the private spaces of family. Vladimir Nabokov writes in *Speak, Memory* of small spaces that he calls "the primordial cave" and the importance of such.[5] Gaston Bachelard writes about a small, protected space where the child learns to dream and where the artist goes in to imagine. It is interesting to consider the child's need for boundaries balanced with freedom. This balance may be found in fantasy worlds; as Goodenough writes, "the place may be literary or psychic, local or exotic, but every children's book provides a sense to a world apart" (12). The courage to imagine lends itself, therefore, to a safe space in which to explore childhood creativity, where anxious states of feeling and thinking can arise with a minimum of fear.

2

# The Construction of the Creative Child

There was a time when meadow, grove, and stream,
The earth, and every common sight,
To me did seem
Apparelled in celestial light,
The glory and the freshness of a dream ...
The things which I have seen I now can see no more.... .

Whither is fled the visionary gleam?
Where is it now, the glory and the dream?

(from Wordsworth, "Ode: Intimations of Immortality," 1802–4)

When William Wordsworth wrote about the child and his natural imaginative and creative powers, as "thou best Philosopher" and "thou Eye among the blind" adults who desperately try to retrieve that lost glory, he constructed the nineteenth-century Romantic vision of childhood. Of course, Jean-Jacques Rousseau's earlier *Emile, or On Education* (1762) established "impulse and sensation" as inherent in and essential to the healthy child. The notion of the child as a natural creator, about to lose her gift as she develops into an adult with the "philosophic mind," was captured by Wordsworth in this same poem. Phillippe Aries, in his influential *Centuries of Childhood* (1965), claimed childhood as an eighteenth- and nineteenth-century invention. However, since then, scholars have challenged that idea, asserting that Medieval and Renaissance times saw children as valued by parents of various classes and distinguished from adults. Amy Ogata, in her recent *Designing the Creative Child* (2013), discusses the origins and influences of the idea that the child is innately creative. She suggests that in modern times creativity has been "mythologized and commodified" (x). She traces "the invention of the creative child" from the Middle Ages "that acknowledg[ed] the notion that play and encouragement helped children to learn" to John Locke's "sympathy for childish inquisitiveness," and the belief that "curiosity ... should be carefully cherished" in childhood (xii). Although awe at the child's apparently innate creativity has its roots in the Romantic era, these beliefs have been solidified, some might say reified, in the work of twentieth-century psychologists, such as Arnold Gesell, who claimed that "by nature" the child was "a creative artist of sorts ... [noting] his resourcefulness [and] his extraordinary capacity for original activity" (quoted in Ogata, ix).

Kenneth Kidd points to Jacqueline Rose who claims "the fantasy of the child as emblematic of a 'lost truth and/or moment in history' is one we never leave behind but rather repeat endlessly" (43). Kidd notes that Rose sees a more truthful story of childhood in the work of Sigmund Freud and Jacques Lacan, both of whom expose that myth as something created to "give coherence to otherwise alarming experiences as self and otherness" (13). Kidd notes how Klein and Winnicott develop a "poetics of play" and subscribe to the idea of the inner child in us all, the child within the adult, so that children's literature is seen as "child-themed but adult-oriented" (xxiv). Kidd sees the child as a "transhistorical object specific to the sociocultural moment in which it is observed" (11). He goes on to establish a connection between a progressive approach to the "healthy socialized" child (Dr. Spock, Margaret Mead, and Erik Erikson) and associating an "impoverishment of the imagination" with totalitarianism (255). Ogata sees the persistently Romantic concept of childhood creativity—"theorized as innate and at the same time responsive to encouragement—steadily emerg[ing] over [the past] two centuries" (xv). She urges that we analyze "childhood creativity as a[n] historical development, rather than essentializing it as a 'natural fact'" (xvi).

Certainly, it is important to evaluate and establish this historical context, to keep in mind that childhood as a concept has shifted over time. However, for me, this does not detract from or substantially revise the idea of creativity as inherent in the childhood of the human being, though recognizable in an increasing variety of ways. Just as the concept of intelligence has extended to include emotional intelligence (Daniel Goleman) and multiple intelligences—musical, visual, verbal, mathematical, kinesthetic, interpersonal, intrapersonal, and naturalistic (Howard Gardner), recognizing the ways in which children express and act out their imaginative capacities have been recognized and therefore expanded. In other words, there are diverse ways children may be seen to exhibit and experience what I believe *is* their natural creativity and access to the imagination. The broadest sense of this expression can be found in children's books, some of which are presented here, along with the new contemporary themes that need to and have been recently expanded to include stories about children from different backgrounds and families, abilities, and sensibilities.

# 3

# The Freedom to Imagine: Childhood Creativity and Socialization in the Work of William Steig

I remember watching my granddaughter when she was three, four, and five effortlessly create exquisite drawings, paintings, and all kinds of designs. I often thought of asking her where they came from, but I knew that she did not know or need to know or want to be questioned. She took for granted her freedom of expression. Similarly, my grandson seemed to express his creativity effortlessly in the complex and varied rhythms he would tap out with his feet, his hands, and his mouth. But school and the awareness of others—what others think, expect, and evaluate—seem to initiate the intimidation and self-consciousness that impair that wild expanse of early childhood. To some extent, of course, this socialization is necessary. However, I remember learning that eyes should look a certain way; noses, mouths, hands, and feet should be recognizable and conventionally suitable. I remember in the seventh grade our art assignment was to make an animal out of paper mâché. I worked hard on my "gerog," half giraffe and half dog. It received one of the lowest grades in the class. That was it for me. I was not resilient, and I retreated from "art." For most children to feel creative, to have the courage to move into an expressive, imaginative place, they need to be, if not overly encouraged, at least not discouraged, judged, or criticized for their efforts.

As artist and storyteller, William Steig is, for me, the artist who most closely encourages and portrays the expansive freedom of the imagination. Even in his simpler picture books (*Sylvester and the Magic Pebble*, 1969, and *The Amazing Bone*, 1977), the imagination emerges from the unconscious quite inexplicably, dramatically, and spontaneously. And in his more complex narratives, *Dominic* (1984) and *Abel's Island* (1976), Steig most fully develops his theories of art and his representations of the imagination. These two books stand as frames, two poles of the imagination. Dominic is the child artist, intuitive, unquestioning, and matter-of-fact about his creative spirit. Abel, lawfully Abelard Hassam di Chirico Flint of the Mossville Flints, is the excessively civilized adult/mouse, who only discovers his creativity after being thrust into nature and isolated on an island for a full year.

Dominic is in many ways a classical hero, and his hero's journey basically follows Joseph Campbell's hero cycle, from the "call to adventure" to the return of the hero, his adventure replete with the magical helper (a fortune-telling witch-alligator), and the "sacred marriage" with a sleeping beauty/princess. However, Dominic significantly resists the conventionality and predictability suggested by this paradigm. As a hero, Dominic is freewheeling, has no goal, and has "left home to look for whatever it was that was going to happen to him" (14). His path is neither linear nor circular. "He was forever leaving the road, coming back to it and leaving it again, investigating the source of every smell and sound, every sight that intrigued him" (14). This meandering suggests the way the imagination works. For Steig, the imagination remains mysterious and erratic. As Dominic says, "'I like to be taken by surprise'" (7).

Dominic is a musician, inspired to play his piccolo when he feels most free. His "passionate love of liberty" illuminates Steig's belief in the power of creativity to achieve all kinds of transformations. Dominic even frees a yellow jacket from a spider's web—which releases that yellow jacket to become one of his rescuers, a transformation from potential enemy to loyal friend. Freedom and openness allow for the unanswerable and the unknowable nature of life, so that when Dominic asks himself, "Why are there owls?"—questioning the reason for such destructive creatures—he concludes, "Why anything?" (49). He knows intuitively that being open is vital to imagining. His child heart feels connected to the world around him; his ability to feel fosters imagining—imagining another's feelings as well as expressing one's own. We see him empathize deeply with the weepy wild boar Barney Swain, so that in "an upsurge of bountiful feeling" (63), "he had to cry too" (62). Steig's characters embody states of feeling and stages of imagining.

Here the imagination is positioned in a harmonious world where everything has a time, "a time to live, a time to die" (34–5), and a place, where "thought and action were not separate" (23), where "the beauty and the sadness belonged together somehow, though they were not the same at all" (35). There is a reciprocity of kindness between creatures, all of whom serve to complement Dominic on his quest, with the single exception of the Doomsday Gang—their name expressive of their function, their negativity, and their malice.

Steig's characters raise interesting and provocative questions about the nature of of art. A mouse painter claims, "Everything is so beautiful just as it is that I pay my respects to life by painting things just as they are" (83). But Dominic replies, "Since I can see beauty just by looking out my window, why would I want to own [such] a painting[?]" (83). Both have their place, Steig shows, as the verisimilitude of the mouse's paintings serves to distract and fool members of the Doomsday Gang, while Dominic's vision allows for the kind of aesthetic discovery that occurs amid the chaos of creativity. The imagination flourishes where boundaries are blurred. Immersed in a night pastoral, Dominic muses about the magic of moonlight. On a particularly splendid night, Steig tells us, "Everything under its influence was alive, awake, and spellbound … It was not clear where the fireflies ended and the stars began" (90). He creates a miniature pastoral where mice are having "a moonlight revel. There was delicate, stately mouse music produced by tiny zithers, lutes, and tambourines." Dominic is moved to play his piccolo "softly, ever so softly." The mice, like other creatures of nature, do not question "where the piccolo notes were coming from. They too," Steig tells us, "were bewitched" (90–1). The elegance of the mice "ladies in gowns and feathers" dancing "cotillions and polkas" creates a comic pastoral—adorning these small, common creatures. In a Dionysian revelry that "grew more and more ecstatic," Steig suggests a unity where "the music strove nearer and nearer to the elemental truth of being": deep in the imagination lies the basic connection between nature and civilization. Dominic's soul "overflows" with an expanse of spirit and feeling, so that "he couldn't help himself. He raised his head and, straining toward infinity, howled out the burden of his love and longing in sounds more meaningful than words" (92). Dominic, child/dog/artist, embodies the spiritual and the infinite, as he exults, "Oh, Life, I am yours. Whatever it is you want of me, I am ready to give." This is Steig's ultimate vision, the imagination inspired by all kinds of sources, animate and inanimate, and evoking inexplicable longings.

Along the way, Dominic finds a doll/dog, his dog version of an amulet, and when he sniffs it, "his heart was pierced with a yearning he didn't understand" (107). He accepts the un-understandable nature of the imagination, its irrational spontaneity. Often in Steig's books rescue from danger occurs through a magical and inexplicable event. In *Dominic*, the fire that threatens to destroy the wedding of the wild boars is extinguished when Mwana, the elephant, suddenly remembers a simple magic word: "Presto." In *The Amazing Bone*, the talking bone suddenly speaks the magic jibberish that shrinks the fox who threatens to eat Pearl the Pig, until he is the size of a mouse. When Pearl asks the bone, "What made you say those words?" the bone replies, "I wish I knew … They just came to me, I had to say them." Similarly, in *The Zabajaba Jungle*, Leonard, inspired by a mysterious voice that urges him to "show us who you are," sets off the fireworks that liberate him from the triumvirate of punitive judges, the socialized world of restrictive adults.

Art and creativity are also inspired by love, maybe above all by love, as Ellen Handler Spitz points out in her article on Steig's "connected" child hero. Spitz asserts that the love of Sylvester's parents turns him back into a donkey after he has been imprisoned as a rock. It occurs with their wish and with the randomness and unpredictability of magic. Spitz characterizes the event of a lion initially frightening Sylvester into wishing himself a rock as "spectacularly nonmetaphoric." Interestingly, with Steig's predictable unpredictability, the rock and the wish *are* metaphoric. In his fear of the lion, Sylvester wishes to be as safe as a rock. His wish transforms him from donkey to rock and his parents' desire for his return, along with the magic rock, transforms him back again. Here Steig demonstrates the power of the creative act to connect wishing (an act of the spirit) with a rock (the static body, the earth, the ordinary), and to intimately and inexplicably infuse the ordinary with the extraordinary.

For Steig, truth and meaning are symbolically portrayed in the various stages of the hero's journey, and come from the unconscious imagination. When Dominic watches a play about his heroic "exploits" at a celebration, he notes that the scripted play, "The Exploits of Dominic," "isn't the way it was at all" (121). The truth is illuminated in his dreams where the duality and complexity of feeling reside. There, Dominic observes, it was "as if he were sitting alone in a theater watching a play, in which he is split into a Dominic who runs away from the alligator-witch because he "didn't want to hear the rest of his life story and a Dominic sitting in the theater who was afraid that the witch might catch the Dominic on stage" (133). When he awakens to reality, he realizes he's badly hurt and stands warned about the closeness of the Doomsday Gang.

The ending of Dominic is designed to be inclusive and healing of all wounds, physical and psychological. The Doomsday Gang reforms, "convinced that Nature itself could no longer abide their destructive, criminal ways"; thus, the attempt to "get into Nature's good graces … as every wanton one of them had been in his original childhood" (137). For Steig, childhood originally contains the power and benevolence of the natural world. Dominic is led to his "sleeping beauty," who has been, fairy tale like, waiting for him. In an enchanted garden where the flowers "never grow old," where it is never winter, she asks, "Are you the one?" As Dominic plays his piccolo, with "soft, yodeling ululations," Steig "affirm[s] … an ancient yet young universe" (141–2). This sense of cosmic harmony is, of course, not the whole of life. Steig returns Dominic and his sleeping beauty to the ordinary world as she asserts her individuality; her name is Evelyn, and though it hints at the mythical Eve, it is, also, ordinary.

In his introduction to *The World of William Steig*, John Updike points to his favorite Steig drawing, which he owns, of a woman rocking face to face with the moon smiling down on her. It depicts the back and forth movement of inspiration, the moon as the source of creativity that connects the earthly and the heavenly, in "the dauntless energy of prelapsarian innocence" (6). Arlene Wilner notes that Steig's protagonists are children "for whom nature and art, innocence and creativity, do not conflict," that there is magic "in the nature of things and the transforming power of one's imagination is a fact of life" (32). The matter-of-factness of his exquisite vision avoids the cloying sentimentality familiar to many romantic representations of childhood innocence. In addition, with humor and the elegant language of beautiful, sensuous detail, he infuses the worldly with a scintillating energy. Exquisite flaming desserts like pumpkin jubilee, the lush green velvet of Dominic's wedding attire, and all kinds of flora and fauna hover somewhere between the ordinary and the fantastic. For Steig, our senses are boundaryless; smell and sight, sound and smell mix in a synesthesia of new metaphors. Dominic's adventures begin with a tune he creates from "The odors ... [of] single notes, or percussion shots ... fused together in wonderful harmonies." He names his tune "The Psalm of Sweet Smells" (9)—his images intensified by synesthesia. At the end of his journey, in the enchanted garden, Dominic touches each flower, producing an "orchestration [of] strings, soft brasses, reeds, light percussion" (140). As the natural world extends into a fantastic world where anything is possible, real surprise is treated matter-of-factly, and transformation is shown to be a natural birthright.

It seems that, for Steig, being creative is antagonistic to socialization—that the hero must leave behind the riches and comforts he inherits in *Dominic* or has acquired in *Abel's Island*. Abel cannot become a sculptor/artist until he is blown away in a storm onto an island where he is forced to live isolated from society in nature. As an aristocrat, Abel has no sense of nature. He is "indignant" at the rain that threatens his rarified picnic lunch of "hard-boiled quail egg, onions, olives, black caviar" (3–4). Nor has he any sense of his nature—his mouseness, which is thrust on him as he survives his natural enemies, an owl and a cat, only by eventually recognizing that the cat was doing what cats "had to" do. "She was being a cat. It was up to him to be the mouse" (112).

Throughout *Abel's Island*, Steig meticulously depicts Abel's journey, which has been forced on him, to retrieve his lost innocence, gradually through the seasons on the island. At first he has no survival skills, "he had never built anything or done a day's work" (23). His epiphanies evolve with living in the heart of nature. Abel begins to notice "how much was going on in the seeming stillness. Plants grew and bore fruit, branches proliferated, buds became flowers, clouds formed in ever-new ways and patterns, colors changed. He felt a strong need to participate in the designing and arranging of things" (54). Thus, Abel discovers his artistic drive and, eventually, develops his talent as a sculptor.

Abel's creative process begins with the need to preserve and be close to his past: he sculpts a statue of his wife, Amanda, "trying again and again, profiting from his mistakes, [until] he had a likeness of his wife real enough to embrace" (54). He then sculpts his mother, sisters, brothers, and, finally, he is able to capture "the proud, stern, aloof, strong, honest look" (55) of his father. Carving out of "tough wood," he has had to make use of his natural but newly discovered gnawing ability. These totems along with Amanda's scarf help maintain Abel's sense of self as it is challenged in nature bit by bit. Abel's discovery of two icons of civilization, a book and a watch, help preserve his connection to his past. With his wit and critique of civilization, Steig informs us that the book is about "masked balls," the artifice and disguises of society, and, most telling, about the wars that persist, "even though, on both sides, everyone wanted peace." "This was something," Abel notes, "to think about, with so much time to think" (64).

So Abel becomes reflective. As he gets the watch to tick, he notices the sounds that he had become accustomed to: "the roaring and gurgling of the river, the wailing and whining of the wind, the pattering and dripping of rain, the chirruping of birds and the chirring of insects"—all "natural, irregular rhythms," which are contrasted with "the steady, mechanical tempo of the watch [that] gave him something he had been wanting in this wild place … He had no use for the time the watch could tell, but he needed the ticking" (60). The sounds of nature, spontaneous and wild, are tempered by the orderly and predictable ticking. Together they represent the integration of the wild and the socialized that Abel must achieve as an adult.

As Abel becomes more reflective, he wonders about good and evil. He writes his first verse to still his fear of the darkness and the dangerous owl. He has gathered owl feathers as talismans against the powerful bird. His incantation comes, Steig-like, without knowing "where the words came from" (66):

Foul owl, ugly you,
You'll never get me,
Whatever you do.
You cannot hurt me,
You cannot kill,
You're in my power,
I have your quill!

Abel asks the same question Dominic raised. He wonders, "Why did God make owls … and other such loathsome, abominable creatures? He felt there had to be a reason" (69). His insistence on rationality emphasizes his sophistication, the adult methodology with which he approaches the world, while Dominic, in his innocence, accepts the random nature of life. Owls in both stories exist as part of nature. "Why anything?" Dominic could tell him. But Abel is not ready to accept this. We are reminded that as an adult he will need to reintegrate the rational with the imaginative and creative. Here Steig seems to address his adult readers as well as nod to his child readers. Steig, in fact, does not seem to retreat from the adult reading over the child's shoulder, as Hans Christian Andersen thought of his readers.

As Abel's observations become more astute, his feelings also deepen. He notes, "How deeply one felt when alone!" (77). Clearly he has not been introspective when immersed in his upper-class life. He begins to plumb his own depths when, out of the darkness of winter, he exults in the visibility produced by the melting of snow. With intensity, Abel begins to address himself, becomes his own witness to the beauty of the natural world. "'Abel,' he shouted, 'do you hear me? I can see!' How beautiful everything looked after the prolonged darkness. How unspeakably beautiful even the shells on the floor. How vividly actual and therefore marvelous!" (76). Finally, with spring, he surrenders to the wild natural world. Steig writes, "When the flowers appeared in May, he went crazy. Violets, dandelions, pinks, forget-me-nots bedecked the island ... and [Abel] ran about everywhere like a wild animal, shouting and yodeling. How it would surprise his family to see him now" (84–5).

What he considers his best artistic piece comes about from indulging his senses, and from being in the present. He releases himself from the social barriers of class with his new friend, the frog Gower Glackens, clearly a creature of the lower orders, one Abel now embraces, and as his friendship grows, he creates his best work. With his careful observation of Gower's natural frog-ness, Abel captured "a perfect representation of stupefied repose. Every wart was lovingly modeled: the eyes bulged properly, the full throat with the delicate wrinkles of age was definitely Gower's. The fulsome belly, the haunches and feet, rested firmly on the ground. There was a vague smile on the broad mouth, and in the lines of the closed eyelids that made the frog appear to be meditating on a homey universe" (92).

After Gower returns to his home, Abel is ultimately forced to face the nature of the frog's trances that insure that Gower, true to nature, will not remember to look up Amanda for Abel. Abel must escape the island with his own wit and will. When he is finally reunited with Amanda in the privacy of his home, where they "covered each other with kisses ... Abel's final words return him full circle to the beginning of his journey. He says, 'I've brought you back your scarf'" (117).

The book does not end here, but rather with four half-page illustrations that capture their reunion: Abel fully dressed in aristocratic garb, Amanda in full dress, though in the final frame, she has left her hat on the floor. Such feeling is best captured, Steig seems to say, in image, beyond words. Also, Steig leaves us, as adults, with questions. What will happen to the artistic Abel, the creature who has reclaimed his animal nature? How will he integrate new and old selves? According to Anita Moss, both Dominic and Abel "retain their innocence, as well as their imaginations" (138). I think Steig leaves it open to speculation whether Abel will be able to integrate his artistic side with his social side. I suspect, however, that children will happily embrace the united couple wholeheartedly and more unreservedly than the adults who read with the worldly knowledge that this integration will be difficult to achieve. For Steig, the imagination is the place where child and adult connect, where innocence is retained into adulthood. Though it takes Abel isolation and immersion in the natural world to find his creativity, we wonder what will happen to him with his reentry into domesticity and into civilization.

# 4

# Imagining Difference and Diversity

In a photo my sister and I stand together, defined by difference. We laugh at my small face, long and thin, which I refer to as "pinhead." She sees her broad cheekbones as wide and flat, which she calls "moonface." Our denigration of our differences illustrates our discomfort with the standards by which we were measured. Difference goes way back, the expectations and aspirations of generations illuminated and projected as legacy. And family difference, no matter how idiosyncratically constructed, reflects the values and assumptions of a larger community, a culture, an era. As a child I learned that my identity defined difference as hierarchy: if I was the pretty one, my sister could not be as pretty—or even pretty at all. She was the smart one, coming second in the family, and therefore inheriting the second most important defining trait for a girl of this culture—which also meant that I was not as smart. Looking at pictures of my sister, it is obvious to me that she was a pretty child, even by conventional standards. And I was smart, even if I did not do as well in school.

In her Ted lecture of July 2009, Adimamanda Ngozi warned about what she termed "The Danger of the Single Story." She was talking about the etiology of her own imagination, how the children's books she read shaped her imagination so dramatically, so completely, that as a young African girl, she wrote about snow and girls with ponytails and blue eyes, nothing about Africa, or about poverty, or about her own life. She urged the importance of a diversity of stories, a balance, so that the stories children read reflect who they are and even "repair broken dignity."

In this chapter difference is explored as an investigation into representations of class, gender, and cultural differences—to set the stage for the acceptance of difference that does not position one group over another.

Representing difference as awareness of groups that have been "othered" by society—this is central to a vision of equality—of difference as interesting, inspiring, and without which children may be discouraged from trying out new ways of thinking, expressing themselves, and imagining. Books for children that suggest the importance of becoming familiar with the unfamiliar, with different cultures and different positions within cultures without hierarchy, can be for children far-reaching.

Exploring the use of the term "liminality," Homi Bhabha uses the metaphor of the stairwell as the space in which people can move between cultures. He writes, "The stairwell as liminal space, in-between the designations of identity, becomes the process of symbolic interaction, the connective tissue that constructs the difference between upper and lower, black and white ... The temporal movement and passage that [the stairwell] allows, prevents identities at either end ... This interstitial passage between fixed identifications opens up the possibility of a cultural hybridity that entertains difference without an assumed or imposed hierarchy" (quoted in Bradford, 158).

Many contemporary stories that embrace and explore difference are autobiographical, stories of survival, generated by the unresolved feelings that stuck in the throat of the author or illustrator. They respond to an urgent call for expression. These are the experiences that seem to resist integration. They are threads of stories that are not woven into a conventional fabric. Excluded from traditional patterns, they require a change of paradigm, a vision that admits multiple perspectives. They may not depict a synthesis of differences, but rather present a Bakhtinian "dialogic" that keeps each voice, each cultural utterance clear so that the dominant paradigm shifts from either/or to both/and, thus dealing with ambivalence, perceiving struggle, and suggesting new kinds of resolution.

The autobiographical or fictionalized informational stories for young children are picture books where the authors' voices sound authentic and where illustrators confirm and expand on the authors' visions. I am thinking of the children's books where the authors address children at the end of their story, like Tony Medina does with *DeShawn Days*, when he writes, "DeShawn uses his imagination to see things differently and to help others. Maybe his experiences will inspire you to write poems, paint pictures, sing songs, or help others, too!" Their personal stories may convince children that what happens to them is within the range of "normal" human experience, no matter how that experience has been denied expression or has otherwise gone unrepresented. Normalizing children's experiences can encourage them to express themselves more freely and imaginatively.

Authors and illustrators of autobiographical stories for children have become more experimental, as contemporary autobiographies depict the self in radically different ways. For example, stories that portray possibility, rather than a strictly cohesive construction, embrace the dialogism that Mikhail Bakhtin articulates. Dialogism, Susanna Egan noted, "a recurring feature of contemporary autobiographies" (25), has burgeoned from feminists and theorists of 'minority' literature" (24), that the " 'I' in many cultures is inherently polyvocal and [that] the construction of the individual subject is always a collaborative social activity" (25). This is obviously true of children whose voices are formed by the adults in their family, school, and cultural communities—before they have developed a fairly consistent or even inconsistent voice of their own. I believe that most children, like Lewis Carroll's Alice, are polyvocal in that they speak the voices they hear, those that represent the adult world, and, at the same time, consciously or unconsciously, those that question it. They are constructed in social context as they struggle to find their own shifting identities, the beginnings of what is known as "the multifaceted concept of self" (Fisher, 196), a paradigm of the self that allows for the widest range of feelings, ideas, and beliefs that resist integration, but, nonetheless, need to be acknowledged. This idea is reflected in different ways in the following autobiographical stories for young children.

## The picture book and life story

In *Two Mrs. Gibsons*, by Toyomi Igus, illustrated by Daryl Wells, the two most important women in the author's life, her mother and her grandmother, are portrayed in difference—one with "skin the color of vanilla" and one with "skin the color of chocolate." Igus tells the story of her Japanese mother and her African American grandmother, a testament to her love for them. The narrator is a child who notes the differences in the way each comforts her, one with bear hugs, the other "stroking her hair and humming before bedtime."

They laugh differently, the food they cook is different, the way they dress her and do her hair is different, and their creative ways are totally different: one makes the "littlest, prettiest strokes of a pen when she would write our names in Japanese," and the other plays the piano and sings, "This little light of mine, I'm gonna let it shine!" The simple, elegant parallel construction portrays difference without hierarchy, and neither loses her vitality in a forced synthesis. While the focus here is on difference, connection is just as strong, in text and illustration. Similar language and cadence, similar colors and positioning of illustrations indicate the love of the child for both her mother and grandmother.

Picture books also represent the various states of dreaming and imagining, not only captured in voices, in the external features of landscape and community, but also in the images that depict internal shifting between states of mind. Words tend to move the plot forward into the outside world and its effect on the child; this is chronological and linear in construct. As Joseph H. Schwarcz said, "Language discloses its contents in time ... The picture, on the other hand, confronts the viewer all at once, as a *surface* . . . We see its content simultaneously, as an immediate whole" (9). The mind of the child moves more comfortably, I want to assert here, than the adult mind, back and forth, in and out of linear progression and the still moment captured in the illustration.

Artists and authors of these new picture books move beyond binaries, beyond the either/or of verbal/visual, movement/stasis, beyond "categories [that] are considered to be opposite and mutually exclusive," as Rebecca Rabinowitz suggests in her article "Queer Theory and Children's Literature." She reminds us that we need to take in, examine, and expand our way of thinking in many areas of scholarship. This compels us to look at difference in new ways: to consider what gets foregrounded, what gets marginalized, and, again, how to embrace incongruity, ambivalence, and ambiguity as acceptable and significant. To obliterate the shame children often feel at being marginalized, we need to normalize difference. And as teachers, parents, critics, writers, and readers, we need to stay open, to be fluid so that we do not recreate boundaries, new binaries, in the face of changing perspectives. These ways of imagining keep the imagination broad, wide, and deep.

Most children grow up assuming their family, school, or community is "normal," that their life is "the way things are." That is until they come up against what may clash with that way. Hopefully, this might be experienced as just another way of being or doing. However, when the child notices that her family is poor compared with other families, that his family looks different from the majority of others, is rarely seen on television or is seen in particularly stereotypical or negative ways, or is treated badly by schoolmates and other peers, then this is not just the way things are. This child may see his life and ways of seeing as inferior or unacceptable.

A powerful example of a children's book that normalizes a minority family is Carmen Lomas Garza's *In My Family* (1996), a portrait of a Mexican American girl. The harmony between Garza's paintings and her words reflects the balance between the Spanish and English in her bilingual text. She writes, "When I was growing up, a lot of us were punished for speaking Spanish. We were punished for being who we were, and we were made to feel ashamed of our culture … My art is a way of healing these wounds, like the sávila plant (aloe vera) heals burns and scrapes when applied by a loving parent or grandparent." Here family, culture, and art together heal and inspire. Garza includes interesting details about the natural world in which she grew up, like the horned toads she loved and the fire ants that "can really sting," along with the food that represented fasting and other rituals and ceremonies that separated daily life from the special moments. Details that define each culture, details that separate one culture from another, also serve to point out the diverse ways that cultures distinguish holidays from ordinary days, and, therefore, also suggest a deep similarity, serving to broaden the imagination of the children who are not familiar with this culture. The similarities may serve as the bridge for children to enter the differences.

Garza illuminates her Mexican American culture with some of its mythic stories like the myth of *La Llorona*, the shadow side of the popular Virgin of Guadalupe. Both are beautifully illustrated along with festival dances and celebrations. Here, as in many cultures, the light and the dark exist as two sides of human nature, the sacred and the profane. As Carl Jung, Joseph Campbell, and other archetypal and psychological critics have demonstrated, in addition to the differences and the diversity of cultural myths, there are also basic similar patterns that connect "majority" and minority

**Figure 1** Benny Len dreams. From *Home to Medicine Mountain*. Courtesy of Children's Book Press, an Imprint of Lee and Low Publishing.

cultures. Whether similar or different—whether different yet similar or similar yet different—these details suggest openings for the imagination, which encourage new stories, new ways of imagining, and all kinds of creative expression.

A darker story of minority culture, one in which children are sent away to boarding schools to "unlearn their Indian ways," is *Home to Medicine Mountain*. Chiori Santiago's words and Judith Lowry's illustrations tell the story of Lowry's father and uncle whose comfortable childhood was abruptly ended when they were taken away to boarding schools "to live apart from their families." Their early childhoods were located in the mountains of northern California where "they hunted deer and gathered roots, vegetables and acorns in the beautiful baskets they made. Everything they needed to make a good life around them." The children arrive barefoot at the boarding school to be forced into "uniforms and stiff new shoes" in which they march military style "in square." Everything is foreign—the clothing, the food, the language—not only the words themselves, but also the narrative patterns. Benny Len and Stanley learned about the world through grandmother's stories, lessons embedded in stories about the Moon, who stole the grandchild of Old Frog Woman, and "how Old Frog Woman went to rescue the boy from Moon's ice-covered house" (8). Benny Len is punished for "daydreaming," which is his way of using his imagination, and for speaking in his Native language. He is robbed of expression not in keeping with the tenets of the school and its colonialist teachings, illustrated on the blackboards as "1492 Discovery of America," "Manifest Destiny," and the "Louisiana Purchase." These doctrines reference aspects of American history that robbed Native children of their culture. The drawings further dramatize the differences between the dormitory—beds lined up like equidistant slabs of tombstones, the teacher at the door casting a long dark shadow; this image is in contrast to Benny Len's dreamscape of his grandmother's house in which one path circles down the page in blue made by water and one circle in white made by smoke—gentle and airy, images of the natural world. Included are a bear, deer, and a wolf in conversation, dragonflies flying down a river ending in a pond with a frog, all surrounded by cattails, and to the right is a cat on a blue circle of rug. Here nature is in harmony; no distinction is made between outdoor and indoor, between animal and insect, mammal and amphibian, or the elements. This is where Benny Len travels at night, where he lives most vitally, in dreamtime that "didn't march in neat rows, like the chronological time of the clock." In his imagination he is able to preserve his sense of things, where "some days were slow as a waterbug drifting downstream in summers. Others slipped by as quickly as a coyote melting into the shadows" (14). His metaphoric language, constructed from the natural world and his dreaming, draws a double audience close to his inner life. He speaks to those children who have had similar experiences and to those who are unfamiliar with this marginalized, often suppressed knowledge. The description of the dream state may be familiar though its representation may differ. This is what I am looking for in books about minority cultures—those that bring readers in so close that they have what Alison Landsberg calls "prosthetic memory," so close that though it is not actually their own memory, it begins to feel like one.[1]

The story is also the true adventure of the boys' return as they jump a train and, thus, go "home to Medicine Mountain." In the wordless double-page spread, the two boys ride the train, arms outstretched to the sky, echoed by an eagle's wide expanse of open wings, and in the smoke the face of the grandmother with leaves in her hair flows—gorgeous, joyous, and sky free. Once home, the three animal icons are repeated in the fire's smoke as the two children are reunited with their grandmother.

Now, as adults, father and uncle answer their children's question, "Did you have to go back?" "Yes," they say, but they did not mind so much "because now they knew the way home" (30). Considering the powerlessness of children and of some minorities at various times in history, this profound message offers "the way home," for those seeking a way to mitigate pain and frustration. Whatever the journey, here home evokes the way to the source of comfort and renewal. The courage to go home to where these children feel free is retained in dream and the imagination, so that it is always available—articulated by the adults here as a testament to the power of the imagination.

Even within the neighborhood where minority children are the majority, there are aspects both inside and outside the neighborhood that threaten to disrupt a child's sense of equilibrium, and to remind the child of what he is missing. In *DeShawn Days*, Tony Medina portrays, through multiple voices and the images of R. Gregory Christie, the world of DeShawn, which opens with a strong self-identification and an invitation:

> I'm DeShawn Williams
> I'm ten years old
> Come see who I live with
> Who I love!

Medina establishes an intimacy between the text and the reader, as the book presents a reciprocity between author and illustrator. DeShawn is our guide into his world: the world of his family, his neighborhood, his school, and beyond to his sense of nation and globe.

DeShawn's neighborhood inspires his creativity. Life in the "hood," expressed in short poems, defines his environment. Each poem captures a mood, a perspective, and the hood is a mixed bag. DeShawn loves the community where everybody just hangs out and plays, where winter is Christmas with the beauty of the park outside and hot chocolate inside. He loves rap, the improvisational expression of his culture. He says, it is

> Not just … the beats
> that make you move your feet
> but the words'cause they talk about reality'cause they talk about me
> and my block.

He loves the "rhyming, the timing," where he pretends he is a deejay "wavin' my hands … in front of the mirror / making believe I'm in a video / wearing a baseball cap / and my uncle's shades and … I'll have me some braids." Christie's images, painted over several pages, vividly depict DeShawn's inner life, his desires, a little boy's vision of what he's extracted from his neighborhood, the styles and art forms he would like to grow into. We see the foundations of DeShawn's creativity, a glimpse into what provides the courage for his imagination to develop.

DeShawn is also aware of difference within his neighborhood. In an upbeat story, DeShawn tells about his friend Johnny Tse who is Chinese, and from whom he learns "new things … like different food … new words," acknowledging that he learns "karate," but that it is Japanese, not Chinese, that there are distinct differences between the two and that difference requires attention. Medina does not assume all Asian cultures are the same; he maintains the distinction between cultures and suggests that being mindful of those differences can be expansive.

There are also things he does not like about his neighborhood—the smells of "dog mess," "cop cars and ambulances screaming … real loud at you"—and not just kids playing around but "big people fighting." There are other frightening aspects of his life, like the graffiti that disturbs him, which contains the violence he dreams about. And he is aware of war and of children who are victims of the bombings. He acknowledges that it helps to write letters "to the kids in the war," even if they do not answer them. Medina asserts here the right of children to know, and notes that in fact they *do* know about the horrors of the world. And they also need to feel hopeful, without falsifying their relative helplessness and without pretending to solve the problem or minimize its significance.

Medina portrays DeShawn as an honest and open child and the story is told through his feelings. He is sad but also accepting that his mother "is hardly ever home" as she works and goes to college; he reports matter-of-factly that his dad is missing. His closest person is his grandmother who is in poor health. DeShawn says, "I love talking to her / I could tell her anything / she never tells my secrets." Trust is central in this depiction of the bonding between child and grandmother. Though each character occupies a unique position in DeShawn's life, his relationship with his grandmother is central, his rock and stability. And, naturally, the most significant experience of DeShawn's story is the death of his grandmother. In his heartbreaking voice, he says, "She was my everything / my protector and friend / ... When my grandmother died / I cried and cried." In the illustration, he appears with the significant men in his community, one with his arm circled around DeShawn, clearly men with whom he can express his deep sorrow. In another painting, he sits on his mother's lap, comforted by her in his sadness. The mother, who is often away and busy, holds him in her arms "and didn't let go / for a long long time." Medina drawing on his life experience strikes what feels like an uncompromisingly honest note.

What voice, what genre can follow such grief? DeShawn tells his final story as a fantasy in which he saves a princess from bullies. Dressed in the same blue depicted as his grandmother's tombstone and his comforting mother's dress, in other words, buoyed up and identified with them, he flies "higher than the tallest tree / and the biggest building / in the project in my / neighborhood." The princess kisses him on the cheek and although "the whole class laughed," he writes, "we all lived happily ever after." His imagination provides the inspiration for DeShawn; the death of his grandmother is devastating, but the story he creates is heartening.

DeShawn's story comes full circle with Tony Medina's "Afterword," much like DeShawn's opening with his self-identification and an invitation. He writes, "I come from a similar world as DeShawn. I was a skinny brown boy from the projects with asthma, an active imagination, and a grandmother who was there for me." He invites his readers to consider that "[a] writer is a great thing to be because you get to paint pictures, tell stories, create worlds, and express your feelings—all with words. It just takes imagination. DeShawn uses his imagination to see things differently and to help others. Maybe his experiences will inspire you to write poems, paint pictures, sign songs, or help others, too!" The story encompasses, as shifting and multifaceted, the various voices, moods, and genres, a full expression of self and other—whether that be friend, neighborhood, or the world. Medina's emphasis on the imagination not only encourages self-expression and creativity, but also suggests the help writing, in particular, might offer others as DeShawn's story can, a gift that extends outward and values difference in terms of creating a community. Medina's message includes the power of the imagination "to see things differently," and the benefit of opening the child's world through the imagination.

## Difference and the species: *Owen & Mzee*

In 2006, with the publication of *Owen & Mzee*, Scholastic Press unleashed into the children's book world a fascination with the pairing of couples from different species. I have seen many images of a cat riding the back of an elephant, a pig and a horse playing together, the affection between species depicted in tiger and bear snuggling, and so on. The popularity of these images suggests longing for a harmony where difference is accepted, even in surprising and unconventional ways.

*Owen & Mzee: The True Story of a Remarkable Friendship* is the tale of an orphaned baby hippo who was rescued from the devastating tsunami that occurred in the Indian Ocean on December 26, 2004. The rescue is an adventure in itself. Owen was left behind, "a baby without his mother, stranded on a sandy coral reef ... tired and frightened ... unable to reach the shore on his own." The story of how this hippo developed a friendship with a 130-year-old tortoise captivated people everywhere. After initially rejecting Owen, within a day Mzee was found snuggling with him—an image now familiar to children all over the world. In effect, Mzee mothered the baby hippo.

Mothers and baby animals have always struck a chord in children's books. I still remember *The Story of Babar, the Little Elephant* and *Bambi*, their mothers' deaths deeply embedded in my memory, and when I mention those books in class, there is an uproar from my students—affirming the vivid and painful childhood memories of those early books. The same holds true for *Dumbo*, the baby elephant, who is separated from his mother; she is locked up and humiliated because of her long ears. The image of Owen and Mzee recalled here suggests to me a realistic replacement for the painful stories of Babar, Dumbo, and Bambi. These earlier stories may retain their popularity, but Owen and Mzee encourage the possibility of animals, though spectacularly different, finding comfort in each other.

The story of Owen and Mzee is a joyful one; their coupling is dynamic. At first, Mzee "wasn't happy about this attention" from Owen, and she hissed and crawled away. Owen was persistent, the two became inseparable, and the book is filled with large photographs that chronicle the growth of this relationship. The authors Isabella and Craig Hatkoff and Paula Kahumbu speculate on what the book offers children: "Science can't always explain what the heart already knows: our most important friends are sometimes those we least expected." Haller Park became one of the most visited places on the globe, as people the world over were charmed by the two friends. In the last picture Owen, substantially grown, leans his head on Mzee's front paws, both blissfully resting.

The excitement over this pair generated a sequel, *Owen & Mzee, The Language of Friendship*, in which Mzee has to be separated from Owen in order to have his shell repaired. How Owen survives, how another tortoise is brought in as a substitute, and how the three wind up together, is fascinating. Equally intriguing is the way they communicate. "When Mzee wants Owen to walk with him, he will gently nip Owen's tail with his sharp beak. When Owen wants Mzee to move, he will nudge Mzee's feet. To direct Mzee to the right, he will nudge Mzee's back right foot. To direct him to the left, he will nudge Mzee's back left foot. If Mzee doesn't respond right away, Owen may squeeze Mzee's foot between his teeth until he starts to move. But neither ever hurts the other." The language between the species is clear and expressed in such detail—clear to children hearing/reading this story—that it places children inside the story. Beneath the story line, simple and quietly dramatic, is a pastoral vision. It implies that beyond species, and by extension, beyond other differences like gender, class, age, and race, we are linked as sentient beings.

## The young adult novel: Representing the cultural "other"

Two contemporary award-winning novels for young adults, Gene Luen Yang's *American Born Chinese* and Sherman Alexie's *The Absolutely True Diary of a Part-Time Indian,* imaginatively portray the experience of being the ethnic minority in mainstream white America. Yang's Jin Wang is Chinese American living in an essentially white suburb and Alexie's Junior is a Spokane Indian living on a reservation who attends an all-white high school. Both are treated and experience themselves as culturally "other." And although there are many similarities—both books are illustrated, semiautobiographical, and, most significantly, challenge the racial stereotypes of their culture—they employ imaginatively different approaches and offer two opposite resolutions. One suggests the possibility of integrating cultural heritage, family, peer culture, and self-acceptance. The other explores the necessity of separation from heritage, family, and friends in order to survive. Both books grapple with questions about what constitutes identity and community. They are courageous stories, told by successful authors who have struggled through some of the pitfalls of being minority creative artists with original and compelling ways of storytelling.

### American Born Chinese

When I first thought of teaching Yang's *American Born Chinese*, I shuddered. The book reaches for the ugliest of Chinese stereotypes—in its attempt to directly and unabashedly portray and address the fears of many Chinese immigrants and children of Chinese immigrants about how they are seen by mainstream America. I thought about what allows us to approach the most disturbing cultural issues. Humor is a way of exploring controversy and the comic book format of *American Born Chinese* easily embraces exaggeration. Chin-Kee (note his derogatory name) is the most offensive characterization. He is the main character in a sit-com, "Everyone Ruvs Chin-Kee," with applause and laughs at the bottom of the pages in which he appears, suggesting the worst of popular mainstream television. Features of visual humor here include Chin-Kee's arrival from China with luggage in the form of take-out containers, with his buck teeth, yellow face, long braid, all cartoonish. He speaks with the l/r reversals attributed to stereotyped Chinese immigrant speech: "Harro Amellica," he says, bowing obsequiously, announcing: "such pletty Amellican girl wiff bountiful Amellican bosom? Must bind feet and bear Chin-Kee's children!"—all of which is tolerated as this caricature is hilarious, but as we laugh, Gene Yang hits us with the horror of such stereotyping in his complex triad of storytelling.

*American Born Chinese* begins with three discrete narrative lines: the myth of the Chinese monkey king, recreated with a comic book superhero; the bildungsroman of Jin Wang, an Asian American boy, who rejects all things Asian in his desire to fit in with his white classmates; and the TV sit-com about two cousins, Danny, the white representation of Jin's desire, and his shadow, Chin-Kee, the representation of his shame. The themes of desire and shame are borne out in each of the three strands.

In the first story, the monkey king only wants to be a human god after he is rejected from a dinner party hosted for the "gods, the goddesses, the demons, and the spirits gathered in heaven" (7). When he is shamed by the other deities who claim, "you may be a king–you may even be a deity—but you are still a monkey" (15), he is transformed from a ruler who rules "with a firm but gentle hand" into a fierce, violent dictator. We are told that "when he entered his royal chamber, the thick smell of monkey fur greeted him. He'd never noticed it before" (20). He then insists that all monkeys wear shoes as he envisions himself as one of "the Great Sages, Equal of Heaven." As epic hero he visits the underworld where he comes before Tzi-Yo-Tzuh, He Who Is, the supreme ruler, depicted here as an old wise man with a huge cane, who reminds him, "I created you, I say that you are a monkey, therefore, you are a monkey" (69). The monkey king tries to escape his shape and nature. However, he does not recognize that the godly embodies "the heights of heaven and ... the depths of the underworld" (80).

To embrace the animal and the human, the profane and the sacred, is at the heart of Yang's graphic novel of acceptance of all parts of the self. His depiction of the four monks of legendary status (133) is a hilarious satire of the other extreme (the monkey as body; the monks as spirit): the first monk who focused only on meditations "could not meditate for more than twenty minutes without developing an itch in his seat"; the second fasted so much that when "he fasted for more than half a day, he would faint"; the third's "sermons were of such eloquence that even the bamboo wept in repentance." In a cartoon bubble—"I'm so sorry! Boo-Hoo!" He preaches, "It's as if your heart had a door on it. No, wait—perhaps it's more like an eye. No, hold on..." (135). But the fourth "unremarkable by all accounts," committed to helping and sharing, and received with extreme hostility, is sent on a quest to inspire the monkey king to escape from the mountain of rock under which he is imprisoned. Yang shows the absurdity of the monkey king's fighting and fart-ing, and, finally, "the monkey king accompanied the fourth monk on his jour-ney to the West and served him faithfully until the very end" (160). Monkey and monk walk off together, without shoes—as both are released from their mutual imprisonment of exclusive selflessness and selfishness, emblematic of balance and integration. Here is a transformative image of two parts of the self, destructive when isolated from each other, powerful and harmonious when accepted.

The second story portrays Jin's longing for acceptance. He has been humil-iated by ignorant teachers—"Class, I'd like us all to give a warm Mayflower Elementary welcome to your new friend and classmate Jing Jang … [who has] moved all the way from China" (30), his teacher says, oblivious to his correc-tions, "Jin Wang from San Francisco." She responds to another child's com-ment, "My momma says Chinese people eat dogs," with, "Now be nice … I'm sure Jin doesn't do that! In fact, Jin's family probably stopped that sort of thing as soon as they came to the United States!" (31). When Wei-Chen Sun from Tai-Wan enters, similarly introduced to the class, Jin wants nothing to do with him. He acknowledges, "Something made me want to beat him up" (36). Yang's portrayal of Jin's projection of self-hatred here, his internalized anger at the school's racism turned outward, feels convincing and significant as one of the most insidious effects of racism. As Jin covets Wei-Chen's transformer toy, they eventually become friends. We learn, in the end, that Wei-Chen himself *is* a transformation from monkey to human, that he is the Monkey King's son.

Jin Wang's shame is most intensely dramatized in the third narrative. Yang's representation of shame here suggests that shame fractures us, as Jin splits into the idealized Danny and the humiliating Chin-Kee, the star of "Everyone Ruvs Chin-Kee," a satirical lurch at "Everyone Loves Raymond," with its "everyperson" hero. The bunch of laughs at the bottom of the "funni-est" frames is the humor of racism and sexism, as Chin-Kee revels shamelessly, wallowing in stereotypical behavior. Yang was courageous in his audacious, gritty depiction of the way many Chinese Americans are regarded. His is a kind of "take back the night" approach, illuminating the horrors of his expe-rience, making explicit those stereotypes that have been projected onto him, those he has incorporated, and those he has had to overcome.

**Figure 2** "Harro Amellica." From *American Born Chinese* by Gene Luen Yang. Reprinted by permission of Roaring Brook Press, a division of Holtzbrinck Publishing Holdings.

Yang also challenges some of the most egregious aspects of male culture with Jin's story. A traditional Chinese herbalist warns against Jin's childhood desire to be a "transformer," a superhero like the toy he shares with Wei-Chen. She says, "It's easy to become anything you wish ... so long as you're willing to forfeit your soul" (29). And it is Jin's soul that is at stake in his betrayal of himself and of his friend, Wei-Chen. In his painful rejection by a girl, Jin grabs Wei-Chen's girl, without regard for her or his friend. This feels like an important part of Yang's rejection of male culture and his emphasis on how crippling and dehumanizing it can be.

Finally, Jin has been transformed into Danny, who cannot get rid of Chin-Kee, and the monkey king is revealed as Chin-Kee's true self. Danny turns back into Jin Wang and Wei-Chen is revealed as the monkey king's son. In his travels, Wei-Chen has found humans "to be petty, soulless creatures [and decides that he] will spend the remainder of my days in the mortal world using it for my pleasure ... anything is better than a lifetime of servitude to humans" (219–20). In rebellion, Wei-Chen has turned into a hipster with signature cigarettes, earrings, and shades. An integration occurs when Wei-Chen and Jin Wang meet at a cafe, Wei-Chen removes his hipster accouterments, and the landscape appears free from laughs or applause on the bottom of the page.

In *American Born Chinese,* Yang suggests that integration means acknowledging feelings of shame and anger, and accepting all things human, of monks and monkeys, a balance of body and soul. And in his satirical representation of super heroes, Yang challenges the harmful and inhibiting aspects of racism and male popular culture.

*American Born Chinese* ends with a moment of companionship between two boys: Jin Wang and Wei-Chen and all that they represent, a resolution of the duality of being Chinese and American, and an acceptance of desire and shame, of the many sides of the self, which is often at the heart of the adolescent quest, and an urgent need to find a community for this new identity. The last cartoon-box is of the two Chinese boys, one dressed in a basketball shirt marked with number 11, which belonged to NBA star, Yao Ming. Jin and Wei-Chen do not reject Chinese or American culture, this small singular image suggests; rather, they incorporate or select that which they appreciate in each culture, even with the touch of irony that satire here affords. This transformative tale, where these fractured stories are brought together, inspires an understanding of the feelings evoked by stereotyping. Beginning with depicting the most grotesque images, Yang develops a healing synthesis, one that evokes new images that encourage minorities to tell their stories and envision their own healing.

## *The Absolutely True Diary of a Part-Time Indian*

*The Absolutely True Diary of a Part-Time Indian* is also a healing story and creates a new kind of hero, one who also challenges male chauvinism and redefines the concept of community. The title alone suggests the irony of believing in the absolute truth of a diary—though it engages the reader in accepting the narrator's subjectivity. So, while Junior is "othered" in an already othered minority—he describes himself as atypical and freakish. Somehow, his self-deprecating humor, acknowledging, even exaggerating his flaws and weaknesses, establishes his authenticity and we serve as witness to his story. We laugh with him as he writes: "I ended up having forty-two teeth. The typical human has thirty-two, right? But I had forty-two. Ten more than usual. Ten more than normal. Ten teeth past human" (2). "With my big feet and pencil body, I looked like a capital *L* walking down the road ... I had seizures. At least two a week. So I was damaging my brain on a regular basis. But ... I was having those seizures because I *already* had brain damage, so ... whenever I had a seizure, I was *damaging my damage*" (3).

Humor underscores Alexie's entire novel, particularly in the post-Holden Caulfield engaging voice of Junior, the first-person narrator. He describes the constant harassment he endures: "One bully, Micah, made me beat up myself. Yes, he made me punch myself in the face three times. I am the only Indian in the history of the world who ever lost a fight *with himself.*" Self-deprecating humor, which is a familiar Alexie technique, also allows for deep ripping at the foundations of racism, while maintaining the gravity of such experiences. At the same time, he directly addresses poverty and the inability to feed one more mouth in the childhood tragedy of his dog dying of starvation. He says: "It sucks to be poor, and it sucks to feel that you somehow *deserve* to be poor ... Poverty doesn't give you strength or teach you lessons about perseverance. No, poverty only teaches you how to be poor" (13). His insights here provide encouragement for children who suffer with poverty to understand that they are not guilty or inferior to those who are more fortunate. His honesty about the effects of poverty not only allows other children insight into his condition, but also affords space in books for honest expression of other difficult things children live with.

Junior's sketches further illuminate his complex awareness of his family: his parents' dreams, of who they could have been with support; of his sister "Mary Runs Away," with her look of "tough and pretty at the same time"; and of his grandmother, his hero, who manages her life without stealing, without corruption, and with dignity. The discrepancy between what it means to be white and what it means to be Indian is depicted in his drawings and signal words. White is defined by words in squares like "a bright future," "positive role models," and "hope," while Indian is identified by "a vanishing past," "a family history of diabetes and cancer," and "bone-crushing reality" (57). The boy in the illustration is part-white and part-Indian, each detail of clothing matched, which illuminates the struggles of Junior as he enters the all-white Reardan High School.

One of the major challenges for Junior is to resolve this duality: his culture as an utter failure and white culture as singular and idealized. He needs to humanize the "other"—on both sides. Although his view of Indian culture is dismal, clearly there are aspects of his family he loves and respects—and there is his grandmother whose values he embraces. His sister, who hides in the basement for a good part of the book and then escapes to another Indian reservation to live in a trailer, was "Too Freaking Drunk to feel any pain when she Burned To Death" (205), he explains; but he learns to understand that she tried to find a place where she could "write some romance novel"—the only escape and self-assertive pursuit she can imagine. He also learns to acknowledge his parents' love for him, even though his father is an alcoholic in denial—to accept their limitations, the horrors of the reservation, and the strengths he has acquired from his culture. He needs to embrace his Indianness, just as he needs to leave behind the reservation, even his best friend Rowdy, though there is an interesting reconciliation at the end: Rowdy acknowledges, "You're an old-time nomad ... You're going to keep moving all over the world in search of food and water and grazing land. That's pretty cool ... Just make sure you send me post-cards, you asshole." And Junior replies, "From everywhere" (228).

At the all-white high school, Junior's friendship with Gordy, an intellectual like Junior, resists idealization. Gordy is selfish, pedantic—capable of only limited friendship. And with Junior's dream-girl, the popular Penelope, Alexie confronts the internalized racism of sexual attraction to the "other." Junior reports: "Penelope was serving the ball and I watched her like she was a work of art ... Her skin was pale white. Milky white. Cloud white. So she was all white on white on white, like the most perfect kind of vanilla dessert cake you've ever seen. I wanted to be her chocolate topping" (114). This perfect girl is bulimic and insecure, also kind, even courageous as she moves against the racism of her family and culture when she comes to care for Junior. She is humanized, as are other white characters—which does not deny the cruelty of the hardened racists, like her father, just as Mr. P, the white teacher who pushes Junior to leave the Reservation, is at once courageous and weak, even unappealing. But he warns, "You know that Rowdy's dad hits him, don't you? ... Rowdy is just going to get meaner and meaner ... You have to leave this reservation ... *forever*" (41–2).

Heroically, Junior learns to navigate his disability, reconcile his differences with himself and others, integrate positive aspects of both cultures along with his own talents, and to reconstruct identity in a new vision of community. He proclaims:

> I realized that I might be a lonely Indian boy, but I was not alone in my loneliness. There were millions of other Americans who had left their birthplaces in search of a dream. I realized that, sure, I was a Spokane Indian. I belonged to that tribe. But I also belonged to the tribe of American immigrants.

> And to the tribe of basketball players.
> And to the tribe of bookworms.
> And the tribe of cartoonists.
> And the tribe of chronic masturbators.
> And the tribe of teenage boys.
> And the tribe of small-town kids.
> And the tribe of Pacific Northwesterners.
> And the tribe of tortilla chips-and-salsa lovers.
> And the tribe of poverty.
> And the tribe of funeral-goers.
> And the tribe of beloved sons.
> And the tribe of boys who really missed their best friends (217).

Such a litany is inclusive—of ethnicities, of daily life choices and tastes, of the high and the low, the solemn and the comic, the sacred and the profane, an expression of the broad and complex imagination of an adolescent boy.

The novel ends with an intensely pastoral scene where Junior and Rowdy climb into the highest tree, "not the summit. But close enough to call it the summit," where they can see "from one end of the reservation to the other... our entire world," which "at that moment was green and golden and perfect"—Rowdy breaks "the spell" by farting. The sacredness of the pastoral fused with the scatological humor of teenage boys speaks again to the essential inclusivity of Alexie's novel. The final scene is a night pastoral of harmony; they are playing on the courts until dark, "until the moon was huge and golden and perfect in the dark sky" (228). And, we are told, they did not keep score. In this resistance to conventional male competition, Alexie challenges other aspects of chauvinism as well: Junior notes how "boys can hold hands until they turn nine" (218), and that "only after winning the champion-ship can men and boys get to cry and not get punched in the face" (196). After that their affection is suspect. Rowdy says, "We'll kick your asses next year … and you'll cry like the little faggot you are," but Junior understands: "Now that might just sound … homophobic … but I think it was also a little bit friendly … I was a happy faggot!" (197–8).

Alexie's humor—ironic, scatological, and hyperbolic—is familiar to read-ers of children's literature and, as Maria Nikolajeva points out, draws on Bakhtin's theory of Carnival and its "socially liberating, subversive … interro-gation of authorities" (10). Much of the post-Holden Caulfield voice of adoles-cent narratives, established earlier in the voice of Huckleberry Finn, ruptures the conventions of the world of the adolescent. It is he who sees through the inauthentic adults in his world, though the adolescent may, of course, exhibit his own limitations and pretentions.

## A Wish after Midnight

A new and refreshingly vibrant minority voice comes from Genna, Zetta Elliott's fifteen-year-old hero of *A Wish after Midnight* (2010). Elliott articu-lates her minority position:

> I am an immigrant. I grew up in a former British colony, dreaming of mag-ical wardrobes and secret gardens. Doors figured rather prominently in my imagination, and books were indeed windows into other worlds. They were not, however, much of a mirror for my young black female self. I learned early on that only white children had wonderful adventures in distant lands; only white children were magically transported through time and space; only white children found the buried key that unlocked their own private Eden … I had to develop the capacity *to dream myself into existence* (Zetta Elliott, The Writer's Page, "Decolonizing the Imagination").

The idea of "dreaming [oneself] into existence" is particularly significant in the literature of "others," minorities that have not seen themselves mirrored in their books. And, of course, children of all cultures can find their own imaginations broadened by diverse visions of childhood. New and unfamiliar perspectives offer to all children the courage to express their own imaginative visions.

Elliott published her essay in response to the dearth of books about children and youth of color. Although winning Lee & Low's New Voices Honor Award for *Bird*, her beautiful picture book, she had trouble publishing her many other books. Thus, she continues to publish a full range of books for children and youth as an indie author, a writer who comes from marginalized groups to publish her work independently, without the help of an agent or editor employed at a traditional publishing house.

*A Wish after Midnight*, her young adult speculative novel, features the sharp and feisty African American girl, Genna, who travels back in time to Civil War era–Brooklyn. This shift in time is jolting to us, her readers, but not more so than to Genna herself, whose shock, related through her senses, takes us with her. The moment is prepared for by the first quarter of the book, in which we meet her family, portrayed with all the complexities of the ghetto life of three burgeoning adolescents in a single-parent family. Making her way through her neighborhood is often harrowing for Genna, who is a good student, a thoughtful girl who wants to leave the ghetto and become a psychiatrist. The plot includes her budding relationship with her Rastafarian boyfriend, Judah, along with the family dramas. The novel is compelling as it portrays a diversity of black characters and cultures.

Genna's sanctuary, her place of beauty and peace, is the Brooklyn Botanical Gardens and the fountain where she wishes on pennies, and where she is thrown back in time. By the time this happens in the novel, we are thoroughly invested in her journey through Civil War–Brooklyn. Her narrow escape as a fugitive slave and the horrors of being black and female are vividly and historically presented with accuracy in Weeksville, the black community cited as "Brooklyn in Civil War" times.

To present fully formed characters is most important to Elliott's purpose. In a superb lecture in my Children's Literature seminar, Elliott used the metaphors mentioned earlier, suggested by Rudine Sims Bishop (1990), to describe three ways in which African American children might find their images in children's books: mirrors suggest the reflection where African American children do not find themselves in the overwhelming majority of children's books. Windows suggest the position of looking into the children's books at the white majority characters and their worlds. Finally, sliding glass doors suggest entry into a diverse world where they can participate and see themselves reflected. Elliott writes all her children's books from this cultural perspective.

As a time-travel novel, *A Wish after Midnight* portrays Genna as "an individual constructed through history, culture and circumstances" (McCallum, quoted in Stewart, 232). Robyn McCallum suggests that "displacing character (spatial, temporal, cultural, and ideational factors) can destabilize sense of identity [and] can undermine essentialist notions of selfhood" (in Stewart, 232–3). To make Genna real, for her to develop beyond essentialist portrayals of African American adolescent girls, Elliott establishes Genna as a complex character who goes through changes, some not so wide or dramatic, that lead to a subtle stabilizing of earlier ideas solidified and fleshed out in her time travel. For example, the act that propels her into running away is her mother's slap in her face, something that can occur in any domestic clash between adolescents and parents. However, when Genna tells the truth about her brother and the reason for his arrest, a truth that her mother is set on denying, Elliott situates the struggle in a particular culture with Genna's characteristic voice. Her mother's slap feels like a betrayal to this girl who tries so hard to be honest and fair. She says, "What I want to know is, why is Mama yelling at me? She's got one son locked up for dealing drugs. [Her sister] Toshi's about to drop out of school and she's gonna get herself in trouble if she don't stop switching her butt like that. I'm a straight A student. I help out at home, I'm working part-time so I can move us out of here, and Mama's yelling at *me*?" (43). As Genna leaves, she hears her mother crying "on the other side of the door." She says, "Part of me wants to go back inside and tell her everything's going to be alright. But another part of me is stinging, and I need someone to put their arms around *me* and tell *me* it's going to be alright" (71).

This is a sad and beautifully drawn moment of conflict, which becomes intensified in the world of 1863 Brooklyn. There, in the war-torn landscape of violence, racism, and poverty, Genna encounters life-threatening attacks by racist mobs. The parallel that Elliott constructs between the two worlds develops the concept of the construction of self through history. In her chosen epigraph, Elliott quotes Dionne Brand, "History is already seated in the chair in the empty room when one arrives." And Elliott demonstrates that the people Genna meets are formed by their race and class, in the chaos of 1863 Brooklyn, as we all are constructed in our contemporary culture.

Genna's early words about her sense of self feel naive compared to the way she views herself during and after her time travel. Introducing herself to her readers, she says, "I'm just plain, and dark, and too tall, and too smart, and too shy to talk to anybody. Except I'm not shy, really. I just don't fit in" (1). Elliott connects her family story with the racism and injustices of her contemporary world. Genna is acutely aware of the various cultures of black women. In contrast to her sister and the popular high school crowd of girls who do not seem particularly interested, she notes the group of nannies in the gardens who take care of white people's children, and she wonders: who's taking care of their children? She's aware of the separation of Blacks and Latinos from Asians and the distance between Black and White cultures. She says, "Whites might live near us, but they don't live with us." When her friend Mr. Christiansen talks about "the great melting pot," Genna says, "I want to ask Mr. Christiansen what happens to the folks who get left at the bottom of the pot" (28).

Genna tries to distinguish her views from those of her mother, who is embittered and suspicious not just of whites, but of her own beloved growing children as well. Genna is able to be more enlightened because she has been raised with the love her mother never had and because she lives in a more diverse and accepting world. While it is certainly a world of poverty and prejudice, she is able to distinguish the good and kind white people from the cruel and dismissive ones. And she asserts, "I want people to accept me for who I am, with my own ways, and my own ideas, and my own future that's separate from everything else that's going on" (38). She finds Judah, who most satisfyingly tells her, "I like you Genna. Because you're different" (48). But the painful barrier between her and her mother and her general displacement in her world make her fervently wish to go somewhere "different, another country, someplace far away," and when her wish is granted, it is brutal and shocking.

As in many time-travel novels, parallels are drawn between the characters of the contemporary world and those of the historical past. Her baby brother, Tyjuan, is particularly vivid; she describes his "warm baby breath" on her neck and says, "I don't know what I'd do without Tyjuan. He's the other half of my heart" (7). Tyjuan's place is drawn in juxtaposition with the white baby, Henry, who serves as an emotional touchstone for Genna in the home of the 1863

Brant family. She says, "I hold Henry close to me … I love Henry like I love Tyjuan. It doesn't matter that he's white and his mother's a crazy bitch. It doesn't even matter that they pay me to look after him. Henry belongs to me, same as Tyjuan" (138). Nannie, the black servant, is in many ways similar to Mama in her powerlessness to rise above her circumstances. She is warm, sharp, and loyal, however firmly rooted in Civil War consciousness. But with compassion, she tells Genna, "Let 'em go, honey. All the things they done to you don't matter no more … Let go the hurt so you can put somethin' good inside … You got to let go all that sorrow, 'cause it's too heavy a load to bear" (131).

In addition to her love for Henry, Genna is buoyed emotionally by being effective: she teaches Nannie to read and she serves as a nurse who goes on the hospital rounds with Dr. Brant. Of both worlds, however, Genna says, "Seems someone's always telling me about the things I can't do—because I'm not white, or because I'm a girl" (143). Teaching Nannie to read, then, becomes something she can do. There are other characters that parallel each other: her white and privileged friend Hannah and her poor white Irish friend Martha; a thin thread connects her romantic interest in Paul, a mixed-race boy, to Judah. All of this draws comparison to Genna's naiveté with her growing understanding of what lies beneath the surface of the Botanical Gardens and the racism of contemporary Brooklyn. And she has come to understand that there will be scars from this experience, that she's not the same person she was before her time travel. Genna has been seriously wounded physically and psychologically. She also sees that Judah, who has entered this world, has been tortured, and has escaped as a slave, is also different. His back to Africa wish is urgent and his bitterness hardened.

The characters, particularly Genna, are drawn with specificity, their voices strong and distinct. Judah feels most interestingly voiced in the succinct haiku he writes for Genna: in the first world he writes:

My love is the sun
and you are a blue lotus
turning toward me (61).
And from the time-travel world, he writes:
Freedom is more than
a bright star in the night sky
it's our destiny (217).

There are vivid descriptions that situate the landscapes. Of her entry into the night pastoral of the gardens, Genna says, "I swim through the shadows without making a sound" (73). "The moon slides out of the clouds like a hand pulled from a glove" (79). Establishing the landscape of the time-travel world, she says, "This ain't Brooklyn. They keep calling it that, but this just *can't* be Brooklyn. Bushes and trees and hills and fields ... Brooklyn in 1863 doesn't look like a city ... When we get downtown, closer to where the Brants live, things start to change. But the houses are still scattered all over the place. Brooklyn is like a mouth that's missing half its teeth" (122).

The history of slavery is captured and reimagined with vitality that makes it hard to ignore, deny, or push aside its horrific truths—those that extend to the present in Genna's acute observations are revealing of the past and present struggles of young black women.

As a stand-alone work, *A Wish after Midnight* succeeds in claiming a diversity of African American characters and cultures. This novel, however, is meant to be followed up and is, by the sequel, *The Door at the Crossroads*. So we are left at the end where Genna is just as mysteriously propelled back to her original world as she was taken away from her original family, and all the issues she ran from. We wait to discover Judah's journey, her place in his story, and to what extent the themes are resolved, how, and by whom. But even as a stand-alone novel, *A Wish after Midnight* represents a challenge to the field of children's literature; it encourages minority writers and all readers, children and young adults, to broaden the range of expression, and to offer more minority cultures a place in imaginative literature for children.

### *Fun Home*

Queer Studies has influenced some of our most experimental books for children and young adults in recent years. For example, *Fun Home*, Alison Bechdel's graphic autobiography, which won fame and success, not only as a graphic novel, but also as a Broadway play, extends the representation of diversity in the field of children's and youth literature. It is, as Hilary Chute and Marianne DeKoven contend, a work of "hybridity, [a] challenge to the structure of binary classification that opposes a set of terms, privileging one" (quoted in Tolmie, 81). Even as parts of Bechdel's self-exploration go beyond what I imagine young people will find accessible, some of which may even be deeply disturbing, *Fun Home* is a paradigm of complexity, portraying what it can mean to see shades and nuances. It offers what I believe is essential to the education of youth. As young people are presented often with black and white portraits of characters or plot solutions to problems, in the belief that they cannot handle subtlety, significant truths with which they may be struggling may be excluded. Imaginative thinking and creativity need to be part of their education. With imaginative thinking that moves to the edges, beyond the boundaries of the known into unfamiliar territory, an exciting though at times frightening place, the reader is encouraged to see possible alternatives as normative.

The graphic novel is in itself a hybrid form that "opens up numerous possibilities for dialogue" between visual and verbal narratives. And the subtitle, "A Family Tragicomic," reinforces the concept of paradox. It establishes that the tragic and comic lie within the intimate domains of family. This seems so logical and yet the extremes of tragic and comic are often set apart. Bechdel presents her tragicomic story by acknowledging the ultimate subjectivity—that not even she knows the truth of her own story. She says, "How did I know that the things I was writing were absolutely, objectively true? All I could speak for was my own perceptions, and perhaps not even those. My simple, declarative sentences began to strike me as hubristic at best, utter lies at worst" (141). By acknowledging the subjective nature of her truth, paradoxically she asserts the truth of her truths, plural and contradictory though they may seem, and in fact may be. Even discovering the range of her truths is a process.

As she notes the signs of the gaps and her lies in her diaries, she depicts one's own relationship with the self as fluid and unsteady, accessible in fragments and at various times, depending on what she is ready to know and to what extent she can hold onto the pieces of truth. She tells her story in nonlinear patterns, circling back and forth into the plot of her father's suicide and her own coming-out story, which are at times conflated. It is not even clear that her father's death was a suicide, though we are left to think that she believes that it was. And at times her own story is the background to her father's story—the discovery of his own homosexuality, primarily, so that it is impossible to tell her narrative without featuring his story—as is often the truth of a family history. In his overwhelming narcissism, her father takes center stage so often that her own coming-out announcement is overshadowed by the announcement of his affairs with other men and by his death. About her coming out, she says:

> I'd been upstaged, demoted from a protagonist in my own drama to comic relief in my parents' tragedy ... I had imagined my confession as an emancipation from my parents, but instead I was pulled back into their orbit. And with my father's death following so hard on the heels of this doleful coming-out party, I could not help but assume a cause-and-effect relationship (59).

One's story is never just one's own. Especially during adolescence, it is difficult to separate the narratives of individual family members. Her father is the artist in her mythic litany; he is Daedalus and she is Icarus, doomed to fall into the sea on the wings he built. However, she is also a verbal and visual artist, the creator of *Fun Home*. While her father creates beautiful stages, his landscapes with his "embellishment ... [are] lies ... his skillful artifice not to make things, but to make things appear to be what they were not" (16). Even his children serve as "the air of authenticity" to his art, "a sort of still life with children" (13). And Bechdel presents his death as "possibly his consummate artifice, his masterstroke" (27) to hide his suicide at the same time as he leaves hints around the house that reveal it.

Bechdel characterizes her process as a search for lost time, which she sees as an analogue to Marcel Proust's *A la Recerche du Temps Perdu*. With adolescence often comes the young person's search for the past, a family history that helps her to understand how she came to be who she is struggling to be, or struggling not to be. Several other literary works are also interwoven into her story as she remembers those books that became part of her imagination. She identifies strongly with different fictional characters: literary (Proust's, F. Scott Fitzgerald's), children's literature (A. A. Milne's, Roald Dahl's), and pulp works like *The Well of Loneliness* and other Lesbian fiction and essays. High and low cultures are integrally part of the story.

Bechdel writes and draws *Fun Home* with her particular way of "rememorying"—what Jane Tolmie calls "the deliberate reconstruction of memory to voice fixed categories" (77). Of course, she is aware of the irony that remembering and representing that process does not bring back the lost

**Figure 3** "He appeared to be an ideal husband." From *Fun Home A Family Tragicomic* by Alison Bechdel. Copyright © 2006 by Alison Bechdel. Reprinted by permission of Houghton Mifflin Harcourt.

time of her childhood. But this is a significant part of her search. Her sophistication, like her many allusions to complex adult literary texts, might be lost on young adult readers. Nonetheless, her visual representations of her story and the discovery of her own sexuality are engaging in ways both hilarious and serious. Youth may identify with her transgressive thoughts and her rebellion against her father's ornateness. The comic book aspects and the coming of age story may be especially liberating for those lesbian, gay, bisexual, transgender, questioning young people who are looking to see their story represented. As a beautifully drawn and powerful graphic memoir, *Fun Home* was nominated for several awards, including the National Book Critics Circle Award in the memoir/autobiography category among many others. It has also incurred the wrath of conservatives on religious grounds. However, it is a noteworthy tribute to diversity. Coming out is clearly the focus of this memoir, along with the dangers of *not* coming out that shaped the father's life. And it stands as a dramatic challenge to conventional gender roles.

# 5

# Reimagining Fear and Trauma

Many years ago, I was riding to the ocean in California with my goddaugh-ter, who was seven at the time. She was telling me about her fear of the waves. I saw from her wide eyes and serious face just how overwhelming the ocean was for her. I heard it in her voice, as she asked, "I think people should face their fears, don't you?" I was amazed at this wonderful child who had lost her mother to suicide three years earlier. I most heartily agreed. I said, "Let's stand at the shore and dig our feet into the sand, and then the waves can't hurt us"—which is what we did.

Also years ago, I was teaching a class in which we were using recurring dreams as a basis for writing. One student talked about her dream of being chased and the terror she experienced almost nightly. The class was riveted and clamored for a "solution." They asked, "Who are you running from?" The student had no idea. As a class, we came up with this: "Next time you have this dream, turn and face him/her/it and ask, 'Who are you?'" Acting on this idea of lucid dreaming, the student did this, and she did not have the dream again—at least not that summer.

Fears are an everyday and important part of our lives and stories. Whether they are real fears or fantasy monsters, they suggest the importance of talking about them and finding concrete ways of responding, especially for children. Obviously, some fears are difficult to pin down as they shift in shape and inten-sity and persist. Literature provides a way of approaching them at a safe distance.

Maurice Sendak pointed out years ago, in response to the furor his "mon-sters" created among some parents and many librarians, that it is crucial not to pretty up the witch so that her power is denied. If so, the child may believe that when he meets the monster in his dreams, that he is alone in his fear, that there is something wrong with *him*. To alleviate fear, it has to be presented in its intensity so that it can be recognized and confronted, but at a more comfortable distance. In his introduction to *Outfoxing Fear: Folktales from around the World* (2006), Jack Zipes asserts that "it is the tyranny of fear that [the editor] wants to 'outfox'" (xix). He affirms that folktales not only explore the most frightening aspect of fear, its unknown-ness, but also "unmask it" (xxii).

Perhaps the courage to imagine or reimagine is most needed for those who have had trauma in their young lives. Imagining can be tricky, a double-edged sword. On the one hand, the imagination is often exactly what saves the young person, providing an escape from or a safe space set off from the painful traumatic scene. In severe cases, dissociation may occur, as in reported cases of multiple personality or dissociative identity disorder—now recognized as an imaginative tool for survival.

One of the difficulties of reverting to the imagination as a cure or helpful tool for terror was revealed to me when, as a young person, I read Joanne Greenberg's semiautobiographical novel, *I Never Promised You a Rose Garden* (1964), the fictionalized story of a traumatized girl. Her imaginary world, the safe place she created, becomes dangerous and threatening as her trauma penetrates that world. The very creatures that she created to support her ultimately betray her in mocking tones familiar from her trauma. The imagination can be treacherous, and children's literature can address this paradoxical process of imagining for the child reader.

## Bearing witness

Reading stories about trauma may offer the child hope, a recognition that this terrible thing has happened to others and that they have survived. A story in which a character becomes a witness to the pain of the traumatized young person and the journey where the child learns again how to trust can be illuminating and reassuring. Storytelling itself, a construction of teller and listener, offers a way of alleviating the loneliness of trauma. Having a witness to the experience, whether that means sharing it with a friend, parent, or other adult, or reading about it, can lessen its hold on the victim. Even speaking the story of the trauma helps to break the cycle repeatedly spinning itself out in the conscious or unconscious. The reader bears witness.

Of utmost importance is the battle against isolation and shame that often accompanies trauma, which may be mollified by reading similar stories. Shame and guilt are painfully woven into the abuse—the victimizing of victims—the idea that somehow this awful thing has happened because it is the fault of the victim, which is part of the silencing and coercion of victimizing. Leslie Marmon Silko, writing from her Laguna culture, urges, in the face of trauma, not to withdraw. She says:

> The stories are always bringing us together ... "Don't go away, don't isolate yourself, but come here, because we have all had these kinds of experiences." And so there is this constant pulling together to resist the tendency to run or hide or separate oneself during a traumatic emotional experience. This separation not only endangers the group but the individual as well— one does not recover by oneself" (86).

Here the significance of community is paramount—there is not just a single witness, but a protective circle of witnesses.

Trauma disrupts coherence; creating narrative restores it. Judith Lewis Herman, in her pivotal work, *Trauma and Recovery* (1992), claims that the goal of treatment for the trauma survivor is to "speak the unspeakable." She emphasizes the importance of taking the shattered, incoherent pieces of the trauma and deliberately, painstakingly weaving them into a cohesive narrative. She provides evidence to suggest that traumatic memories are neurochemically stored in a different way from traditional narrative memory, and that those with post-traumatic stress disorder (PTSD) are hardwired and chemically coded to reexperience trauma when triggered. At the time she wrote the work, evidence-based research on PTSD was in its early stages, but her words about "speaking the unspeakable" remain startlingly prescient.

## Art, creativity, and agency

Storytelling also can alter and transform experience where it can provide a holding environment that contains the trauma. Writing one's own story may serve as a self-witness. As an object, the story is separate from the writer, removed from ugly origins, possibly lifted into an aesthetic place, though here, as always, the horror needs to be represented in some authentic way, not trivialized, oversimplified, or otherwise weakened and made unrecognizable, even to the unconscious. Doing something creative with the feelings evoked offers the young person agency, something to do, to read about a transformation as an alternative to feeling overwhelmed, wiped out, and further traumatized. As healing may take time, creating a story, drawing, or other art form suggests ways of acknowledging and containing it. It offers a meaningfulness to the experience—not that *it* was beautiful or meaningful, but that the expression of such experience can be transformative and aesthetically satisfying. The process of healing involves a gradual movement of incorporation: details from the moment-to-moment movement through the day, unconscious mostly, in which images of the trauma come into contact with everyday images. This allows for the wound to become integrated, slowly, as slowly as necessary. For children this integration is especially important. Part of the trauma will persist into adulthood, perhaps through adulthood. Psychologists and therapists seem to agree that creative expression for children can transform trauma and may prevent an emotional and intellectual shutdown.[1]

## Fear and denial

Often for children the most frightening thing about fear is its denial in the family and in the general culture. This can isolate the young person and further evoke shame along with fear. In Neil Gaiman's *The Wolves in the Walls*, for example, the child Lucy's insistence that there are wolves in the walls is denied by her mother, father, and brother. The family is finally forced to acknowledge the truth of Lucy's fears, when they see the wolves romping through their house. They witness the childish and anarchic behavior of the wolves through the holes in the eyes of the children's paintings on the wall—in other words, through the eyes of a child. Lucy is vindicated. Further, the wolves are revealed as childish rather than frightening; in fact, they are frightened of the people as they chant, "The people have come out of the walls." Finally, when Lucy tells her witness pig-puppet that she now hears elephants in the walls, he assures her that her family will learn the truth of that sooner or later. It is not her responsibility to warn them—particularly as it is unlikely that she will be believed. Interestingly, Gaiman's ending here does not leave Lucy quite so vulnerable as she was originally. Even without her family's concurrence, she seems more sure of herself. Dave McKean's illustrations match the ways in which Gaiman's story hovers on the edge of realistic with distorted and eccentric images, as with most of his stories, asserting a dark but playful landscape.

In a more realistic mode, Maya Angelou's written text for the book *Life Doesn't Frighten Me* articulates the very real fears of many children as they play on the streets—in such daily contact with threats of bullying, violence, and drugs that they often have to deny them. At the same time they are clearly aware of them. Here they are beautifully, frighteningly imagined in Jean-Michel Basquiat's paintings that accompany each of Angelou's claims that she is not frightened. She repeatedly says, "Life doesn't frighten me." The incantation allows for that paradoxical experience—acknowledging the frightening images as well as denying them. The images are also abstracted so that while streets and characters are recognizable, their shapes heighten and suggest rather than clearly delineate. This also allows space for acknowledging the fear while defending against it. Encouraging such a paradox that children often find hard to live with—adults clearly do as well—can enable creative expression. Such a picture book for young children can lessen the fear that something is wrong with the individual child for having these complicated feelings. Here Maya Angelou can speak the lines that accommodate familiar fears; however, Basquiat's images remind the reader that his daily experiences may not need to be verbally acknowledged. They are acknowledged but contained in images. Without dispelling the very real fears—an impossible task really—the words that Maya Angelou writes in response provide the child with strength and hope. The doublespeak of Angelou's words and Basquiat's accompanying pictures articulates and dramatizes Judith Herman's theory, where she claims, "The conflict between the will to deny horrible events and the will to proclaim them aloud is the central dialectic of psychological trauma."

## The role of nature in healing from sexual trauma

It is not surprising that healing from the violence of rape is connected in art and literature with images of nature. Recovery can reimagine a time when childhood was safe, or when the world felt more natural. Andrew V. Ettin tells us that pastoral images "link us to our earliest, purest, most natural condition, and to the protected ... way of life that we imagine we remember from our own childhood" (45). Pastoral implies longing: the loss of something, perhaps from childhood. Wordsworth understood that the natural world, experienced by the infant with the body of the mother, is the earliest and most primal, and that the natural world, experienced in the body of the world, becomes a holding environment. But for children who were not raised in nature, the pastoral may be held in the imagination, in language and image, so that what was disrupted, denied, rejected, and destroyed of the natural world and of natural connection can be reimagined. Two recent books for young people imagine this green world as the healer in situations of rape—one of father-daughter incest and one of a thirteen-year-old girl by an older teenage boy. Clearly they are very different and are handled differently, but both involve betrayal, serious and damaging. Lois Kuznets tells us that "pastoral literature traditionally demonstrates the human need for the healing powers of the simple, rural, or rustic life ... Urban novels [as well as suburban novels] bur[y] the pastoral imagery deep within the psyches of the protagonists ... Pastoral imagery emerges from the individual psyche in dream and fantasy ... in exaggerated and distorted forms" (156–7).

### *The Tale of One Bad Rat*

This is certainly true of *The Tale of One Bad Rat* (1994), a graphic novel by Bryan Talbot, about Helen Potter, a runaway teen who has been incested by her father from the time she was a young girl. The pastoral imagery comes to her through the Beatrix Potter books given to her as a young child. Her name connects her to Beatrix Potter with whom she identifies as a victim of parental abuse and cloistering. Talbot writes in the afterword, using as his main source Margaret Lane's *The Tale of Beatrix Potter*, that "Potter was an oppressed child ... starved of affection, not sent to school ... a virtual prisoner on the third story of the family house ... [that] as a young girl, she was 'unnaturally lonely' ... her only true friends ... the small animals she accumulated, studied, and drew." Linda Lear contradicts this in her 2007 book, *Beatrix Potter: A Life in Nature*, saying, "There was nothing to obstruct the view from the third-floor nursery window ... nor was there anything to restrict the physical or intellectual freedom of the little girl who occupied the nursery ... In terms of exposure to the world of art, literature, science, fantasy, travel and natural history [Potter's childhood] was a rich and enviable one" (25). About school Potter wrote, "Thank goodness, my education was neglected ... I have always found my own pleasure in nature and books" (42). "Nature, she knew, was not immutable, but nature as revealed in the Lake District, and etched in her mind's eye, was the closest to everlasting as she could come" (7–8). Whatever the truth of that childhood, Helen becomes focused on the Lake Country as a pastoral medallion, an icon of peace and safety. In this story of Helen's escape into the horrors of homelessness, where she is vulnerable to all kinds of predators, her main source of comfort comes from her pet rat, which she has rescued from a lab at school. The rat itself becomes a strangely distorted image of pastoral. She identifies with the rat in critical ways: like Beatrix Potter's farm animals, the rat is a small creature, preyed on by larger ones; but here the predators are humans, the most vicious of all. Helen deeply identifies with the rat's victimization: the rat is imprisoned, caged by the school; Helen is trapped in the brutality of her parents. After she moves into a grim squatters' flat of runaway teen boys, her rat is killed by a cat. So Helen leaves for town, always accosted along the way. The rat, her alter ego, is now depicted as large in her imagination, where it remains until she is actually in Beatrix Potter territory, the beautiful Lake Country of the Romantics who understood the healing nature of pastoral. As Wordsworth wrote about the Lake Country in "Tintern Abbey":

> Oft, in lonely rooms, and 'mid the din
> Of towns and cities, I have owed to them,
> In hours of weariness, sensations sweet,
> Felt in the blood, and felt along the heart;
> And passing even into my purer mind,
> With tranquil restoration (ll. 26–31).

It is the tranquility Wordsworth seeks in memories of the pastoral Lake Country, when overwhelmed with the busyness of "towns and cities." It will be restorative to Helen, as it was to Beatrix Potter, as her quest to survive her trauma takes her there.

In the foreword to *The Tale of One Bad Rat*, Stephen Gallagher writes, "Rats, like wolves, have been forced to carry a certain burden of the human imagination." He connects this demonizing with child abuse, when he writes:

So how do you handle it, then, if you happen to be brought up in an atmosphere of certainty that the demon is *you?* And children, of course, believe what they're told … because they simply haven't the data to know otherwise. Make them think that they're guilty, and they'll wonder what it was they did. Let them think they're worthless, and they'll assume it must be … true… Bad rats, all. When a soul's been starved in this way and kept in darkness, its only hope lies in making its own journey out of there. And when the darkness is your entire world, even starting such a journey requires a faith in yourself that can be very hard to muster.

The clarity and passion of this statement is addressed to young readers and could encourage such a journey. This book describes in detail the process of Helen's quest to find faith in herself—how she comes to trust enough to break the silence of her abuse that she's held all these years. Not until Helen establishes safe boundaries with a supportive couple, who serve as an alternative family, is she strong enough to confront her father. At this time she believes she needs to say goodbye to the rat, her imagined companion, while she works back to the actual source of the trauma. Predictably, when she does confront her father, his defense moves from denial to self-pity, pointing the blame elsewhere (to his unemployment, his failing marriage, even to Helen herself)—and, predictably, such a person refuses/is incapable of seeing his child as a separate person with an integrity of her own. The mother's jealousy and emotional cruelty has supported him all along.

However, Helen has found a new home. In the mountains of Lake Country, in the light of the pastoral landscape, Helen shrieks out her pain and feels freer of the dark oppressive "visions" of her father that have followed her everywhere. Here, most significantly, the rat reappears as her muse, in a profound realization that she can transform that darkness into a source of inner light. She says of the night pastoral, lit by the stars, "We're so fragile … so precious … eh, Rat?" She begins to believe that her dark and frightening "visions" are not a curse but a talent, "a blessing really." This is an extremely important aspect of healing from abuse, the belief that something positive can be salvaged from all that pain. Like Beatrix Potter, who called her talent "the seeing eye," Helen comes to understand that her talent for "seeing" with the inner eye allows for all parts of the self: the Rat as her muse, her artistic power *and* her fragility, that which she must protect and feed—metaphorically, if no longer literally. And by internalizing Beatrix Potter, she creates her own story of *The Tale of One Bad Rat*, with the Rat as hero, closely identified with but also separate and transformed from a former self.

Kuznets reminds us that the pastoral plot is a story of "retreat and regrowth" (158). Talbot's story, *The Tale of One Bad Rat*, begins with a full-page image of gorgeous Beatrix Potter country, and appears as a retreat into fantasy. He writes, "Once upon a time, there was a very bad rat." Set against the realistic harsh urban landscape of Helen's homelessness and her pet, a figure of fear and horror to passersby, the story begins in two distinct modes. There is no attempt to conflate realistic and fantastic elements, as often occurs in fairy tale literature. We know when the rat is "real" and when he is part of her imagination. The fantastic is depicted as dream sequences—nightmares of the most grotesque kind where Helen envisions her suicide at the train station and when she imagines herself naked running from an attack cat, huge and black with fangs against a landscape of cave, rocks, and lightning. The images convey her terror, but Helen is not confused. She knows where she is and when her companion is alive, when he is dead, and when he is imagined. When she is hungry and without money, she addresses the fantasy rat, "Good job you don't need anything to eat." Here the fairy-tale tag "once upon a time" signals the distance between the images that continue to haunt her, and the pastoral she dreams of—where her healing eventually takes place.

Helen's own story, the tale within the tale, is a synthesis of her real abuse transformed into art, her story illustrated with the soft colors of Potter's tales. She speaks to her abuse when she adds to Talbot's beginning, "Once upon a time, there was a very bad rat. Her name was Helen Barnrat. She knew that she must be a very bad rat because everybody told her so." At the end of her story, she understands that since she is no longer terrified of her father, who appears as the aggressive and brutal cat, "that she was a very good rat indeed." And at the end of Talbot's tale, Helen is depicted as having achieved the harmony she sought in nature. She has integrated the lessons of Beatrix Potter, the rat, and the Lake Country, as she is seen in the mountainous landscape, pad in hand, painting with the rat positioned, large and muse-like, behind her.

*The Tale of One Bad Rat* speaks, as all graphic novels do, through both image and word, which layer the text. Here the literal plot level of the novel is interrupted by her past, presented vividly with immediacy of the image. We are there with her. No need to announce a time shift, as we see her child-like hair, her girlish dress, her vulnerability juxtaposed against her father's leering and her mother's snarling, streaked drunken face; we recognize the urgency of the pastoral of her imagination with which the story begins—foreshadowing the future integration of this landscape and her healing. And the entire story is framed by the realistic format of the informational book in its direct address to the readers. The foreword explains how children incorporate abuse into a dangerously negative self-image of blame and shame; the afterword describes the genesis of the story, the creative process, the real children who served as models, and, finally, where to go for help—all aspects necessary to telling this complex and chilling tale of survival.

## Speak

The title of Laurie Halse Anderson's novel, *Speak* (1999), also suggests a journey—from silence to healing where the heroine speaks out, which involves a variety of ways of speaking along the way to recovering words. This includes speaking through writing, her artwork, and internal dialogue, to help the reader understand the process of recovery through the imagination. Elizabeth Rose Gruner notes that only after writing the story of her rape can Melinda speak (12). *Speak* is teenage Melinda's tale of survival. It begins, "It is my first morning of high school. I have seven notebooks, a skirt I hate, and a stomachache," establishing Melinda's strong voice and her pain. For the most part, her voice is internal, withheld from the outside world. She tells us that she is "the only person sitting alone" (3), her isolation due to the story of her trauma, which unravels slowly throughout the novel. Melinda has stopped speaking because in addition to her traumatic rape, when she spoke out she was not believed, and, even worse, was shunned by her peers for calling the police, which resulted in secrets revealed to the parents of the teenagers at a party. She had welcomed the attention by this popular boy at the party, but was unprepared for his violence when he lures her out behind a tree. When she called 911, and the police came and broke up the party, Melina ran home, further unprepared to talk about what had happened, leaving the enraged teenagers bewildered by this interruption to their party. They get into trouble with their parents, they find out that it was she who called the police, and she is shunned by all except one new girl, an outcast like herself, who, in her desire for acceptance, promptly betrays her. From a girl with many friends, happily integrated in her school's young teen culture, she virtually becomes a pariah. It does not take much imagination to understand the dissociation, the silence into which Melinda retreats. "I am Outcast" (4), she tells us. She feels further betrayed by a school full of "lies they tell you," which she lists, such as "1. We are here to help you ... [through to] 10. These will be the years you look back on fondly" (6); she concludes, "It is easier not to say anything" (9).

In an interview that appears at the end of the book, Anderson describes herself as "like Melinda," that she "found a piece of Melinda's voice in my own high school experience." She mentions the absurdities of high school culture. She says, "When I was a teenager I dreamed about escaping. I was lucky. I succeeded." But nothing about rape. She claims that "*Speak* is not just a book about rape. *Speak* is a book about depression." She also mentions, "I have heard from hundreds and hundreds of survivors of sexual assault, male as well as female." She has recommended hotlines and where to go for help. When asked, "How did the character of Melinda come to you?" she says, "In a nightmare ... I could hear a girl sobbing ... The crying girl was in my head ... When I first started writing, I had no idea what had happened to her. It wasn't until she was comfortable with me that she let her secret out." Powerful, intimate—*Speak* is a portrait that invites a close look at high school culture and its deep psychological effects on sensitive teens.

Therefore, *Speak* is organized around marking periods, rather than the four seasons, a more natural order of life as this book is about the violent interruption of the natural. Here school is the dominant ordering structure, where peer culture and chaos are everywhere, where nothing is stable, including your own body and self-image. Melinda describes her school culture as "no-cultural," noting how at holiday time, "The orchestra plays an unrecognizable tune ... The school board won't let them perform Christmas carols or Hanukkah songs or Kwanza tunes. Instead of multicultural, we have no-cultural" (69). No-cultural captures Melinda's world at home as well. About her parents she says, "My family has a good system. We communicate with notes on the kitchen counter. I write when I need school supplies or a ride to the mall. They write what time they'll be home from work and if I should thaw anything. What else is there to say?" (14). She says, sizing up herself and her family, "I bet they'd be divorced by now if I hadn't been born. I'm sure I was a huge disappointment. I'm not pretty or smart or athletic. I'm just like them—an ordinary drone dressed in secrets and lies" (70). Her low self-esteem, generated, at least in part, by a lack of family nurturing and support, helps to keep her silenced about the rape.

As her grades drop, her parents respond, as Melinda captures them in dialogue:

> **Mom**: [creepy smile] "Thought you could put one over on us, did you
>              Melinda? …
> **Dad**: [Bangs table, silverware jumps] "Cut the crap. She knows what's up.…
>              You get those grades up or your name is mud" (36).

When Melinda goes so far as to scrape the inside of her wrist till it bleeds, her mother, noting the wrist, says, "I don't have time for this, Melinda."

> She says suicide is for cowards … Tough love. Sour sugar. Barbed velvet.
> Silent talk … She has figured out that I don't say too much. It bugs her (88).

Melinda's internal voice—defensive and sarcastic—eloquently expresses her sense of alienation. She says, "I just thought of a great theory that explains everything. When I went to that party, I was abducted by aliens. They have created a fake Earth and fake high school to study me and my reactions" (42), articulating the "fake"ness of the way everything feels since the trauma.

Only Mr. Freeman, her art teacher, seems to notice her pain and is able to help her. The combination of his interest in her and in her imagination works through a pastoral scene of a tree that indicates her healing process. Although she is at first dismissive of him, describing him as a "big ugly grasshopper," his words are prescient. He says, "Welcome to the only class that will teach you how to survive" (10). In his challenging initial assignment, each student selects a word from a globe—one object from the world on which to focus. He says, "You will spend the rest of the year learning how to turn that object into a piece of art. You will sculpt it. You will sketch it, papier-maché it, carve it … By the end of the year, you must figure out how to make your object … speak to every person who looks at it" (12).

Melinda picks the word "tree," but she complains that it is "too easy. I learned how to draw a tree in second grade" (12). Perhaps, but this journey involves relearning, or learning for real, creating her own version of pastoral. Her healing emerges as she works hard in art class, trusting Mr. Freeman, and, finally, revisiting the tree under which the rape took place, before she is able to speak about the truth of the crime.

Healing here involves a kind of hitting bottom. Deciding that her "room belongs to an alien … a postcard of who I was in the fifth grade" (15), Melinda retreats into an underground room in the basement of her school to rebuild her life, like Maya Angelou, one of her heroes, did after her rape—and there in the darkness she decorates it with her paintings and drawings, and with her posters of the voices that speak for her. She says, "There is a beast in my gut, I can hear it scraping away at the inside of my ribs. Even if I dump the memory, it will stay with me … My closet is a good thing, a quiet place that helps me hold these thoughts inside my head where no one can hear them" (51). She's been "painting watercolors of trees that have been hit by lightning … One picture is so dark you can barely see the tree at all" (30–1). The evolution of the tree painting parallels the darkness she must enter and the various stages of repair.

Melinda's creative work becomes more elaborate and more revealing as Mr. Freeman encourages and approves: she constructs a sculpture out of the bones of the turkey from the failed family Thanksgiving dinner, "a half-melted palm tree from a Lego set … I pop the head off a Barbie doll and set it inside the turkey's body (63), creating art out of the bones of her life, each object suggestive of family and cultural dysfunction.

Melinda's strength also comes from learning about art, in particular, reading about Cubism: "Seeing beyond what's on the surface … Dicing bodies and tables and guitars as if they were celery sticks, and rearranging them so that you have to really see them" (119). Her tree is starting to evolve, and the combination of pastoral and art—the artifice of pastoral—imaginatively recasts the distortion and barrenness of the world from which she has retreated. Little by little, the natural world suggests her healing, as it repairs itself. "Seeds are inefficient," Melinda says. "If the seed is planted too deep, it doesn't warm up at the right time. Plant it too close to the surface and a crow eats it. Too much rain and the seed molds. Not enough rain and it never gets started. Even if it does manage to sprout, it can be choked by weeds … It's amazing anything survives" (126). The metaphor extends to leaves and finally to the tree. Mr. Freeman advises: "This looks like a tree, but it is an average, ordinary, everyday, boring tree. Breathe life into it.

Make it bend—trees are flexible, so they don't snap. Scar it, give it a twisted branch—perfect trees don't exist. Nothing is perfect. Flaws are interesting. Be the tree" (153). And she is—flawed, scarred, twisted, and needs to accept, even embrace these traits. To make something beautiful out of all her pain.

Healing often requires reconnection, finding an early image of beauty, of the natural, a memory that can serve as a medallion of hope. In this novel, this memory surfaces in biology class, her other relatively safe environment, when she is moved through the smell of apples to remember one lovely childhood moment:

> One time when I was little, my parents took me to an orchard. Daddy set me high in an apple tree. It was like falling up into a storybook, yummy and red and leaf and the branch not shaking a bit. Bees bumbled through the air, so stuffed with apple they couldn't be bothered to sting me. The sun warmed my hair, and a wind pushed my mother into my father's arms, and all the apple-picking parents and children smiled for a long, long minute (66).

This moment, itself an emblem of timelessness, suggests the ways in which pastoral alters time and space, conflates with memory, and becomes an icon of healing. Nature here is benign. The bees slow down and are harmless, the branch ceases to shake, Melinda falls up into a storybook, parents embrace. It also foreshadows the restoration of family connectedness.

Juxtaposed against the stillness of memory, time rushes ahead in the chronology of the plot, as the rapist, IT, pursues and terrorizes her: "'Freshmeat.' That's what IT whispers. IT found me again. I thought I could ignore IT ... I can smell him over the noise of the metal shop" (86). At the end of the book, when IT attacks her in her underground dwelling, she slams the wood base of her turkey-bone sculpture against the poster of Maya Angelou, which crunches, as "IT breathes like a dragon. ITs hand leaves my throat, attacks my body. I hit the wood against the post, and the mirror under it, again. Shards of glass slip down the wall and into the sink ... I reach in and wrap my fingers around a triangle of glass. I hold it to Andy Evans's neck" (195). She names him, defeats him, and if this scene is not totally believable, it is rendered in such vivid smells and textures that, in the long run, it convinces. As the voices of the women come together—from Oprah, "You can't keep this inside forever," from Sally Jessy (talk show host) "listen to me, listen to me, listen to me. It was not your fault" (164)—the reader finally can breathe a sigh of relief.

And now the internal work. In order to reconstruct her identity, Melinda struggles with the two Melinda voices she has incorporated at war inside her head, neither accepting nor supportive. She wonders, "If I kick both of them out of my head, who would be left?" (132). An important question. A new voice needs to sprout out of the decay, like the seeds, like the leaves that are "suffocating the bushes ... They look harmless and dry on top, but under that top layer they're wet and slimy," which she rakes so that "pale green shoots of something alive [that] have been struggling under the leaves ... straighten to face the sun. [She says,] I swear I can see them grow" (166). And now her father acknowledges that she has done "a lot of work," as they stand together "staring at the little baby plants trying to grow in the shade of the house-eating bushes" (167). Melinda says, "The time has come to arm-wrestle some demons" (180). All this propels her to return to the scene of trauma, the tree under which the rape occurred, where she says, "I crouch by the trunk, my fingers stroking the bark, seeking a Braille code, a clue, a message on how to come back to life ... I have survived ... Is there a chain saw of the soul, an ax I can take to my memories or fears?" She becomes "the seed I will care for" (189). She does not deny that "IT happened. There is no avoiding it, no forgetting. No running away, or flying, or burying, or hiding. Andy Evans raped me in August when I was drunk and too young to know what was happening. It wasn't my fault ... And I'm not going to let it kill me. I can grow" (198).

She notes, "My tree [in the backyard] is definitely breathing; little shallow breaths like it just shot up through the ground this morning ... The bark is rough ... One of the lower branches is sick." (196). About her drawing, she says, "My tree needs something" (197). She decides to draw birds, "little dashes of color on paper ... without thinking—flight, flight, feather, wing" (197). Images of pastoral transform into words as she tells Mr. Freeman her story. "The tears dissolve the last block of ice in my throat. I feel the frozen stillness melt down through the inside of me, dripping shards of ice that vanish in a puddle of sunlight on the stained floor. Words float up" (198).

The plots come together: what was fractured is restored and synthesized so that the original landscape of pastoral damage from trauma, the pruned tree in her backyard, and her art project, the tree of her imagination, are brought into a kind of harmony. This could be Blake's higher innocence, that which grows from the loss of innocence into experience—new growth, certainly new life for Melinda as she repairs broken friendships and will again join the high school community—without denying its absurdities, but with the full power of speech. As Gruner points out, the book ends with Melinda saying to Mr. Freeman, "Let me tell you about it" (16).

Both *Speak* and *The Tale of One Bad Rat* depict the way pastoral can retain the healing image in the imagination as a beacon of hope until the wound can be healed and the sufferer has integrated the trauma and is ready for the story to resurface. Readiness also depends on one encouraging adult who can serve in place of inept or cruel parents for the young person. In classical hero stories, the helpers who assist the young hero in his quest are often Hermes, who serves as the connectors of gods and men, and Athena, a source of wisdom. In contemporary realistic literature for young people, the helper is transformed into an ordinary person. For Helen Potter the new family, the McGregors, she finds in the Lake Country, offer to serve as support when confronting her father—a modern-day connector of the innocent to the forces of destruction. Ruth McGregor, the figure of wisdom here, urges Helen to seek solace and affirmation in books about victimization and abuse. For Melinda, Mr. Freeman, her art teacher, urges creativity, honesty, and the courage to reimagine her trauma.

## The trauma of death, the ultimate loss

The finality of death is for children, even for us, almost unimaginable—that a central person in your life will not ever be in your life again, that you can never see this person again, and that, in fact, this will happen to you as well at some point is inevitable, and devastating. My grandson, Max, at four, asked my son, Jonathan, if he was going to die. Jonathan answered, "Yes, but not for a very very long time." This was followed by Max's next question, "Will I die?" and, again, Jonathan answered, "Yes, but not for a very very long time." At this, Max began to wail, "I don't want to die." It was terrible—and, again, natural, inevitable.

That summer as Max and I were looking at some flowers, he told me that he and his babysitter had once planted a flower. "It was purple," he said. "It was beautiful. I loved it. And then it died." Looking mournful, he said, "I'll never see it again." When I tried to comfort him with the idea that some flowers come back, he would not have it. His narrative had solidified.

Death has become a regular topic in children's literature, even for the very young. I remember teaching *The Tenth Good Thing about Barney* (1971), the story of a cat who died and the litany of good things recited at his burial. Memorializing was an approach for children, particularly dealing with the common event of pets dying.

For older children there are two recent and prize-winning books that take opposite tacts. Neil Gaiman's *The Graveyard Book* (2008) is an elaborate fantasy replete with a range of night vultures—ghosts, werewolves, witches, vampires—each treated with originality that avoids the stereotypical treatment of such popular creatures. And like all really good fantasies, *The Graveyard Book* is rooted in the real world, here the world of corruption and cruelty.

Patrick Ness's *A Monster Calls* (2011) is a realistic novel, though it features a monster that appears, to the protagonist, Conor, in all its enormity as a yew tree. It shape-shifts as it is revealed over the story as a projection of Conor's psyche. *A Monster Calls* is an elaborate treatment of Conor's feelings about his mother's deterioration from cancer and imminent death.

## The Graveyard Book

Always working with ideas of freedom, of childhood and the dark imagination, Neil Gaiman opens *The Graveyard Book* on the most chilling scene imaginable—the murder of a baby's entire family. Gaiman writes on a black page in white letters, "There was a hand in the darkness and it held a knife. The knife had done almost everything it was brought to that house to do, and both the blade and the handle were wet" (7).

The murderer, called "the man Jack," wears shoes with "such a shine ... like dark mirrors, you could see the room reflected in them" (9). Indeed, the man Jack and his crime reflect the ugliness and corruption of the world. We learn midway through the book that he is part of a group of powerful men—European, African, Indian, Chinese, South American, Filipino, American—from all parts of the globe, and from whom the baby survivor of the murdered family has escaped into the dark pastoral of the graveyard to safety, where he is adopted by ghost-parents and the ghost community. So comforting and engaging are the graveyard characters that by the middle of the book, we have forgotten about the image of the hand in the darkness and the knife it held. But the return of the black page and the white lettering, which tells the story of the "Convocation" of world leaders and their meeting, reminds us that "Every Man Jack" is still searching for the child.

Gaiman pulls no punches here. Rather than a single man Jack, Gaiman asserts that there are Jacks everywhere in our society. Corruption is ancient, traditional, and ongoing. Although the child will have to claim his place in this real world as every living person does, first he needs the nurturing of the graveyard world—the transformation and flight from the darkness of the living world into the light of the dark pastoral. This child will live in a fantasy world (though not labeled as such by Gaiman) until he is able to enter the "real" world less painfully, more safely.

In the graveyard community, the child is renamed Nobody, Bod for short. The name suggests a reversal of the everyman hero. Bod's no-name name strips him clean of the real world and plunges him into this lovely pastoral. There he remains protected for his early childhood. *The Graveyard Book* is, however, a bildungsroman, and, growing up, Bod will be journeying through unsafe territory, reflecting the dangers of the world he must learn to recognize. This graveyard world itself contains dangers, as all dark pastorals do, manifestations of the powerful leaders of the real world. The child's task is to protect himself *from* and prepare himself *for* the real world.

The first of these dangers are the ghouls, who disguise themselves as judges, dukes, and bishops; one claims to be the thirty-third president of the United States, another Lord Mayor of London, another emperor of China, and one even introduces himself as Victor Hugo. They represent the treachery, misrepresentations, and pretentions of the "civilized" world. They live in Ghûlheim, a city "like a huge mouth of jutting teeth" (82). They "slip from shadow to shadow, never seen, never suspected ... fast as thought, cold as frost, hard as nails, dangerous" (81). And they represent the beginning of Bod's education, at the heart of which is learning to differentiate the authentic from the false. During his imprisonment with the ghouls, the sky is "an angry, glowering red, the color of an infected wound" (79), "the color of bad blood" (87). There a "dead sun set, and two moons rose ... one pitted ... one the bluish-green color of the veins of mold in a cheese" (83), signs of disease, nature denatured, in contrast with the green pastoral graveyard, where "bumblebees explored the wildflowers that grew in the corner of the graveyard ... [where] Bod lay in the spring sunlight watching a bronze-colored beetle wandering across" a gravestone (39). His meeting with Scarlett, a lonely child from the living, a soulmate, takes place on "a perfect spring day … the air … alive with bird-song and bee hum … daffodils bustl[ing] in the breeze … a few early tulips nodd[ing] … [a] blue powdering of forget-me-nots and fine, fat yellow prim-roses" (49–50). Once Bod is rescued from the ghouls by Miss Lepescu, a lovely werewolf, he looks up and sees a glorious dark pastoral, "the Milky Way … as if he had never seen it before, a glimmering shroud across the arch of the sky … filled with stars" (95). The darkness is described as "gentle," a good place in which to rest. The child Bod has the freedom of the graveyard to roam in as he pleases with the gift to see in the darkness, "like the dead"—a metaphor for the intuitive ability of children before they learn to distrust their hunches and feelings. He can "fade from awareness" and "slip through shadows." He can make himself invisible—all metaphors for the ways in which the powerless in the world are actually invisible to those in power. Bod has been taught to empty his mind … [so that he is] "an empty alleyway … a vacant doorway … nothing" (106). This does not quite work for him. What *does* work is a poetic incantation of the dark pastoral, a movement in imaginative practice from the state of being the verb "to be" to the action verbs "slip" and "slide":

Be hole, be dust, be dream, be wind
Be night, be dark, be wish, be mind
Now slip, now slide, now move unseen
Above, beneath, betwixt, between (132).

This particularly contemplative moment in the book offers the message that finding yourself, being heroic, means embodying various aspects of the imagination that will provide movement into the real world. Bod's quest is to leave his nameless state, to discover his real name. Gaiman asserts some very real creative and inspiring aspects of the real world, such as the possibility for change. The graveyard creatures remain fixed as whoever and whatever they were at their deaths; the markings on their gravestones reflect the retrospec-tive gaze afforded the dead: Thomas Pennyworth "(here he lyes in the cer-tainty of the most glorious resurrection)" still waiting, and Nehemiah Trot, poet, tagged by his epitaph, "Swans sing before they die." The living Bod must move toward integration.

The evils of the graveyard are essentially tied to the worldly world and posited against the graveyard pastoral. Everything lively and loving belongs to this dark pastoral, with the exception of the child, Scarlett. However, even the graveyard shows the signs of the prejudice of the living social world, like those relegated to the edge of the graveyard, buried in "unconsecrated land" (100)—the criminals, suicides, "those who were not of the faith" (103), who are "not our sort of people" (106). Like traditional heroes, Bod must go to many corners of experience: to the underworld and the earth, to the powerful and the powerless, and to the outcasts. He befriends and is befriended by the witch, Liza Hempstock, whose story harkens back to traditional witch burnings—she has been tested by drowning and burned by her community. As horrible as those crimes are, Gaiman does not present her as simply innocent. When Bod assumes she did not have magic powers, was not in fact a witch, she says, "What nonsense. Of course I was a witch" (111). She acknowledges that cursing came easily to her, and that she was responsible for having those who drowned and burned her themselves drowned and burned. But her description of them burning her body "on the Green until I was nothing but blackened charcoal ... [and then] popped ... into a hole in the Potter's Field without so much as a headstone to mark my name" (111) inspires Bod to find a headstone and provide her with a naming marker. And though as a child he is powerless to purchase the costly headstone, he finds a paper weight, on which he carves her initials, "E. H.," and touchingly adds, "we never forget," which resounds with the cry from the Holocaust, as a testament to all those who have been forgotten by society.

The central pastoral scene, juxtaposed against the Convocation of the Jacks, is an inclusive and original tableau: an extraordinary moment in the Old Town's history where the living and the dead come together in a Danse Macabre. But even this dark idyll is imperfect. Gaiman resists such a harmonic vision. The beauty and the magic of the night, "when the winter flowers bloom ... and are cut and given out to everybody, man or woman, young or old, rich or poor" (154) excludes Silas, Bod's guardian. He says, "You must be alive or dead to dance. I am neither" (149). He is one of the liminal characters who embodies the greatest wisdom, and represents the knowledge of both worlds, beyond a simplistic reading of dark and light, good and evil. Silas has seen and been part of it all. He understands that even the man called Jack is, rather than innately a monster, a pawn in the game of power. Further, there is a silence about the evening—an unspoken taboo against acknowledging this most extraordinary event. The Lady on the Grey, the figure of death who rides through the graveyard, represents the only real sense of democracy: Death is the great leveler. She is a reminder that death, at the end, comes for everyone. Gaiman's fantasy reflects the very dark reality of death in *The Graveyard Book*. Even with the fun and frolic of Carnival with its reversals (the graveyard as the most vitally alive place, the danse macabre and the white flowers of death bringing life in this moment of union for the community), Gaiman does not leave Bod or the town there. He returns the story to the real world with its criminals—world leaders as well as violent bullies in the schools. Children will recognize the darkness, even as the satirical thrust runs throughout the story; the Jacks of the world may remain murky. However, adults will not miss this vision. And like most of Gaiman's work for young people, like many other fantasies, his stories reach a double audience of child and adult. In its refusal to deny the larger political picture, Gaiman is courageous in his imaginative depiction of corruption. Although we may have forgotten the murders of Bod's parents with all the humor and pleasure of the graveyard, the murders have only been submerged. The murders open the book—we get to see the knife and the blood—so that when we are returned to the world it is not quite so shocking. Corruption has been there all along.

When Bod travels to the real world, he comes to understand that as hard as he tries to challenge injustice with the school bullies, he must accept limitations, his own as a human being, and the world's imperfections—and they are serious. And although Bod learns the name of his birth, something he has been searching for, he asserts that Nobody Owens is, in fact, his real name. Like other orphans in literature whose origins are not formative, he discovers that he was really raised by the graveyard community.

Bod loses his graveyard powers as he more fully enters the real world and he loses Scarlett. Silas wisely and sadly tells him, "People want to forget the impossible. It makes their world safer" (289). Silas has taken Scarlett's memories so that she will not remember the trauma of the last battle with the Jacks, but Bod will be wiped from her consciousness as well. In other words, if we wipe out knowledge of one disturbing aspect of life, other knowledge will also be repressed. In this way, Gaiman asserts the complexity of the imagination and the courage it takes to go back to its original site.

Although Gaiman's heroic vision includes the prophecy of a child born who would "walk the borderland between the living and the dead" (271), and that this child will destroy the Jacks of power and tradition, he also suggests that there will be Jacks of all trades to replace those Bod manages to destroy. Essentially Gaiman urges—and all this is done subtly—that you must believe what you know and have seen to be true, even if the entire world denies its possibility. His vision of a real democracy remains only a vision. He leaves us in the world, "A bigger place than a little graveyard on a hill," with "dangers in it and mysteries ... mistakes to be made and many paths to be walked before [Bod] would, finally, return to the graveyard or ride with the Lady on the broad back of her great grey stallion. But between now and then [Gaiman concludes], there was Life; and Bod walked into it with his eyes and his heart wide open" (307). Perhaps being "open" is what Bod can extract and retain from his experiences; this is Gaiman's closure here. Bod represents the potential power of childhood—that its potency is in the future, what Clementine Beauvais, in her work on child power, calls "might," as opposed to "authority," the present power that looks toward the past. As his choice of name suggests, he will bring the graveyard of his innocence into the future of his "Life."

### A Monster Calls

Patrick Ness's *A Monster Calls* is a deep and authentic treatment of children's healing from fear of the severest loss, the death of the mother. Its focus is the feeling of guilt that often accompanies this loss—or incipient loss. Siobhan Dowd, who is credited with the initial idea for this novel, died of cancer before she could write it. In emails to her editor, Denise Johnstone-Burt, she wrote:

> I believe I have quite a lot of quality time left to me ... The story's theme is healing. It is really my paeon to the great, ancient tree, the yew, without which I might not be alive today, as all the Taxol drugs that so successfully treat breast cancers are derived from it. The yew tree is the oldest tree in the United Kingdom ... The tree is known to be poisonous, especially the red berries on the female variety, but its healing properties were only appreciated in recent decades.

Perhaps the genuine quality of the story derives from the tragic nature of Dowd's death, that she died before she could write it, and Patrick Ness's story retains that quality. He writes, "Almost before I could help it, Siobhan's ideas were suggesting new ones to me ... I felt—and feel—as if I've been handed a baton, like a particularly fine writer has given me her story and said, 'Go. Run with it. Make trouble.'" His guideline: "to write a book ... Siobhan would have liked."

In this novel, a monster appears to Conor as his mother is dying of cancer in the form of a nightmare—a nightmare that does not frighten him because, as he says, it is not *the* nightmare. We come to understand that in the truly terrifying nightmare Conor is holding onto his mother who is dangling over the edge of a cliff, and it is about his fear/wish to let her go. He describes the nightmare as "the one with the darkness and the wind and the screaming. The one with the hands slipping from his grasp, no matter how hard he tried to hold on. The one that always ended with—" (11). He cannot finish the sequence, so crushing is this desire to rid himself of this horror that he lives with daily, of his denial that his beloved mother is dying—so crushing that he wants it to be over.

The black and white illustrations of Jim Kay figure prominently in this gripping story. The monster "of his dreams" begins as an inkblot, emerges into a giant/yew tree, and, finally, as Conor gets closer to recognizing the monster as a contorted inner self, takes more and more of a human shape. Kay's illustrations are fascinating and subtle as they morph into drawings of the monster as a comforting figure. When Patrick Ness was asked if he had a clear visual sense of the story before Jim Kay got involved, he replied:

> Not a visual sense, no, more of an emotional feeling ... how the spaciousness and the darkness/lightness might go ... Black and white, shadowy, suggestive. Then the most amazing thing happened ... we asked Jim to do a test drawing just to see what he might come up with. He sent back that incredible illustration of the monster leaning into Conor's bedroom window. That drawing never changed and is in the book as I first saw it. He was instantly the obvious choice, and he came up with things I never could have dreamed of.

The operative word here is "suggestive"—as the monster, we come to understand, is a representation of Conor's guilt. Even the font, the italics in which all the monster's words appear, mark the singular nature of his words and the state of consciousness he represents. That he does not seem to appear to anyone else establishes him as a projection. He emerges from Conor's own unacknowledged actions, most notably when Conor wreaks havoc in his grandmother's house and brutally attacks the school bully who taunts him, both presented as the work of the monster. It becomes obvious at that point that it is Conor who has asserted himself in these outbreaks of rage.

Jim Kay claimed he wanted to "work starting from a black canvas and pull the light out, which makes for a much darker image ... to give the reader[s] the room to create their own characters and images in their mind ... putting suggestions of the Monster and Conor in there to help them along the way; darkness and ambiguity allow the readers to illuminate the scenes internally."[2] And ambiguity is the dominant emotional state in this novel. It characterizes Conor's feelings, conscious and unconscious.

The novel chronicles Conor's journey from denial to acceptance. It begins with his isolation—from his grandmother, his father, his friends at school, as he retreats deeper and deeper into a dream state. He resists the limited support of his grandmother, whom he does not really like or feel empathic toward; his father, who has abandoned him in favor of his new family in America; and his friends—particularly his friend Lily who knows about his mother's illness and has apparently shared this dark secret with other children. In addition, as is often the case, there is the accompanying shame he feels about the difference between the lives of the other kids at school and his own tragic life, so that he tells no one at school. He seems to tolerate, or even encourage, the bullying of Harry and the school bullies. Unconsciously, Conor seeks the punishment Harry and the others inflict on him because he is guilty—of wishing it were over, of letting her go in his nightmare, *the* nightmare, the monster of his own unconscious guilt. Jim Kay said he "imagine[d] the story as a moving film or piece of theatre, and ... start[ed] building the props and setting the scenery around the characters." So that the story seems filmic, in its black and white suggestive scenes of the old yew tree shifting into the monster as a figure of Conor's internal struggle, it is portrayed in particular in the several dark double-page spreads that speak the unconscious and the double narrative. These illustrations arrest the time and pace of the main realistic, chronological narrative, which tells the story of the monster's appearance as a nightmare, the incidents of school and home, and the mother's slipping into death. Visual texts resist the linear time-bound nature of the verbal; they are closer to the world of dream and the imagination, in which the monster is both tree and human, in which time is frozen still or distorted, layering the text so that it portrays an internal as well as external reality. Both Ness and Kay, with their vivid images, both visual and verbal, have the ability to engage the child hero as well as the child reader in understanding the seemingly paradoxical complexity of internal feelings and external reality.

Another way that Ness complicates the story is to play the main narrative against the three interpolated tales told by the monster. These short and often shocking tales serve to disguise and simultaneously reveal the main narrative, as they mirror Conor's struggles. The first tale begins in fairy-tale time of "long ago" and in the pastoral "green place" where "trees covered every hill and bordered every path." Characters are the anticipated prince, princess, king, and queen. But "the king was just a king," and when he dies the prince's step-grandmother wants to marry him. Conor, understandably moralistic in his attempt to simplify his painful reality, and in his predictably thirteen-year-old voice says, "That's disgusting ... she was his grandmother" (65). However, that is just the beginning of the unconventional and turned about events of the stories. Each of the three tales takes two chapters: the first part begins a fairly conventional tale; however, the second part, what Ness titles "The Rest of the Tale," reverses our expectations in a shocking turn of events. In the first tale, when it turns out that the [good] prince killed his beloved princess, the monster reverses all expectations as the prince not only goes unpunished but also "ruled happily until the end of his long days." Conor challenges, "So the good prince was a murderer and the evil queen wasn't a witch ... Is that supposed to be the lesson of all this after all? ... Who's the good guy here?" The monster answers, *"There is not always a good guy. Nor is there always a bad one. Most people are somewhere in between."* When Conor insists, "That's a terrible story. And a cheat." The monster answers—and here is the real moral—*"It is a **true** story ... Many things that are true feel like a cheat"* (73–4). This indirectly addresses the terrible unfairness of death and illness. And to help prepare Conor for the impending devastation, he needs to understand that the world is not fair and reasonable, and that his grandmother, with whom he will be left, has her good and bad points, "like most people."

The stories get increasingly more realistic, as the second one is located in a specific time (fifty years ago), a time of industrialization, when "factories grew on the landscape like weeds. Trees fell, fields were up-ended, rivers blackened ... Villages grew into towns, towns into cities. And people began to live **on** the earth rather than **within** it. But there was still green, if you knew where to look" (109). This tale is marked by boundaries between the natural and unnatural, the pastoral and the industrial, and between people with self-ishness as a defining and destructive feature. Conor is challenged to redefine the protagonist he believes is "evil," as the monster/tree explains, "*He was greedy and rude and bitter, but he was still a healer ... Belief is half of all heal-ing*" (119). Conor's mother insists, as she's dying, that she still believes in the "green things of this world" (140), which challenges the nature of truthfulness and emphasizes the necessity of believing.

The third story raises the issue of Conor's "invisibility," a state he both wants and does not want. The monster/tree has taught him that "stories were wild, wild animals and went off in directions you wouldn't expect," like the imagination, like life. The double-page spread that most subtly and symbol-ically reimagines the state of Conor's unconscious is of a rabbit on the left-hand side of the page sitting on a weathervane facing away from the center, where the monster on the right-hand side, now human with twigs growing out of his head and body, sits facing the opposite way, head in hands. The natural and the unnatural are in opposition here, mirroring Conor's inability

**Figure 4** The natural and the unnatural. From *A Monster Calls*. Text copyright © 2011 by Patrick Ness. From an original idea by Siobhan Dowd. Illustrations copyright © 2011 by Jim Kay. Reproduced by permission of Candlewick Press, Somerville, MA, on behalf of Walker Books, London.

to connect school and home with the world of his imagination and dreams. When the monster first appears, he asks, "What are you?" and the monster responds, "*I am not a 'what' ... I am a 'who.'*" The monster roars:

> *I am the spine that the mountains hang upon! I am the tears that the rivers cry! I am the lungs that breathe the wind! I am the wolf that kills the stag, the hawk that kills the mouse, the spider that kills the fly! I am the stag, the mouse and the fly that are eaten! I am the snake of the world devouring its tail! I am everything untamed and untamable! ... I am this wild earth, come for you, Conor O'Malley* (44).

These incantatory images in the language of poetry connect the dark nature of life—what is unreasonable, uncivilized, desperate—like his mother's illness and the unconscious feelings Conor harbors. When such engulfing, overpowering pain inherent in the universe comes to those too young to grasp it, it may be presented as a narrative or poem (like the language the monster speaks here), held in the imagination and contained, separate from everyday language, the language of "real life." In this book, Ness engages different kinds of language and different genres—to express levels of consciousness. The main narrative establishes the story, the characters, and the events in time and place. The interpolated tales, short and didactic, set in an emblematic past, mix narrative and the poetic in their concentrated form. And the last tale most closely mirrors Conor's state of mind. It is about an invisible man, "*not that he was **actually** invisible,* the monster said ... "*It was that people had become used to not seeing him*" (156). The monster raises the issue of identity, Conor's need to be acknowledged as a grounded and real self. He says, "*And if no one sees you ... are you really there at all?*" (156). In the story, the invisible man decides to assert himself. "*I will make them see me,*" he says, which propels Conor to challenge Harry's taunt, "I no longer see you" (155), until Conor assaults Harry landing him in the hospital. Ness presents storytelling as increasingly actualizing, forcing Conor into action, even action that he does not recognize as his own. The monster's stories "*chase and bite and hunt,*" though they seem to divert the expected, moral ending, they tell "a truth." The fourth story, the monster demands, will be Conor's to tell. These stories lead up to and prepare Conor for his teacher's request that all students write life stories, something Conor fiercely resists. Conor's tale, the fourth one, the monster insists, will be the truth and "not just any truth. Your truth" (46). This is most painful for him, what he has been avoiding, noting:

> The hill, the church, the graveyard were all gone, even the sun had disappeared, leaving them in the middle of a cold darkness, one that had followed Conor ever since his mother had first been hospitalized ... it felt like the nightmare had been there, stalking him, surrounding him, cutting him off ... It felt like he'd never been anywhere else (185).

Here Conor is forced (and ready) to speak the horror of his nightmare, and to finally let it go. He asserts, "'I don't want you to go' ... leaning forward onto his mother's bed, [h]olding her ... He knew it would come, and soon ... The moment she would slip from his grasp, no matter how tightly he held on ... [And by holding] tightly onto his mother ... he could finally let her go" (215).

The ending is, naturally, inevitably, terribly sad. There is no lying or diffusing the pain here. When the monster tells Conor that he has come, not to heal his mother, but to heal him, he speaks the excruciating truth—that no one can heal his mother. She will die and soon, but the book addresses, through story and illustration, the process of healing and the complexity of feelings that emerge from and respond to that most basic and undeniable truth. Ness and Kay have used visual, poetic, fictional, fantastic, and autobiographical modes to tell Conor's story, suggesting that one genre, voice, or mode could not portray the truth of Conor's internal and external world—the truth about a mother dying and its effects on the child, and the manifestations of the child's rage and despair on the other people in his world. The author, illustrator, and the character Conor all required courage to powerfully imagine the various aspects of this story and the simultaneity of complex and paradoxical feelings represented.

## Contextualizing: Beyond individual trauma

In his preface to *The Future of Trauma Theory: Contemporary Literary and Cultural Criticism* (2013), Michael Rothberg notes that trauma is "perhaps best thought of not as any kind of singular object ... [His interest is in exploring how] the problem of individual psychic suffering became 'tangled up' with an array of the larger problems of modernity, including industrialization, bureaucracy, and war" (xi). He points to "questions of science, law, technology, capitalism, politics, medicine and risk," in an attempt to extend trauma study beyond a "eurocentric, monocultural orientation … to nuance our notions of trauma by revealing their cultural and historical specificity" (xii). Rothberg believes that "the 'new' trauma theory is still in the process of developing paradigms to match those of its classical, psychoanalysis-inspired predecessors" (xiii).

The American Psychological Association has been criticized for its "western" formulation of PTSD, defined as a "sudden, unexpected, catastrophic event … a single devastating blow" (Craps, 49). According to Craps, "many feminist and multicultural clinicians and researchers have argued that this criterion is too narrow because it makes some important sources of trauma invisible and unknowable. In particular, it tends to ignore 'the normative, quotidian aspects of trauma in the lives of many oppressed and disempowered persons" (49). Definitions have been expanded to include "oppression-based trauma … postcolonial traumatic stress disorder … and post-traumatic slavery syndrome … [These definitions attempt to include] the impact of everyday racism, sexism, homophobia, classism … and other forms of structural oppression" (49), to emphasize the "traumatic abuse" of "economic domination, or political oppression" (50). Sam Durrant points to culture and literary critic Judith Butler's urgent call that rather than view the 9/11 trauma individualistically and psychoanalytically, that stresses "a reconstitution of the subjects borders," in other words withdrawing from others, such trauma invites broadening a commitment, an *ethical* commitment to others (92). As Walter Benjamin wrote, "The tradition of the oppressed teaches us that the 'state of emergency' in which we live is not the exception but the rule" (quoted by Jenny Edkins in *The Future of Trauma Theory*, 127). This shift from trauma as unusual to the usual suggests a need for new approaches as we acknowledge the power of cultural wounds.

For us, here, the focus is on children and their experience of trauma and its representation, those events that are individual as well as those that lend themselves to an historical/cultural lens. I am aware that all events, including those that seem singular and idiosyncratic, have an historical and cultural context. And since children as a group have often been and continue to be exploited in so many different ways, this is an important insight. Children's feelings of powerlessness and oppression have been approached in much of children's literature: in the parodies of teachers, parents, all kinds of adult authority; in visions of super-heroic strength; and in the fantasies of other worlds that seem to be alternative to normative visions of power. It is important, however, to question: How many of these representations reinforce the same paradigms they set out to challenge? How many actually offer new visions one might see as beyond power and powerlessness?

## The culture of bullying

Some trauma, like the trauma of bullying, is ubiquitous, culturally prevalent, and often remains unacknowledged by the larger community of parents and teachers. I doubt if any of us has escaped bullying—as victim and/or as victimizer. It seems an integral part of childhood. Until fairly recently bullying was accepted, if not openly, then covertly, as "normal," "natural," along with "kids will be kids" and other seemingly innocuous cultural aphorisms. Many parents advise their children to fight back so the bully will not continue his/her bullying. Though some children are able to ward off further attacks with this advice, the issue of bullying essentially goes unaddressed. Many children continue to get harassed, sometimes for years, because they do not have the necessary strength or support to resist victimization. I am heartened by programs created to address the subject that offer alternative ways of dealing with both the bully and the victim. However, with the burgeoning internet and public exposure, the problem has shifted and in many ways intensified the fear and shame at the heart of bullying. We are aware of the teen suicides linked to cyberbullying; these are the extremes but such horrifying incidents are growing in number and reflect the turn the culture has taken. The issue is in need of broader and more urgent attention.

Among the many reasons for bullying, these major ingredients prepare children for victimization: their vulnerability, their need to be part of a group, and general denial and violence in the larger culture. Power is a central issue in this section, what children learn about power.

## The victim: *The Goats*

Although published in 1987, Brock Cole's beautifully written novel, *The Goats*, authentically portrays today's culture of bullying. What lifts this book above the many books written for adolescents and preadolescents is Cole's portrayal of the emotional complexity and the exposure of the sexist, classist, and racist culture that produces such abuse. Cole's focus is on two victims, thirteen-year-old Laura and Howie, who are stripped bare and abandoned on an island by their fellow campers. What prepares these two children to be victims begins with their sense of powerlessness in their families, though the neglectful families themselves are not vilified here. Howie's parents, archaeologists on a dig in Turkey, are essentially unreachable. Coming late in his parents' lives, Howie feels like he "'was an accident maybe' ... [that] he never seemed to fit ... They loved him ... but they didn't know what to do with him. He had to be careful not to get in the way" (128). Laura, on the other hand, is being raised by her single working mother who is anxious for some time of her own, who laments, when Laura calls from camp to urge her to take her home, "You know you shouldn't call me at the office unless it is really important. I mean an emergency or something." She wonders, "Why can't Laura adjust to camp? ... What had she done to raise a child so stiff and unbending? She was a little prude, that was part of the problem. No wonder the other kids gave her a rough time" (36). She tells Laura, "I know that some people aren't very nice, but you have to learn to deal with them, not just at camp, but everywhere" (37).

Camp can be a hotbed of bullying as evidenced here, where the camp director and administrator call the treatment "an old camp tradition." Miss Haskell, an administrator, says, "I was a goat," as the scapegoats are called. This is the familiar parental apologia; when confronted with their own violence against their children—smacking around, the threat of the belt, etc.—these parents will often say, "I got smacked around, whipped with my father's belt, and it didn't do me any harm." When I hear this I think, and sometimes say, "Really?" I can see the gaping wound in gestures, in all kinds of defensive behaviors. I am especially sensitive to this issue as my sister and I got plenty of beatings as young teenagers. And I remember the way we got blamed: "Look what they made me do," was one of the most lethal maternal legacies of my childhood.

*The Goats* is clearly meant to focus on scapegoating. Cole also suggests, with the sexual symbol of the goat, the sexuality of early adolescence and the ease of scapegoating the vulnerable and self-conscious adolescent whose body is changing. The literal nakedness of Howie and Laura leaves them exposed, physically and psychologically. Laura gets her period and Howie has been teased about his late development. The culture of shaming is focused here on sexuality—on the children's innocence and the projections of the adult world.

When Laura's mother confronts the camp director about her missing daughter, she receives this cultural wisdom:

> Sometimes there are boys and girls who are a bit, well, judgmental about their fellows. And some of the other campers might decide, mistakenly, that things could be improved if a boy and girl were put in a situation where they might realize that we are all just people. That there's nothing wrong, for example, in a healthy interest in members of the opposite sex … [that] most kids teased in this way would come back, well, a little proud of themselves, actually … It's perfectly safe. It's just the other campers' way of saying, "Hey kids, come on! Get with it!" (65).

Shaming and suspicion ripple through the various adult comments in this novel. The cleaning woman who discovers that they have been sleeping together in a motel and finds Laura's tampons, calls Laura and Howie "wicked wild things" (148). This image of her humiliating them is juxtaposed against the author's clearly sympathetic portrait of two innocent children trying to survive the cruelty of their abandonment. An earlier image, a centerfold of a woman "with her legs spread" (21) on the ceiling in an abandoned cottage where they seek shelter, suggests the ugly objectifying of women's bodies by adult culture. And the man who picks them up in his truck that smells of goats, and has a gold goat's head hanging inside his jeep, sneers at Howie and makes sexual innuendos. These creepy adults fill out the larger picture of adult suspicion and lewd projection onto adolescents who, Cole understands, are still innocent in their budding sexuality.

In the beginning of the novel, Cole establishes Laura and Howie themselves as complicit in the tradition of bullying. They want to be accepted, popular, part of the crowd that picks out a victim, before they realize that they have been chosen. Howie says of Laura when he first finds her on the island, "She was one of the real dogs," accepting this evaluation by the lead bully. Laura herself assumes that another girl was going to be the goat. She says, "They told me Julie Christiansen was going to be the goat. We were all supposed to come out and go skinny-dipping, and then we were going to lose her." Howie thinks that "she was an even bigger jerk than he was, thinking that Julie Christiansen could *ever* be a goat" (9). She says, starting to cry, "I thought they liked me" (9).

The story is a two-child hero cycle, where the bonding provides for a heroic reconfiguration of the story of scapegoating. They will run away from the island and not go back to camp. The story follows their gradual intimacy as they learn to really care about each other, and head from "The Island" to "The Woods," outlined metaphorically in the chapter titles. The first chapter "The Island" stresses their isolation. It also suggests a kind of poisoned Eden where the two naked figures are freezing, hungry, and eaten up by mosquitos—a grotesque pastoral. Their growing intimacy is portrayed physically, but not sexually—as they are young and not ready for sexual contact. As they bump shoulders walking along together, "[Howie] thought he would like to hold her hand, but he couldn't because she would think he liked her in that way" (47). As they take turns drinking out of a can, Laura notices that she was "putting her mouth on the same place [as Howie's]. It meant that she was getting his germs ... he was getting hers. She didn't mind. If they had the same germs, she reasoned, they would be all right" (53).

As Howie takes refuge in pastoral images of trees, leaves, the woods, he thinks about what it would be like "for them to live alone somewhere in the woods ... He could see the girl, dressed in the color of fallen leaves, the smile at the corners of her mouth" (55)—a particularly sweet moment that is juxtaposed against the ominous images of camps and beaches.

On their journey they learn to steal, to lie, and to break into cabins—all desperate and acceptable acts of survival as presented by Cole, which harken back to a "Hansel and Gretel" archetype. In the folktale, the two children must lie to the witch and throw her into the oven. We listen as she crackles and burns, thrilled that when the two children return to their weak father, the stepmother, initiator of their abandonment, is magically gone. All this is to say that although the folktale is presented as fantasy (the witch can be killed without remorse), the story of Laura and Howie has an established precedence for acceptable child-heroic survival tactics.

At the center of the journey are three chapters that present alternative teenage culture: "The bus" (that takes Laura and Howie to the camp for poor, mostly black children), "The Dining Hall," and "The Cabins." There they meet two teens, Calvin and Tiwanda, who are kind and caretaking. Among these and several of the other children, Howie is able for the first time to feature himself as the hero of his own story about going into a mysterious cave in Greece with his father, a scary mythic tale, about the possibility of goat sacrifice, even the possibility of a god at the center. His story is a success with the other kids, and the fact that he and Laura are on the run invites the kids to name them Bonnie and Clyde, the infamous bandit pair. In this section of the story, they transform from goats to bandits. Although they cannot be heroic let alone respected in their own social group, here they are revered as outlaw heroes, particularly when Howie unwittingly knocks down Pardoe, a particularly disturbed boy, who is threatening Laura; Laura says, "I will kill him" (90). Tiwanda, thoughtful and savvy, explains to Laura:

> He's got a bad family history … He's been hurt bad deep down inside. It makes him all queer. That's why Mr. Carlson [camp leader] lets him come camping with us. He thinks he can fix the hurt. Mr. Carlson, he's a good man, and he won't see how bad Pardoe is.
>
> But someday somebody's going to see. They're going to say, "Oh man, we hurt this thing so bad, we can't let it live. We got to kill it." But that don't have to be you, honey. That don't have to be you (90–1).

Cole lets this sad account stand—without any attempt to sweeten it. He also portrays Calvin, another abused child, one who has been burned with cigarettes by his father, as a constructive child, one with a positive vision, who offers this advice:

> I'm going to tell you the first bandit rule … If you see you're going to get popped in a fair fight, don't fight fair … It's like society, don't you see? They got all these rules that everybody's supposed to play by. But sometimes you see that those rules are going to cut you up. That makes you a bandit. You're a smart bandit when you know you don't have to play that game no more (89).

Though Howie does not fully understand this, given the wide distance between his upbringing and Calvin's—"he didn't think he was a bandit"—he concludes, "But then maybe he wasn't a goat either" (89).

Though Laura and Howie gain confidence from their experience with kids from the lower classes, they decide, "They were really strong only when they were alone" (101). However, they are too young to be totally on their own. And they cannot resort to living together in the woods—affirming the sad impossibility of pastoral. They need to return to the social world. Fortunately, Maddy, Laura's mother, undergoes a transformation from a critical and somewhat lax parent to a concerned and empathic mother. Once Laura goes missing, she realizes how little she knows about the place she sent her, how unsupportive she has been, and she counters Margo's conventional, gender-biased warning against keeping the two together: they could "develop a dependency which would interfere with their re-socialization later" (112). Maddy's intuition tells her, "If you found someone you liked and trusted, you held on for dear life" (112). At the end, in conclusion, she is accepting and empathic toward Laura. And they will take Howie home with them so the two can be together in a healing adult place.

The values of the social world that produced the bullying behavior will continue. Cole does not, and knows he cannot, solve the problems of race, class, and gender discrimination, the deep suspicion of the adult world toward adolescents, or the violence and neglect in families. But he offers a believable and moving alternative, a vision of trust between an adolescent boy and girl, between girls and boys of a different class, and a healing relationship between mother and daughter.

### The bully: *The Elizabeth Stories*

I had asked my freshmen to write freely in reaction to a quote about bullying—specifically about being part of the bullying, rather than its victim. These were some of my students' one-sentence/paragraph responses:

> "You're such a nerd," I hear them calling out to him, as he sits quietly in the corner minding his own business ... I struggled for the words to come out of my mouth. I wanted to help. But I didn't. They outnumbered us and I turned away, leaving my friend with a broken spirit.
>
> They laughed. I said nothing. They teased. I said nothing. They yelled. I said nothing. I should've said something.
>
> I laughed with them.
>
> He's so stupid. What a weirdo. Who picked out his outfit today?
>
> These were common statements that I heard in the seventh and eighth grade. I knew exactly how it felt because I used to come home crying in fourth grade from similar comments that were thrown at me ... The saying "sticks and stones may break my bones but words will never hurt me"

is so far from the truth. I wish I had the power to stand up to bullying, but I wasn't strong enough. It's very easy to say you would do it, but in reality it takes a lot of courage, much more than I had then. Instead, I rationalized what the bullies were doing and stood silently and watched.

Clearly, power is the issue here and the fear that renders you powerless. You know that though you are not marked as the primary target, you have escaped only momentarily. But now you are engaged in the culture of bullying.

What children believe they have avoided is often accompanied by guilt and shame. When these painful feelings are suppressed, pushed into the subconscious or driven deep into the unconscious, they take their place along with other injustices. They contribute to and are evoked by the socially constructed racial, gender, and class components that diminish a child's sense of safety and well-being.

One of the most potent portrayals of bullying through the eyes and in the voice of the bully is Isabel Huggan's *The Elizabeth Stories* (1984), particularly the opening story "Celia Behind Me." Celia is a diabetic, near-sighted, chubby child, perhaps intellectually damaged, who becomes the butt of a group of children living in a puritanical Canadian town, where rage and guilt are layered into growing up female. As Liza Potvin notes in her article, "*The Elizabeth Stories* and Women's Autobiographical Strategies," Elizabeth learns "that she must resort to duplicity and secretiveness to survive, as her mother has always done." Potvin points to the whole book, this story, "Celia Behind Me," and those stories that follow, as a portrayal of the "process" of becoming a woman, and that Elizabeth is torn between sympathizing with her mother and hating her "with all [her] heart" (70).

It is significant, then, that this first story about Elizabeth's elementary school experience leads off with this story that suggests that crucial to female development in this social environment is victimization. Third and fourth grade, the age of Elizabeth in this opening story, seems particularly poignant when children become reflective, conscious, and articulate about their feelings. Elizabeth is both cruel and sad, and as she feels helpless to escape the focus of group bullying only by becoming the bully herself, her anger and fear spiral into a dangerous cycle. She is acutely aware of this, as she says, "I knew, deep in my wretched heart, that were it not for Celia I was next in line for humiliation" (8).

Her mother's warning—"You just remember I'm watching ... And if I see one more snowball thrown in her direction, by you or by anybody else, I'm coming right out there and spanking you in front of them all" (7)— threatens an equally brutal humiliation. Either way, Elizabeth is trapped. And, as she says, "The awesome responsibility of now making sure the other kids stopped snowballing Celia made me weep with rage and despair" (7). She has already suffered abuse by the others as she cries easily. She has "prayed ... not to become pretty or smart or popular, all aims too far and out of my or God's reach, but simply not to cry when I got called Sucky" (8). When that inevitably occurs, Elizabeth desperately prays, "Dear God and Jesus, I would please like very much not to cry. Please help me. Amen." Helpless to escape shame, she turns to brutalizing Celia, is beaten by both parents, and humiliated in isolation from her peers. Without depicting this trap in which the bullied child is caught, there is little room to move beyond the moralistic simplicity of good and bad children—here Huggan depicts how quickly the position of victim and bully can turn from one to the other. How poignant this insight that may help children to imagine, even consider another possible scenario.

Elizabeth's voice powerfully conveys and evokes the complexity of childhood fear and anger. Celia forgives her quickly and easily, but Elizabeth's rage, even after Celia dies at seventeen, is turned inward. As she says, "I never was able to forgive her. She made me discover a darkness far more frightening than the echoing culvert, far more enduring than her pink, smooth face" (14). The helplessness that turns masochistic and sadistic illuminates the truth of the residual devastation of bullying. What Elizabeth discovers, her own inner darkness, is not only the entry into this powerful group of linked stories, but also constructs the book's arc. Elizabeth's cry to her mother, "Why can't I just play with the other kids like everybody else?" (7), resonates with the wishes of most children—to be like everybody else, to belong, not to be isolated from the group—whatever its activities. Without clearly recognizing the power of this wish, adults may not be able to revise bullying behavior. Also, those effective anti-bullying programs used in some schools, those that engage both the bullies and the victims of bullying, underscore the essential connection between the two, and the powerlessness children often feel in schools, camps, and other groups. Boundaries are necessary, but so is understanding. Stories can portray and reflect the double nature of child impulses, beyond the either/ or of simplistic imagining, within the individual child who is, after all, the recipient of the socially damaging situation. She must contain the natural fear and anger with little agency to act in some alternative way. The group often becomes the object of desire, and children's often desperate need to be accepted as part of the crowd needs to be addressed and reimagined in literature. I wonder how the issue of power, unequally distributed and maintained as it is in the adult world, can be transformed imaginatively in the child's world. Isabel Huggan's stories do not provide the hope for an alternative, but they offer a picture of how it feels to be excluded and shamed, particularly as a girl growing into a young woman.

Turning from a middle-class female social world to a dangerous world of young black men, we are presented with the dramatically different kinds of susceptibility of young women and young black men to shame and self-rejection.

## The culture of racism: Youth as *Monster*

As Dean Schneider writes in *Book Links*, "One of the great pleasures of reading young-adult literature is that so many of its authors are willing to tackle big themes and moral issues, and they do so with great inventiveness" (20). In this online piece, Schneider addresses youth in a series of thought-provoking questions and activities in conjunction with the theme and the experimental treatment of a criminalized black youth. Walter Dean Myers's *Monster* illuminates the systemic racism in the ways in which young black men are traumatized in our society. In poor neighborhoods, often the streets, gangs, and prison cultures create horrific conditions surrounding and threatening the survival of many young black men. In this novel, Steve Harmon is being tried for "felony murder." Ultimately, he is judged innocent and therefore will not have to do prison time, though we never fully secure the answer to his innocence, or even what it means to be innocent here. Perhaps this is because Steve himself is confused about his innocence and his guilt. Although he is implicated in the crime that is committed, Myers leaves it open as to the extent of his involvement. He makes it clear that Steve is criminalized and drawn into this ambiguous situation because he is a young black man. The novel focuses on his feelings, the ways in which he suffers awaiting trial, captured in a first-person diary he writes to keep himself from despair and panic. The diary brings us close to his experience, as he writes:

> They say you get used to being in jail, but I don't see how ... We sleep with strangers, wake up with strangers, and go to the bathroom in front of strangers. Sometimes I feel like I have walked into a movie with no plot and no beginning ... It is about being alone when you are not really alone and about being scared all the time (2–4).

Steve decides to write the majority of his story as a movie script, his most powerful tool for surviving this unbearable time. He writes his story from two perspectives: the movie script, in which he appears as a character, is in the third person. The other perspective is his first-person diary. The doubleness here represents his attempt to turn the story of the trauma into a work of art that can separate him, at least temporarily, from the horror and can also represent the complexity of his trauma. As trauma fractures experience, often rendering it sequentially incomprehensible, the use of two different modes, the intimate diary for his immediate feelings and the formality of the dramatic courtroom experience, flesh out his experience that may be foreign and/or repugnant to many readers, as it is foreign and repugnant to himself. However, the combination represents most fully his attempt to stay sane. He says:

> I can hardly think about the movie, I hate this place so much. But if I didn't think about the movie I would go crazy. All they talk about in here is hurting people. If you look at somebody, they say, "What you looking at me for? I'll mess you up!" If you make a noise they don't like, they say they'll mess you up (45–6).

The movie helps to remind Steve of his worth as a human being, which is constantly being eroded. He mentions various scenes that make him feel like he is "a real person" (60). "I want to look like a good person. I want to feel like I'm a good person because I believe I am" (62). He is told by his defense attorney that his job "was to make me look human in the eyes of the jury," that the jury will be prejudiced against him because of his race and youth. "Half of these jurors," he says, "no matter what they said when we questioned them ... believed you were guilty the moment they laid eyes on you. You're young, you're Black, and you're on trial. What else do they need to know?" (78–9). Steve becomes aware that in society's eyes he is a Monster. And he becomes further aware of a distance between him and his father, a space filled by something "like a man looking down to see his son and seeing a monster instead" (116).

In the face of such demonizing, Steve urgently fights to feel valuable, and it is his film teacher who believes in Steve's talent and integrity. As the script develops we see it becoming more artful—less is made explicit to the reader through explanation. Rather, a simple action stands in for the particular experience: as Steve practices answering questions with Miss O'Brien, the defense attorney, she uses a cup to indicate whether his answer will nail him or support his innocence—cup turned down means wrong answer; cup turned up, it's a good answer.

Steve becomes more introspective and conscious of himself as an artist, as well. He writes:

> Nothing is real around me except the panic. The panic and the movies that dance through my mind. I keep editing the movies, making the scenes right. Sharpening the dialog. "A getover? I don't do getovers," I say in the movie in my mind, my chin tilted slightly upward. "I know what right is, what truth is. I don't do tightropes, moral or otherwise." I put strings in the background. Cellos. Violas (271).

The power to create, to reimagine the scene, to dramatically transform his truth into something aesthetically satisfying may be the closest he will come to believing in himself. The world may not open to include him in the way he needs, and clearly the way the author suggests he and other young black men deserve to be believed. But his courage to imagine his story from his own point of view is transformative; it is a kind of creative power.

After the movie ends, after his parents' relief and his own relief, he is left adrift. He writes, "My father is no longer sure of who I am … I want to know who I am … I want to look at myself a thousand times to look for one true image. When Miss O'Brien looked at me, after we had won the case, what did she see that caused her to turn away?" His last line is, "What did she see?" (281).

Healing from trauma requires an affirmation, a belief in the young person, who cannot possibly sustain a sense of self alone. In this powerful novel, Walter Dean Myers stresses the crippling effects of institutionalized racism, its effects on the family and community, and the overwhelming disadvantage of those youth who fight to survive in this world.

## The culture of domestic violence: *When Dad Killed Mom*

Years ago I learned that a man who had been my summer crush when I was a teenager killed his wife and then himself in front of their only child. The shock, the horror—I can never forget. I heard that he was a big drinker and that his wife was going to leave him when he killed her. At that time, I thought this was a very rare occurrence. However, Julius Lester, author of a challenging young adult novel, *When Dad Killed Mom* (2001), writes, "A painful and sad truth of our time is that fathers kill mothers ... and I wonder, What is it like for the children?" (181). "Since childhood," he writes, "I have endured the deaths of many people ... I grew up with children who suffered the death of a parent ... So, as I wrote and cried, I was grieving for them all—and for myself. *When Dad Killed Mom* is fiction, but the emotions it explores are not" (183). Lester creates a credible story here with empathy drawn from "a sense of personal grief." With this novel, he provides a healing place and possibilities for diffusing the accompanying shame and guilt of the survivors.

The two adolescent protagonists, Jeremy and Jenna, are the narrators here. We get quite close to them through their voices and perspectives. Jeremy, twelve, is his mother's favorite. He tells us, "[My mother] says I remind her of herself when she was twelve—serious and hardworking. She says she likes to see things through my eyes, that I see things as they are and that's what it takes to be an artist" (3). Jenna, fourteen, is more rebellious and attached to her father, who is a college psychologist. Lester, who is black, has chosen to portray a middle-class white family here, perhaps to show that domestic violence does not only occur in poor, minority families. This looks like a "good" family from the outside—but what is uncovered is the mother's infidelity and hot temper and the father's attachment to the daughter that the mother suspects has sexual overtones. She does not suspect him of full-blown incest, but she does not trust his judgment. She was the father's patient and is aware that the father has had affairs with students and patients.

By the fifth grade, Jenna is already a bold, courageous feminist, defending a portrait she made of her vagina—which Lester manages to present with both hilarity and seriousness. She tells us:

> Mom ... was impressed by how realistic my drawing was. I had put in the labia major and the labia minor and all the folds of the vaginal lips like petals of a flower ... I had spent a long time sitting on the floor of my room

naked, my legs spread, a mirror between them, looking at my vagina ...
I thought it was beautiful and it was mine! (9).

While teachers and fellow students are freaked out by Jenna's forthright
drawings, she, with her mother's support, remains, nonetheless, committed
to her vision. She is fortified by her mother's belief that "artists show people
what they have not seen and don't want to see." Jenna says:

> What's more unseen and unloved than a vagina? ... When I grow up I'm
> going to hire models and draw their vaginas and have an exhibit in a gal-
> lery in Soho or somewhere and it'll be room after room of nothing but vagi-
> nas and breasts and nipples—African American, Jewish, Asian, white . . .
> and women will come and they'll be amazed at how beautiful vaginas are
> and how different they look. They say no two people have the same finger-
> prints. I bet no two women have vaginas that look alike, either (10).

This is Lester's introduction to Jenna. Jeremy is more reserved. As the novel
unfolds, we listen to the two children, each reporting his or her feelings about
the murder of their mother by their father and on the extreme awkwardness
of everyone around them. Lester stresses the importance of having intimates
in the face of tragedy—someone who understands the need of the young people to process such experience in their own time, in their own way. Jeremy's
teacher, Miss Albright, serves as his witness; Jenna's witness is Karen, her
father's first wife, who has been graciously integrated into the family. All this
speaks to a civilized, sophisticated group of artists, therapists, and teachers.
However, clearly something is wrong here and the truths that are revealed
at the trial are complicated and disturbing. It is established by the father's
seduction of students and patients that he has weak and improper boundaries. At the trial, he accuses his dead wife of having been sexually inappro-
priate with their son, a "bold-faced lie," a projection—it is he who has been
seductive with his daughter and has encouraged her to be seductive with him.
It is the children at the trial who force him into telling the truth—that his wife
was going to expose him and leave him, that he would have lost his position as
well as his family. Several wise and significant messages come from the dramatic scenes: between the two children, between Jenna and a boyfriend, with
the grandparents, and within the courtroom. One narrative strain exemplifies the temptation to fill the emptiness and escape pain and grief. Jenna
becomes involved with Gregory, a boy who has suffered extreme deprivation

and makes guilt-inducing demands on her. He attacks her by saying, "Your mother left you a pile of money and a house. Karen took you in without blinking an eye. My father didn't leave me enough to buy a stamp, and my mother didn't leave me enough spit to lick the stamp if my father had left one, and I don't have any friends of the family living in big houses lined up at the sign that says, 'Gregory Needs a Home'" (135). Jenna concludes, "I hate to leave him here by himself, but all I know is that I've got to get out of here before he drags me down some more" (136). A significant insight comes from Jenna's realization that just because she is wounded, she need not take on the role of healer for anyone else. Jenna quotes the singer Alanis Morissette: "I don't want to be a bandage if the wound is not mine" (131). And drawing her own boundaries and asserting her own identity, she also decides to shed the name her father had chosen—a name associated with two former Jennas, both of whom were killed early in life. Unburdening herself of her father's past losses, Jenna chooses the name Melissa, the name her mother had wanted for her, thus aligning herself with her mother. For Jenna, as a young woman, this new name reflects a reimagined self.

For Jeremy, the end of the novel shows him reflecting with his own clear-sightedness, "It's okay being back in my own room. But it's not like it was before. I'm different now. Everything that happened at the trial ... was in the papers and on television and the other kids seem like they look up to me now, like I know things they don't. And I do" (172).

The children survive the grief, the guilt, and the shame, with the support of friends and family. And their grandfather, their father's father, offers some understanding for the father who has committed this evil act. He asserts:

> This business of being a person is complicated and confusing sometimes ... Who you are and what you are is partly because of who your parents, your grandparents, and even the ones before them were ... We humans like to think we are free to choose our lives. Maybe we are. Maybe we aren't. I'm just not sure anymore (174).

He goes on to tell the story of the father's traumatic life. His attempt is to humanize the father, not to forgive or deny, but to establish that evil acts do not mean the person is evil, nor do they come out of nowhere.

The other voice we hear is the mother speaking through her diary. There we get a picture of her growing suspicion of the father, her concern for her children, and her accusations. We see the dissolution of the marriage through her memory of their arguments. The parents' desperation is established and prepared for over a period of time. For example, she writes:

> I told him I thought his relationship with Jenna was inappropriate, to put it mildly. "If you're accusing me of something, I'm very hurt," he said … The bastard was trying to manipulate me.
>
> "I'm not accusing you … I'm telling you—as a woman and mother Jenna's still a child. All this attention you lavish on her is more than her years and experience can handle. She should be out with boys her own age, not doing a sex tease for her father."
>
> "And where did you get your degree in psychology" he responded coldly … "You talk like she's a stripper and I'm a dirty old man … She's my daughter and I'm her father and I'm also a trained psychologist. If a girl experiences her beauty with her father, her relationships with boys will be far healthier."
>
> But as I turned and walked off the porch, I thought I saw Jeremy … I hope he didn't overhear us (106–7).

The repercussions are serious for all in the family. Clearly Jeremy is affected by what he hears and sees, though he is not the central focus.

The novel takes readers through the healing process—a slow but thoughtful depiction of how each child comes to terms with this tragedy. We see Jeremy struggle to find himself in his new family. And we watch Jenna make amends with her mother at her graveside. At the end, though Jenna and Jeremy choose different homes and are adopted by different people, they remain connected. Together they execute a blog for other children who have lost parents in which all will feel free to express themselves. This engagement with others who have survived similar trauma is enormously therapeutic for the victims. It offers them dignity and helps to normalize their experience—which in the general culture can seem freakish and create an isolating atmosphere of awkwardness. Further, with their understanding about what it feels like to experience such loss, the children can also be most helpful to others. With their blog they create a new community. In this courageous work of fiction, what stands is the healing that comes from a reconstituted family and community. And the children are powerful in creating such a healing place for themselves and for other children.

Although there are more common and less dramatic forms of domestic violence, *When Dad Killed Mom* speaks to many kinds of trauma that evoke shame and guilt, displacement and isolation. It also addresses the beginnings of healing and suggests the function of time. Time itself shifts with trauma. Because it is often experienced differently for each person, the felt experience of time and grieving needs to be open, not set.

The novel speaks to this essential message for children: nothing is too shameful to be written about. You can find your experience reflected in books to deflect the danger of hiddenness. You need not deny your past. Others have been there and this is the story of their survival.

6

# New Heroes: New Visions of Childhood

## Setting the stage: Alice, Jim Hawkins, Dorothy, and Huck

The heroes of classical children's literature demonstrated new ways of looking at children in their time. Lewis Carroll's *Alice* stories, *Alice's Adventure in Wonderland* (1865) and *Through the Looking Glass* (1871), reversed the direction of children's literature in nineteenth-century Britain and the United States. *Alice* inspired stories that moved away from the didactic to entertainment for children. When Carroll wrote *Alice's Adventures in Wonderland*, he had a real child as a model and muse, a spunky girl of seven, who, once fictionalized, became a prototype of a child hero. Alice questions the absurdity of the adult world, often without realizing that she is doing so. She is proud of her knowledge, though she does not really know what she knows—Carroll, for example, suggests that unconsciously Alice is correct when she says that 4 times 5 equals 12 and 4 times 6 equals 13, as these figures function accurately in a base system other than 10. Carroll as a mathematician must have known what Martin Gardner asserts in *The Annotated Alice*. Of course, Alice thinks she has got it all wrong. I wonder here if Carroll is suggesting that children's intuitive knowing, perhaps unconscious or unexplored, is powerful and imaginative. However, by the end of Wonderland, asserting herself against authority, Alice says, "Who cares for you? You're nothing but a pack of cards." And in *Looking Glass*, she is the only stable figure in the face of the constantly changing authority creatures who spout absurdities all around her.

After Alice, a number of child heroes that challenge conventional ways emerged. Rather than the moralistic underpinnings of Victorian ethics, in *Treasure Island* (serialized 1881–82) Robert Louis Stevenson generated a culture of adventure. However, beneath the pleasures espoused in these stories, Stevenson, like Carroll, invoked a critical irony about adult culture. Stevenson's Jim Hawkins, boy hero, is particularly unheroic. He begins his journey in search of a father figure—his own has recently died—and he meets with a group of unsavory pirates, as well as the two conventional, respectable but weak seekers of adventure, Dr. Livesey and Squire Trelawney. The really formidable male, Long John Silver, strikingly unmasculine, a cripple with a "ham face," is the unconventional but powerful villain, who uses his crutch as a lethal weapon, and escapes with a fortune. Jim has the most difficult time coming to terms with Long John's seductive ways. Although his journey includes heroic ventures out on his own, surviving and investigating enemy conspiracies, those risks are foolish and unnecessary. And although he emerges from his journey wiser and more mature, he is left lonely and cynical. Stevenson does not grant him a new leadership role, nor is he integrated into his community. His relationship with adults is only tangential. He is forced to tell the story he most wants to forget—his adventures. Ironically, the book closes with the parrot's words, "Pieces of Eight! Pieces of Eight!"—the piratical refrain, the mantra of the materialistic world into which Jim is fated to grow. Stevenson's courage to imagine an un-Romantic adventure story in which the hero is left isolated is noteworthy, though *Treasure Island* seems likely to be remembered as a boy's adventure story—conventional and heroic. Unless you actually read it, the irony—to my mind its strongest and most original feature—goes overlooked.

In some ways, Dorothy of *The Wizard of Oz* is Alice's later American counterpart. She is grouped with Huckleberry Finn as one of the "audacious kids" (Jerry Griswold) of America's "Golden Age of Children's Books." Dorothy is a spirited girl, pitted against the bleakness of Aunt Em and the dreary Kansas landscape. Kansas has "robbed" Aunt Em

> of her youth and prettiness ... The sun and wind had ... taken the sparkle from her eyes and left them a sober gray ... She was thin and gaunt, and never smiled now. When Dorothy ... first came to her, Aunt Em had been so startled by the child's laughter that she would scream and press her hand upon her heart ... and she still looked at the little girl with wonder that she could find anything to laugh at (1–2).

In this hardworking, joyless Midwestern family, play is only available to Dorothy's dog, Toto. Toto twice spurs her on her journey: once when he jumps out of her arms so that she is prevented from hiding in the cyclone cellar with her aunt and uncle, and at the end when he jumps out of the wizard's balloon, forcing Dorothy to rely on her own way to get home. Toto is Dorothy's helper and her job, then, as child hero and spirit of new life, is to bring color and joy into the lives of her Kansas guardians and, in general, to support playfulness in childhood. Although she does not mean to murder the two wicked witches, she is nonetheless the liberator of the munchkins, the old but childlike figures, who remind her that it does not matter whether she intended it or not, she is the destroyer of the Wicked Witches. And as supporter of the Straw Man, the Tin Man, and the Cowardly Lion, Dorothy discovers, along with her readers, her child power. When she confronts the Wizard as a fake, she is, like Alice, a challenger of authoritarian adult hypocrisy. Dorothy is imagined as a brave and outspoken girl who subverts authority and manages to go home, to domestic safety, without consequences.

As an American boy hero, Huck Finn challenges the convention of boy heroes, and becomes a prototype of a new kind of hero. As Andrew Levy notes, in *Huck Finn's America*, Huck represents a challenge to myths about American children. He credits Steven Mintz in his book about American childhood, *Huck's Raft*, with disputing "the myth of a carefree childhood." Levy further notes that *Huck Finn* affirmed the "international conversation about children and their ability to shape and not just be shaped by the culture around them" (xviii). Azar Nafisi, in *The Republic of Imagination*, claims that "Twain's most effective act of heresy was a literary declaration of independence from all previous forms of fiction ... In most of his work, but most perfectly in *Huckleberry Finn*, he set out to give shape and voice to this mongrel, who was not just on the margins of society but without a space within its literary orbit. This is what fates Huck to be seemingly unable to fully articulate his own story" (62–3). Though the voice of the "mongrel" may seem inarticulate, it fully captures an authentic voice of the outsider and demonstrates the power of imagining children in a new way that became most popular in children's books that followed. Clearly Huck's slangy, expressive voice inspired Salinger's Holden Caulfield, and his exposure of class and race opened a new area of inquiry for authors of children's books. In contemporary books that followed, children often become powerful voices for censuring adult values that seem hypocritical, ungenerous, inhibiting, and threatening of democratic principles, such as racism, sexism, and classism.

# New heroes

### Girl power: *Pippi* and *Matilda*

Girls of the twentieth and twenty-first centuries must have been yearning for strong girl heroes, for girls with superpowers, such as the heroes of *Pippi Longstocking* and *Matilda*, evolved. With the freshness of Astrid Lindgren's child heroes, Pippi Longstocking released a new range of powers in child heroes. Astrid Lindgren's Pippi was wildly popular in her various forms: as hero of the series from 1945 to 1948 that was translated into eighty languages and as hero of several films and television features.

Lindgren was known for her opposition to any kind of abuse of human dignity, particularly exploitation of children. Her best-known radical child power works are the *Pippi Longstocking* series, which transforms girls from passive creatures to agents of their own desires. Pippi embodies the green world of eternal freedom and childness, where she resists civilization, although her story is set in the socialized world with its injustices. She is in opposition to the institutionalized world of parents, school, the police, and bullies of all kinds. Living on her own, she is spontaneous and free, in her little house and yard with her animals. She is the world of play—no rules, chaos without repercussion. As the strongest girl in the world with a trunk full of gold, she is fearless and able to survive on her own, without the vulnerability of the child. She is "wise ignorance"—wise in her instinctual resistance to anything false or moralistic, but moral in her natural kindness, essentially a generous and empathic soul. Her ignorance of social mores maintains her as the voice of Lindgren's attack on the oppressive social order. Earthy, hilarious, and anarchic, she represents Carnival's comic reversal of order and propriety. Often impervious to the disorder she proliferates, she confronts injustice intuitively. My favorite scene is at a social party, where Pippi answers the women's derogatory complaints about their servants:

"If only my Rosa were clean," one says, to which Pippi replies in an extensive narrative invention of Grandmother and her servant, Malin, "Malin was so outrageously dirty that it was a joy to see her, Grandmother said." When another suspects her servant of stealing, Pippi asserts, "Malin stole too … She was very clever with her hands, Grandmother said." As yet another claims, "My Ella … break[s] the china," Pippi retorts, "Speaking of Malin … she set apart one day a week just to break china … There was such a crash bang in the kitchen all morning that it was a joy to hear it, Grandmother said" (Lindgren, 125–7).

A new parental figure, comical and the reversal of authoritarian adulthood, Pippi's father is a cannibal king in a grass skirt, colored beads hanging from his neck, a gold crown on his head, and "a couple of fat, hairy legs [which] stuck out, with thick gold bracelets on the ankles" (108). He is an absurd though kind authority figure, who cannot beat Pippi in a wrestling match, and sees her as resourceful and competent. "Do as you like," he says. "You always have done that … You are right as always, my daughter" (136–7). Pippi also resists hierarchy, and any homage paid to her by the Kurrekurredutt native children, when they worshipfully throw themselves on the ground. In her anti-racist, anti-authority stance, Pippi gets down on her knees and asks them, "Have you lost something? … In any case, it isn't there, so you might as well get up" (74).

Although Pippi is unable to change social institutions and customs in the real world, she remains an image of pastoral—a wild child, untamed and undifferentiated from nature. As a girl, Pippi is not especially female identified. Firmly rooted in the "civilized" world, her friends, Tommy and Annika, are conventional in their gender roles, and aware of time and its association with loss. Pippi, on the other hand, remains focused on playfully rhyming and on her senses and desires:

I do exactly as I wish
And when I walk it goes squish, squish …
For the shoe is wet.
The bull sleeps yet.
And I eat all the rice porridge I can get (88).

However, with one foot in the socialized world—she wants "to be a fine lady," and with the other in the world of fantasy, where she wants to become a pirate—Pippi demonstrates Lindgren's placement of her fantasy hero in the real world. There are two moments in which Pippi seems to recognize that time will catch up with her. She says, "Time flies and one begins to grow old … This autumn I'll be ten, and then I guess I'll have seen my best days" (105)—her humorous but also serious acknowledgment of time passing suggests a movement away from innocence and toward experience. In the other instance, at the very end of the series, Pippi sits "with her head propped against her arms … staring at the little flickering flame of a candle … She seemed to be dreaming." Annika notes that she "looks so alone." Lindgren leaves her readers in the darkness of the time-bound world as "Pippi continued to stare straight ahead with a dreamy look. Then she blew out the light" (197). Lindgren's courage to imagine this original girl hero so full of vitality, so unconventional, established the hero of many children the world over.

One of Pippi's followers, Roald Dahl's Matilda, represents another vision of girl power. First published in 1988, and also set in the real world, *Matilda* features a rebellious superhero child, with extraordinary strength that is entirely mental. Dahl's attack is on the abuse of adult power—at home and at school—children's two basic institutions. Clémentine Beauvais responds to the issue of power, the various critical voices and its various forms, when she asserts that the power of the child is of the future in opposition to adult authority that is of the past. Nonetheless, when I refer to the powerlessness of children, I am speaking about the present, children constricted by authorities of home, school, and other institutions. This does not deny the ways in which children can be resourceful and courageous in their imaginings. In terms of "mighty" child heroes, Pippi and Matilda represent ways of being powerful, though neither is rooted in realism. They do both, however, challenge adult authoritarian power.

Reading is presented in much of children's literature as an expression of power—from which children can escape the adult world and imagine alternatives. Matilda finds safety and stimulation in the library where she reads all the children's books and many adult books. She is a math genius as well. Her intellect offers her a sense of power. Her gifts are put to work at home and at school where she cleverly does damage to her vicious and corrupt father, and in her fury at the injustices of the head of school, Trunchbull, she discovers her strangest gift of telekinesis: with intense concentration, she can move objects.

*Matilda* was extremely popular in the United States as well as in Great Britain where it was first published. Most recently Broadway featured a very popular musical that engaged adult audiences as well as children. Matilda remains a wonderfully inventive girl. Like Pippi, she is hilarious and satirical, bold and audacious.

In the end, Matilda finds comfort and happiness: she goes to live with the kind and supportive teacher Miss Honey, escaping her cruel father and neglectful mother. And she uses her powers to expose the fascistic Trunchbull, restoring Miss Honey's rights to her inheritance, which, it turns out, Trunchbull has stolen. This certainly is the ultimate in child wish-fulfillment. At the end, nothing painful remains, except for the real world from which *Matilda* offers an escape—at the same time it focuses its attack on selfish and malicious adults.

Critics have situated Dahl as a fantasist who uses mostly fairy-tale tropes: Trunchbull and the Wormwoods as evil and Miss Honey as goodness and simplicity, who lives in a cottage in the woods, Snow White-like. Beauvais sees Roald Dahl and *Matilda* as conservative, sexist, and snobbish, and other negative positions in the social realist world. Although I think there are merits to both perspectives—and they seem to live together without too much constraint—I see Matilda as a superhero child, rooted in a particular family in a particular culture (that Beauvais sees as "petty bourgeois"); the family seems archetypally grotesque as crooks as well as heartless and ignorant people. However, Matilda subverts their power, exposing their vulgarity and the vulgarity of Trunchbull, as opposed to Miss Honey's refinement—and her respectable doctor-father's roots. Matilda is neither vulgar nor refined. She is an original, falling into neither group and offering an alternative vision. Of course, as she is a child, we do not know where she will wind up—what will be her position in the real world?

Like Pippi, like all children, Matilda is unfinished business. Unlike Pippi, however, there is nothing lyrical about Matilda. *Matilda* endures, enjoyed by so many children; it is biting, even cynical about some of childhood's institutions. It remains satirical. Lindgren, on the other hand, engages satire as well as depicting subtle longings of the child hero. Pippi, separated from other children by her immense gifts, evokes a sadness. She is essentially without community, though her spirit is free and her father is always somewhere palpably supportive. She remains vibrant and comical, but a subtly complex figure, drawn with a light but penetrating touch. It is interesting how Lindgren was able to imagine this comic, fantastic, and, at the same time, real hero, with a subtle sense of darkness. Nonetheless, hilarious, buoyant, and cheerful, Pippi leads with her vitality.

## Children's ways of knowing: Louise Erdrich's historical fiction for children

When I began reading Louise Erdrich's *Birchbark* series, from the first pages of the first book, *The Birchbark House*, I was mesmerized by the way in which Erdrich assumes and presents children's many ways of knowing. As a child I knew things that I did not know I knew. This is often true of children's experience. And it is often discovered and articulated in adulthood—by authors of children's books, which adds to their complexity and vibrancy. There the adult writer can concretize that which she comes to know. I knew what my parents proudly valued—art and education, along with "being a good person," and I also knew what that meant. It included being well thought of and, in a more subtle and unacknowledged way, being beautiful. I also knew that being beautiful meant having a small nose and big eyes. I knew that they believed they brought up my sister and me to think for ourselves, but I also knew that it did not include disagreeing with them in any substantial way. I do not think I could have articulated, let alone admitted, much of this. I remember feeling conflicted, confused about what I saw and what I was told I saw. I must have resisted an introspection that comes with an early trust in one's feelings, a self-respect that encourages the child's ability to imagine.

Erdrich most clearly and carefully chronicles the evolution of her child hero, Omakayas, as she learns to listen to her instincts. She is attuned to the natural world, as well as to the animals and their ways of telling. I would have loved her as a child, as I did as an adult. I might have grown into consciousness with her, as Erdrich so vividly describes her process of coming into self-knowledge.

In the acknowledgment page of *The Birchbark House*, Louise Erdrich wrote, "This book and those that will follow are an attempt to retrace my own family's history."[1] By going back to her origins, to America's origins, she reclaims the power of children and of her people *for* children. This view of autobiographical writing, recapturing one's own story through fiction, is in accord with feminist challenges to more traditional views of autobiography. According to Leslie Marmon Silko, who grew up on the Laguna reservation, Native storytelling is a synthesis of forms of personal narrative and contemporary Euro-American modes of autobiography: folktales, myths, family stories, cultural stories, and personal stories (Wong, 9). These are the forms that Erdrich draws on in her historical fiction for children. Further, when Erdrich sets her stories in early America, she suggests a view of family that reaches beyond one's particular life span, and that of parents, grandparents, great-grandparents, to historical legacy and a broad sense of community. For Erdrich, family includes the earliest Ojibwe settlers of the West. In her adult fiction as well, Erdrich's "characters' individual lives are always portrayed in the context of community—homecoming, the return to 'a society, a past and a place'" (Stokey, 25).

Erdrich's vision of contemporary life includes age-old traditions. She writes in her memoir, *Books and Islands in Ojibwe Country*, that for her trip with her baby through the lakes and islands of Southern Ontario she took tobacco, "not to smoke but to offer to the spirits of the lake ... [along with] disposable diapers" (6–7). She writes that it does not matter whether she literally believes in the spirits; she wants to project back to an imagined past when that belief system was organic, as a way of writing her childhood story.

It is an interesting blend that she's after both in her work for children and her adult work. She writes, "Ojibwe people were great writers from way back and synthesized the oral and written tradition by keeping mnemonic scrolls of inscribed birch bark. The first paper, the first books" (11). Clearly she associates birch bark with origins, writing, and language. *The Birchbark House* and the two books that follow, *The Game of Silence* and *The Porcupine Year*, are a mixture of English and Ojibwe languages. Throughout the books Ojibwe is contextualized, framed by English for meaning, and a glossary and pronunciation guide of Ojibwe terms and names appear at the end of each book. Using Ojibwe serves to help take us inside the culture so that we get a glimpse from an insider's view—to mix the unfamiliar with the familiar until the unfamiliar becomes familiar. Erdrich contends, "However awkward my nouns, unstable my verbs, however stumbling my delivery, to engage in the language is to engage in the spirit of the words" (87).

In *The Birchbark House*, *The Game of Silence*, and *The Porcupine Year* the hero, Omakayas, is an Ojibwe girl living in mid-nineteenth-century America, much like Laura, the hero of Laura Ingalls Wilder's extremely popular *The Little House* books. Heid Erdrich, Louise's sister, said that their mother, when reading *The Little House* series to them as children, would censor out all the racist parts, and that Louise wrote with the idea of redressing the wrongs done to Indians in those books by rewriting the story of settling the West from an Indian perspective. Set in the same time period, the format of the books and the pencil-look of the illustrations sprinkled throughout the chapters suggest *The Little House* series with Garth Williams's drawings.[2] The themes of family life, sibling stories, survival stories of nature, of the seasons, food, girls' games, toys, and tasks serve to parallel Omakayas's experience with Laura's, reimagining America's girl hero with an internal spirit surviving in a harsh environment.

In Laura Ingalls Wilder's *Little Town*, John E. Miller notes that the "one ethnic conflict that figures prominently in Wilder's books [is] between Indians and whites" (78). He writes that Wilder "endeavoured to present her stories from the point of view of a girl who was the age Laura had been at the time the action occurred." The result, he concludes, "was to eliminate almost completely social conflicts and political controversies which children would not have understood or been aware of [and that] to a considerable degree hers was sanitized history that excluded unpleasant realities" (109).[3] However, the prominent concerns, conversations, and incidents involving Indians in *The Little House* series suggest Laura's awareness. Note her most revealing question to her mother in *The Little House on the Prairie*: "This is Indian country isn't it? ... What did we come to their country for, if you don't like them?" (47). Or to her father, "Will the government make those Indians go west?" When her father replies, "White people are going to settle all this country, and we get the best land because we get here first and take our pick," Laura insists, "But, Pa, I thought this was Indian Territory" (236–7). *The Little House* series does not fully interrogate the stereotypical vision of Indians, although it is the child hero who questions the family's position.

Erdrich goes further. In rewriting the "story" of America's past, she credits children with a full range of knowing and understanding. In *The Birchbark House*, even before Omakayas is able to articulate her experience, before she fully understands when her grandmother, Nokomis, tells her to listen to the animals' ways of talking, she notes that Nokomis "spoke so earnestly, with such emotion in her voice, that Omakayas was always to remember that moment, the bend in the path where they stood with the medicines, her grandmother's kind face and the words she spoke" (104). She intuits, as children can, the significance of a given moment, often with its original depth and richness. Erdrich offers this perspective on children's developing consciousness by focusing on a specific Ojibwe girl with particular gifts and a particular history.

In her portrayal of Omakayas, Erdrich offers this alternative vision of power that encourages children to listen with all their senses, to experience a deep listening similar to Theodore Reik's "listening with the third ear."[4] This third ear hears many kinds of language—language of the senses and the voices of nature, whatever form they take. It requires listening beneath the surface of narratives, those that take the shape of daily anecdotes and those that are more consciously constructed stories. Throughout the series, Erdrich depicts Omakayas listening to her dreams and to her own internal voices. All these languages offer power—the ability to navigate and understand the world.

*The Birchbark House* is set in early America, where Omakayas is "the only person left alive" on Spirit Island, as her home is called. We are told, "It was clear that she had been loved" and that "the family who had loved her was gone" (1). She is rescued by Old Tallow, the strangest and strongest woman in her community, and adopted into the family she assumes is her own. Her name, translated as "Little Frog," given to her ostensibly because of the way she hopped along as a baby, signifies her future as the spiritual leader of her community. "Frogs are like frogs in all stories—transformers," Heid told me. Clearly their ability to live in water and on land, even after their transformation from tadpole into frog, suggests a special knowledge, a gift. "But," Heid continues, "they are also the agents of story spirits to Ojibwe. If you tell a tale out of season, you are threatened with frogs and toads crawling into your bed."[5] Omakayas's name indicates not only her transformational potential but also the importance of telling the tales in context, *in season*, in order to recognize their meaning and value.

Contextualizing storytelling, like contextualizing Ojibwe words, means understanding that "language *is* story," that words are stories themselves, as Silko claims in her essay, "Language and Literature from a Pueblo Indian

Perspective" (84). Entering these "word-stories creat[es] an intricate structure of interpolated tales" (84). This seems true of Ojibwe tales as well, and *The Birchbark House* and its sequels incorporate a broad expanse of interpolated tales. The chronological story of Omakayas's evolution is a linear progression, though it moves against the circular cycle of the seasons. It begins in summer and ends in spring, coming "full circle," as the final chapter's title indicates, into a hopeful clearing from the devastating winter.

Although *The Birchbark House* begins with a prefatory description of Omakayas's rescue as an infant, the lone survivor of small pox, chapter one begins when Omakayas is seven years old. She only comes into knowledge of her birth toward the end of the book, after the second disastrous small pox outbreak, which again kills off a number of her tribe, including her beloved baby brother, Neewo, and leaves her beautiful sister, Angeline, scarred. Reclaiming the story of Spirit Island and the devastation of her people years earlier occurs only after Omakayas has been forced into facing profound and sorrowful truths. This knowledge is part of her preparation for becoming the spiritual leader of her tribe. Her journey involves acquiring awareness and sensitivity, so that she stays close to her instinctual life as she grows into consciousness of herself, her family, her community, and her relationship with the natural world. Her education is provided by the stories of her tribe and by the deep listening that begins in nature.

For example, early in the novel, Omakayas begins to learn the language of bears. She comes across two lovely cubs and is thrown over by the mother, who suddenly appears "with no warning … [leaving] Omakayas flipped over on her back and pinned underneath a huge, powerful, heavy thing that sent down a horrible stink" (29). Although she is terrified, Omakayas waits while the bear "tested her with every sense, staring down with her weak eyes, listening, and most of all smelling her" (30). We are told that Omakayas "couldn't help but smell her back" (31) and explain to her, "I didn't mean any harm. I was only playing with your children. *Gaween onjidah*. Please forgive me" (31). Later, on reflection, she is "convinced that something she did not understand had passed between the two of them. Not words. Perhaps they had communicated in smells. Or maybe in a language of feelings. Her terror, the bear's pity" (34). "Something about what had happened made Omakayas [feel] very quiet" (35). In this space, where she is "empty and peculiar and faint inside," she feels a thought coming. We are told, "A voice approached. This happened to her sometimes ... If she attended to it closely, once it was gone she would know something a little extra, as though she'd overheard two spirits talking" (35). "And as she holds on to her thoughts," she feels "the presence of the powerful mother bear at her shoulder," though there are no words, no odor, "no bear sounds, no tracks" (36).

The bears become her helpers as she heals slowly, grieving Neewo's death. It was with Neewo that Omakayas first spoke the language of love. It was also through Neewo that she learned the language of death. In a sensory description of how the knowledge of his death comes to her, Erdrich writes, "The heat of his body no longer warmed her; then they were the same temperature and then he was colder" (149). After the small pox devastation, somehow Omakayas instinctively knows to ask of the bears, "Will you give me your medicine"? (212). She does not yet know what she means by that question, but she hears the healing voices—"A small sound, a word or two, muffled under the snow and leaves ... The sounds of voices, small and whispery, still floated from the depth of the woods" (203). Nokomis tells Omakayas that bears are "a different kind of people from us. They don't use fire, but they laugh. They hold their children. They eat the same things we do and treat themselves with medicine from certain plants" (207). And then there is Andeg, the crow that Omakayas saves from her own hand, after she has killed enough birds for the family meal. Andeg becomes her companion, and Omakayas learns that although she is close and similar to the creatures, she needs to be differentiated as well—she is a person and cannot reciprocate Andeg's desire to be her mate. She understands that he wants to "make a nest" with her. She tells him, "I can't. I love you, but I'm not a bird" (217), and she is surprised to find "tears form[ing] in her eyes. Andeg loved her so much!" (217). Omakayas notices that he is away for longer and longer periods of time, until one day "[a] group of wheeling, excited black birds passed overhead ... [and] without a good-bye, Andeg jumped off her shoulder ... indistinguishable from the others. [She] felt her heart squeeze shut painfully as the birds passed out of sight" (218). Andeg returns, but "half wild, afraid of humans." Omakayas's knowledge of the ways in which animals and birds are different from humans affects her way of seeing the world and reflects her maturing with the experience embedded in her innocent childlike imagining. This painful acceptance leads her to understand that just as it is fitting that Andeg behaves as the crow that he is, she must be herself, "Omakayas, who heard the voices of plants and went dizzy. Omakayas, who talked to bear boys and received their medicine" (219). The animal spirits speak through dreams, through their gaze, through their smell, offering help and salvation to the tribe.

Omakayas knows to listen to her dreams and to the less rational, the less verbal ways of knowing. These incidents establish the ways in which children feel, sense, understand what they, again, do not know they know. Knowledge seems to come in layers—moving up from the intuitive and the unconscious into the subconscious and into consciousness. Erdrich suggests that it is a natural process when not impeded; she seems to indicate that some children, like Omakayas, are naturally intuitive and attuned to this knowledge. She also comes to accept her ambivalent feelings about her family—the complex love and resentment she feels for her sister and her anger that Pinch, the brother who survived, was not the one she loved. We are told that one day, "looking into the heart of the fire, Omakayas suddenly experienced a strange awareness." And after feeling frightened and disoriented, "she opened her eyes and felt herself gently touch down right where she was, in her own body, here" (220).

Erdrich's portrayal of psychological development is extraordinary: not only does she chronicle Omakayas's learning in detail, convincing and sensuous, so that children can follow and identify the various stages, but she also describes a broader sense of understanding that includes animals, birds, the natural world, and learning through story.

In addition to the voices of those in her daily life, we listen with her to the voices beneath the surface of the interpolated tales she is told. They run throughout the story and reflect her experiences and her states of mind as they are positioned in the main narrative. Storytelling in layers, in direct and linear narrative and in interpolated tales, portrays the ways in which children may experience life—that it does not appear in undeviating lines, that one story intercepts, interrupts, and reflects on another. Native American storytelling, in particular, is rich with such narrative patterns.

Her father, Deydey, is the first storyteller. His story, told with gusto, is an epic-style adventure, which begins in medias res, about overcoming fear and doing battle with ghosts. Like Odysseus he tells a tale of man-eating female figures, whom he must outwit to survive. He has forgotten his mother's advice to respect the spirits, and only in time does he remember his father's advice: "'Never let fear take your mind away,' he said. 'Always think'" (65). Then he outwits the ghostly sisters with his clever trick of turning them against themselves.

With Deydey there is always some ambivalence. In the very beginning Omakayas is both thrilled by and afraid of his return. She loves his humor but it comes with an uneasy laughter. We are told, "At any moment, Deydey's mood could change to barbed annoyance" (52). She knows that although things were more exciting with him home, they were also "less predictable but somehow more secure" (52). Deydey's story communicates all this beneath its surface to Omakayas. His language is sharp, the tale fairly linear in structure, told in a masculinist prose, aggressive in pulse and voice, and distanced from his listeners. Omakayas and her siblings have been drawn into the tale with fear.

In contrast, Nokomis's tale, "Fishing the Dark Side of the Lake," is also an adventure, but includes her audience. She begins, "When I was just a little girl, I was told by my grandfather ... never to fish the dark side of the lake," and then she addresses her listeners, "Why, you wonder?" She goes on to tell how terrifying it was when "[a] hand reached out of the water [and] pulled itself up my fishing line, finger over finger, fist over fist, until suddenly the beautiful face of a woman appeared. 'I am your grandmother,' she said" (136).

This tale of lineage, of the relationship between Nokomis's grandfather and grandmother, is a complex story of struggle and dissatisfaction. It is also a tale of love. When her grandparents are reunited after many years, her grandfather regains his youth: his hair becomes black again; "suddenly he had all of his teeth" (138). For Nokomis, however, it is also a story of loss, as she, an orphan who has been raised by her grandfather, never saw him again. Again we see the complexity of Erdrich's vision—that powerful stories contain loss as well as love, and that truth comes through different modes, and is embedded in cultural and personal stories.

If Deydey's story excites and entertains, Nokomis's offers acceptance and understanding. Deep listening here is prepared for by the way Nokomis speaks—in the language of prayer. First, "in the deep light of the fading afternoon," she raises her arms and everything "grew very quiet around her ... the birds hushed [and] the sky bent to listen" (101). From god figure to animal creature, from the most to the least powerful, all of creation is connected. Nokomis's stories here, as in all three novels, reflect "the integration of daily and sacred experience" (Gargano, 32). The inclusion of the sacred and the quotidian are integral to Erdrich's way of imagining for young people. Her vision suggests ways in which children might imagine their own experiences of disparate knowledges—the integration of the spiritual and the worldly as well as private and publicly shared and acknowledged experience. The story ends with Omakayas listening to the birds' singing and to the voice of her little brother: *"I'm all right,* his voice was saying, *I'm in a peaceful place. You can depend on me"* (239). Omakayas emerges, knowing that she will always be touched by "the tender new buds, opening magically," but there will also "always be a shadow to her laughter, a corner of sadness in her smile" (222).

*The Game of Silence*, the second book in this series, portrays Omakayas's developing ability to understand the language of feeling—through gesture and tone, as well as words. This book, in particular, demonstrates the way language can capture feeling, to help children locate their own experience in words that may have been beyond them when they were younger. Erdrich carefully depicts the development of the middle years of children, with the specificity of a unique individual child. The prologue presents Omakayas as a thoughtful and intensely emotional person. She is deep in thought, distinguishing kinds of love through metaphor. "Her love for the hunter Old Tallow was a fierce and tangled ball of feeling" (x), she tells us. Her love for Pinch "stung the roots of her hair." Her love for Angeline, her mother, and her father, "were strong as earth ... [while] the love loss of her tiniest brother, Neewo ... [was] a deep black hole, bitter and profound" (x). She decides that she will give to the new baby, Bizheens, whom her family rescues and adopts, "all the love she had stored up but could no longer give to her little brother Neewo" (5).

Omakayas, like many healers, finds a way to heal herself and to use her pain to understand the feelings of others. She understands, for example, "the fury of the Angry One," a child who was rescued along with Bizheens, because "he was hungry, always hungry ... He'd starved so badly ... that he would never be completely full" (45). Her journey in *The Game of Silence* involves a deep understanding through wordless language, through the silence of visions and dream spirits that appear. The game of silence involves a contest to see who can resist talking or laughing, and although it is light and playful in the beginning, it suggests what you can learn from silence and from deep listening. It leads to Omakayas's vision quest, which involves isolation, fasting, and turning inward. Erdrich considers the importance of all ways of knowing. Here she presents silence as knowledge that comes through deep listening, the way the imagination can be accessed through listening to one's dreams and waking thoughts, what one knows from the external world of action as well as the internal world of imagining, that using the full self provides access to the imagination, and being part of as well as separate from community. From these different perspectives comes different kinds of knowledge: what it feels like to belong and what it feels like to be alone. Both kinds of knowing broaden and enrich the imagination.

Omakayas observes the world around her from her seat in a tree and drifts into a state "between sleeping and waking … She let herself go." From this liminal position, she "sees herself walking toward the beach with her arms full of bundles," traveling together with her family to "a beautiful lake filled with hundreds of islands … [which] Omakayas saw … as spirits" (231). These scenes, "some small and some big, wrenching, full of great joy … the scenes of emotion, good and bad … [are] the story of her life. She had been shown the shape of it."

She also understands that in the face of uncertainty, the only certainty is that her family must leave their beloved home to escape the white man. Home has been something that is moved, built, and rebuilt around the changes from season to season, as Clare Bradford points out in her study of colonial and postcolonial narratives. She notes that home, the birchbark house as a solid and identity-affirming concept, is replaced by community, which she sees as "deeply relational" (143). Here Erdrich presents a new sense of power, one that is internal, visionary, and dreamlike, not a power to be used *over* others, but rather one that should benefit the community. Omakayas's gift, the gift of the prophetic healer, as Nokomis warns, "is for the good of your people" (221). *The Porcupine Year* is about the search to reunite community.

Erdrich continues to depict stages of psychological development, as Omakayas is now a young adult and therefore her relationship to her community is shifting. For her to understand this shift she will come to the knowledge of her origins and of the people in her community. She also needs to come to a deep awareness of how her community will survive the larger political struggles of the world around her. In *The Porcupine Year*, Omakayas and her family have had to leave their home because the US government wants "to make way for European settlers" (ix). This is the story of their survival, the year Pinch finds a porcupine that seems to bring them luck. The depiction of the porcupine as both naturalistic and spiritual suggests the connection between the physical world and the spiritual world that characterizes Erdrich's work.

In this novel, as Omakayas is maturing, Erdrich describes her, psychologically, as "that creature somewhere between a child and a woman—a person ready to test her intelligence, her hungers. A dreamer who did not yet know her limits" (9). In that liminal space between girlhood and womanhood, the issues of adolescence and of power are illuminated. They involve preparations, rituals, and other techniques of survival—deep listening and observation skills, and dream work. Often in realistic literature for children the dreamworld is depicted as separate from the "real" world. For the most part, it is in fantasy where we get a connection between these spheres of knowledge. Omakayas here remains close to the natural world; as well as dreaming, emergence in nature is part of the way she experiences the world. Omakayas serves as a model of how children might expand, include, and even rely on new parts of the self in their imaginings. Again Erdrich underscores her belief that children's power lies in in their innocence, which is not conceptualized as purity, but rather as the "open heart." The women, particularly the two elders, Nokomis and Old Tallow, have retained this wise innocence through deep listening and knowledge of natural forces. Old Tallow carries the knowledge of the animals as well as that of Omakayas's origins. She feels mythical, primal, and archetypal, though she retains her individual and therefore realistic character.

But Omakayas faces conflicts that lie beneath and alongside the life and death issues of survival, particularly in the interpolated tales of Nokomis in *The Porcupine Year*. Here as in the earlier stories, these tales are particularly powerful. "The Bear Girl Makoons" is a Cinderella tale about the youngest sister who outwits her rejecting sisters and their antagonists. Rather than punishing them, Makoons returns light to the world, and protects them with her kindness. After the prince figure in this story rejects her for her bear-like appearance, she offers to free him of her presence. When she emerges "out of the glowing coals a beautiful young woman," he begs her to marry him, but she asserts, "I found out your true nature ... and I will not have you" (120). She returns to her parents who always loved her—"even when I was a bear" (120). That story illustrates a kind of justice—compassion for those who are not attractive, power for them in their struggle to survive, and forgiveness to those who wrong them. Reimagining this Cinderella tale offers feminist support for this girl hero and for girl readers.

Nokomis's last story relates the painful cruelty of Old Tallow's life. Nokomis had waited to share it but the right moment comes during Omakayas's initiation into womanhood. The story, titled "The Girl Who Lived with the Dogs," contains many lessons about survival—how Old Tallow lived through unbearable cruelty by actually believing she was a dog, as she was thrown to the masters' dogs and treated as if she were one of them. A sad lesson embedded in this story is that like all abused creatures, "No matter how badly they were treated, [the dogs] serve[d] their master" (165). In the end, however, they choose Old Tallow as their master. And she does not have to decide whether or not to kill the cruel master in his weakened state, because the dogs can do this without guilt. "They are not motivated by pity," we are told. "Theirs is the justice of hunger" (168).

With the two elder women, their stories, both inspiring and cautionary, Omakayas's initiation into womanhood is prepared for over time. Nokomis teaches Omakayas how to gather remedies for strength, for a good heart, to heal bruises, to stop bleeding, to cure boils, and for colds and cough, toothaches, cramps, and fevers. We are told that "in her later years, [Omakayas] would realize that this was when she had received the greatest part of her education. She learned all that Nokomis knew. This was how she became a healer" (98).

But here she is still a child, unprepared for her sexual attraction to Aminikiins and her jealousy of Two Strike. When Nokomis tells Omakayas that she is too young to look for a husband, she admits, "I know I am ... but I have these feelings" (147). When Animikiins returns from his year with the Bwanaags, playing "wild and lovely" songs he invented for Omakayas, her mother warns, "Your Deydey played the flute for me, long ago, and won my heart ... My daughter, you must be very careful" (132). "But," we are told,

"Omakayas didn't feel like being careful" (132). Omakayas's feelings are complex and beautifully described. Her jealousy is "a sharp pain dart through her chest." It is "ancient … mean, hot, and vengeful" (139). The rapids are "a dark tunnel that seemed timeless, blind, malevolent. A yawning throat of water" (5). In winter we hear "the roar of ice" (152). Winter is a dangerous spirit that "hid the animals and put the fish to sleep." People could "feel its bitter breath" (107). Erdrich's fresh and arresting metaphors locate perceptions, ways of thinking and of imagining the natural world.

Omakayas is also a sharp observer of other people's feelings. And she learns to understand the motivation behind Two Strike's competitive and destructive nature, that LaPautre, her adoptive father, "has hurt Two Strike's heart, for she adored him" (145), and that "she had been forced to the extreme side of her nature" (152). These subtle psychological insights, a combination of nurture and nature, privilege neither and accept both. These are striking ways of imagining children's and young adults' experience.

In preparation for her "first moon," Omakayas also learns that there are a variety of ways of being a woman. Old Tallow's womanhood was virtually ignored, as she grew into a strange, rough, supremely powerful woman, whose strength was beyond that of most men. Two Strike has "refused her woman's lodge … [and] went out hunting when she had her first moon" (148). Nokomis, softer and more nurturing, tells her, "When your body is ready to bring life into the world, you are a changed being." She offers Omakayas a comforting protection and freedom, though she understands that she is too young to be left alone with her impulses.

Omakayas is specially gifted. But stories of how she acquires an internal power, how she stays close to her feelings attuned to nature and all living things, can inspire all children and offer them hope during periods of loss and despair. There is something soothing about Omakayas's love of nature, about her delight in her surroundings. Her sense of family and her significant role in her community help to alleviate feelings of powerlessness. Learning at an early age that you belong, that you are part of a larger world is most important for children. Hearing tales of survival, of recreating and reclaiming self and community, suggests that others have survived this. Again, as Silko points out, "Stories are always bringing us together." They work against the tendency "to separate oneself during a traumatic emotional experience" (86).

Omakayas emerges from her dark place of isolation when she is needed by her family and her community. And although some of this is heavy fare for children, the stories are rich with childlike humor, child characters, lovely details about nature, and fascinating historical moments many children enjoy. The dark moments are also historically based, as are many of the warm moments of compassion—one dependent on the other, an integral vision of children's literature for children of varied ages and interests.

These are stories that can help children learn to accept their feelings, those of helplessness, sadness, fear, and ambivalence. In this sense, Erdrich's stories offer children a model of wholeness, of connectedness, no matter how different the culture from their own. The fact that the child's journey is inherently one of promise, growth, and fluidity keeps us hopeful. It resists absolute closure since we leave Omakayas, wiser and somewhat older, but still a child. And as the child is connected to and represents the larger community, the story points to a whole world in process.

### The child writer hero: *My Name Is Mina*

When Louisa May Alcott's *Little Women* was published (in 1868 and 1869 in two volumes), it became clear that although Amy, Meg, and Beth were beloved characters, it was Jo who was envisioned as a new female character. As the hero of her story she was the writer, the storyteller whose narrative shaped all that followed. *Little Women* constructed the American girl in each of the March girls as they pass from childhood into young womanhood. Jo is their chronicler who documents their story. She herself is willful and struggles to control her impulsive and strong personality. She is boyish, a model for unconventional womanhood and female individuality. The novel begins when Jo is fifteen and ends when she is twenty-five, accepting a marriage proposal from an older professor, who supports her desire to be a serious writer.

In what I think of as the middle years of modern children's literature, not quite contemporary, but constructed in the wake of the second women's movement (early 1960s), *Harriet the Spy* by Louise Fitzhugh (1964) goes further in featuring a child writer. At eleven years of age, Harriet represents an autonomous girl who writes about anything that is important to her. This includes mean comments on her friends and other children in her notebook, which gets lost and then found and read by the other children, and therefore she is rejected by her friends. Harriet desperately wants her friends back and her nanny, Ole Golly, offers this advice: "You have to apologize and you have to lie." Harriet gets her friends back, but learns to be more careful and to be honest with herself—but not necessarily quite so with other children. It is interesting that these two girl writers, Jo and Harriet, are not gendered as conventional girls. Louise Fitzhugh created Harriet as a girl who dresses like a tomboy and some feminist critics have considered Harriet "queer" (Trites, Bernstein). Harriet continues to dress the way she wants, regardless of her parents' urgings for her to be more ladylike, as Roberta Seelinger Trites points out (4–5). Trites further identifies Harriet as feminist defined, in particular, by her agency.

By the time David Almond published *My Name Is Mina* (2010), women and girl heroes were freed up to be different, not necessarily identified with a particular gender, or a conventional or even unconventional stance. Rather than binary positioning, here is where queer theory is most useful—to expand beyond either/or. Mina is a fully developed child writer, an evolution of a character type. The writings of the child, taken seriously as writing, are not as strikingly featured anywhere as they are in David Almond's *My Name Is Mina*. Mina is a child poet, and rather than construct a conventional plot, as critics and reviewers have noticed, Almond uses Mina's writings to reveal her most interesting mind and the way she sees and expresses her vision of the world. One reviewer wrote, "This is an incredible book. It isn't a story; it is a collection of thoughts and words. Most of the time I was reading it I forgot it was written by David Almond; I read it like it was Mina writing it as she was thinking it."[6] *Publishers Weekly* proclaimed, "Almond gives readers a picture of the joyfully free-form of Mina's mind and her mixed emotions about being an isolated child … This novel will inspire children to let their imaginations soar."[7]

In David Almond's earlier successful novel, *Skellig* (1998), Mina was the homeschooled girl he meets, who spends her time in a tree, discovering and protecting baby owls. The owls are nurturing the wild dust-covered smelly angel, Skellig, who is deteriorating in the garage. As the story of the hero, Michael, winds down, issues resolved, a harmony reached, Mina suggests a central character for this prequel, *My Name Is Mina* (2010).

Mina's name calls to mind Bram Stoker's Mina who breaks the spell of the vampire, Dracula, with her ability to synthesize the mind and the heart. Almond's Mina is a child who represents a synthesis as well—of the light *in* dark, of the mind and the imagination. She is the unconventional child who has her mother's support for wildness and the creative life. She proclaims: "My name is Mina and I love the night." This is her tag, her mantra. She says, "Anything seems possible at night when the rest of the world has gone to sleep."

These words open the story where she continues, "It's dark and silent in the house, but if I listen close, I hear the beat beat beat of my heart" (9). In the dark she feels a deep connection to the inner life. "There's a full moon in the middle of the sky," she continues. "It bathes the world in its silvery light. It shines on Falconer Road and on the houses and the street beyond, and on the city roofs and spires and on the distant mountains and moors. It shines into the room and onto me" (9). Moonlight, rather than sunlight, creates this unity, connects local and global, urban and rural. And in a rejection of the "regular" world, Mina asserts: "Some say that you should turn your face from the light of the moon. They say it makes you mad. I turn my face towards it and I laugh. Make me mad, I whisper. Go on, make Mina mad" (9). Mina welcomes madness, darkness, and the imagination. She is a poet of the dark pastoral and her story bears the courage to imagine the darkest images of childhood.

At the center of this poetic novel is the question of identity: who Mina is, who and what she identifies with. She says: "I look into the night. I see owls and bats that fly and flicker across the moon … Whisper the cat is slipping through the shadows. I close my eyes and it's like those creatures are moving inside me, almost like I'm a kind of weird creature myself, a girl whose name is Mina but more than just a girl whose name is Mina" (10).

As child poet, she speaks for the feelings and thoughts of many children. She loves words and articulates with sophistication and naiveté the wonderings of many children, although, ironically, she is perceived as different and taunted for her "strangeness." In that way, Mina's ideas represent denial of the more conventional child culture. But her quest, in part, is to find friends, to identify with other children—even if they seem strange. Mina's journal contains her retreat from her school, her homeschooling by her mother, and, finally, her visit to the school for troubled children, where she becomes more accepting of difference—her own and others'.

As Mina begins her journal, "My name is Mina and I love the night" (10), she asserts a spontaneity, in what and how she will write. She posits two questions, which link her to birds, the natural creatures associated with the pastoral. Here, as in *Skellig*, she quotes Blake in an assertion of freedom: "How can a bird born for joy / sit in a cage and sing?" And "Do I plan a sentence before I speak it? Does a bird plan its song before it sings?" Followed by large font and caps, "OF COURSE NOT!"

Her journal also contains her dreams and poems in which she closely identifies with birds and other creatures of the natural world—owls, bats, and Whisper, her black cat. Her journal also contains her ideas for activities—those that move her through the light and dark of her imagination, until she reaches some understanding of complexity, of opposites and their sameness, and of an acceptance of her frailties, which encourages a deep descent into the imagination without worrying about the appropriateness of what is found there. It allows for spontaneity and the courage to approach relatively fearlessly the sources from which children may write. However, this journey into the imagination is never for free/without some pain.

For Mina, perhaps the most difficult are her feelings about the death of her father, her greatest loss. Those feelings provoke fear and anger, and a sense of isolation from other children. She raises all kinds of etiological and nihilistic questions: "Why is there anything? Something rather than nothing? Before there was something was there nothing?" (17)—an attempt to make sense of the loss of her father. She writes a story about a "beautiful tree and boring heaven." She wonders if the artist creates things "to look like something that's in the world but can't really be seen at all" (38). She wonders about storytelling, about the difference between writing in the first or third person, and uses black and white fonts, black and white pages, to describe, suggest, and vitalize her stories.[8] In her worry and pain on confronting the loss of her father, Mina does not, however, approach her feelings with trepidation. She continues her focus on her writing and her wonderings.

Mina's first journey into the dark pastoral begins in a park outside her school where she descends down into the earth, into a tunnel. In the face of a snarling dog, she repeats her mantra, "My name is Mina," adding, "I am very brave"— and tames the dog with the lullaby her history teacher sang, "Coorie doon …

my darling, Coorie doon the day." Music, like poetry, speaks to the spirit and can reach beyond the lines of language. On her journey, Mina notes that looking for her father took her to the gates of the Underworld and, like Orpheus, she could not bring him back—could not even find him. Orpheus is replaced in her mythological lexicon by Persephone, who moves between the underworld and the earthly world. Almond suggests a paradigm of fluidity between the two worlds, a back and forth in which each state remains distinct, like the seasons. She invents "Extraordinary Activities," exercises for poets—experiments with movements between oppositional states: writing in the third-person narrative about the self and writing in the first person as someone else.

Looking through a circle made with thumb and finger, into the sky she "contemplates th[e] emptiness" of daytime. And then, in the nighttime version, she urges, "Look through the ring into the sky. See the great abundance there" (100). Remembering how as a little girl she "danced the dance of the wild things with Sendak's Max," she suggests, "Write a page of words for joy. And the 'sad version,' write a page of words for sadness" (133). She recommends writing a page of "UTTER NONSENSE," out of which, as she says, "very fine new words may emerge with 'sensible results.'"

As her ideas for extraordinary activities evolve, the states of perception she connects become more complex: sleep and flying become simultaneous activities. "Go to sleep. Sleep while you fly. Fly while you sleep," she urges. She wills herself to "sleep while [she] fl[ies] tonight!" (195). In her dream she "kept on rising" through the roof, above the house, in the night, with the moon and stars above, and the house and Falconer Road below. She whispers to herself, "Don't be scared, Mina. Don't stop it now." And bravely she laughs, rising again across the sea to Cairo, Amsterdam, The Alps, till "she shivered with the joy of it" (200).

Like a mythical hero, Mina travels through the world, into the underworld, and into the heavens; on earth, she journeys into her tree, connecting with the bird creatures with which she so intimately identifies. She seems to feel closest to owls, the night creatures to whom she devotes a chapter, "Mina and the Owls." With her Mum, she lies in wait for them as the sky opens into moonlight. Her mother, so attuned to her, says: "They're birds of wisdom … the symbol of seeing hidden, secret things" (148).

Mina's poems, prayers, and wishes are about birds, as symbols of freedom and of the soul. She writes, "In Tibet, people believe that the soul breaks free of the body at night, and has journeys that are remembered as dreams ... Imagine flying through the night with the bats and the owls, looking down at the house, the street, the city, the world!" (81). And in her prayer, she writes:

> If my soul, when I die
> Is taken by the body of a beast,
> I pray that the beast will be a bird,
> And that my soul will be uplifted by the body of a lark (83).

Her poems about night creatures are among her most beautiful. About owls, she writes:

> You fly in the velvet night.
> You see what can't be seen,
> You hear what can't be heard.
> Lend me your feathers
> And bones and wings.
> Lend me your eyes
> And ears and claws.
> Lend me the heart
> To leap like you
> Into the astonishing night.

Her greatest wish is to see the unseen, to immerse herself in her dark and vibrant imagination.

Mina writes all kinds of poems, and her poem of creation and birth, what she calls her egg poem, is a concrete poem, a poem shaped like an egg. She writes:

> I sit in my tree,
> my knees to my chest,
> I empty my mind,
> and forget that my name is Mina.
> I have no knowledge of the world ...
> I am inside an egg.
> I am a secret hidden unmade thing. A chick, growing... (178).

She allows herself to be unnamed, to rebirth herself into another species, to become new, empty, to allow space for creativity—the space she needs, without expectation, to be original. Her poems are also rants, full of direct anger against the repressive school. In her response to SATs and other issues of learning levels and tests, she challenges, "Would Shakespeare have been well above average?" (159). She writes another concrete poem, the other side of the previous invocation: "I hated school, I hate school, I will hate school," and notices the power of conjugating the word "hate" and repeating the word "school" until it loses its meaning. She speaks for children in their need for freedom in another poem, "Simple facts about children," where she asserts, "Children have to be left alone sometimes ... no need to keep on saying: learn this, learn that!" This is Mina's sense of child power.

She goes on to express what is, in many ways, at the heart of issues of control: "Why are we so scared of nothingness?" (112). This subtle psychological insight points to the fear of emptiness, the need to fill in all the spaces so that nothing unpredictable, nothing new can get through. But to be creative, as Mina understands, one has to be able to let go of control—to free oneself, to become empty, as Bod learns in Gaiman's *Graveyard Book*, as Erdrich's Omakayas understands.

In addition, writing in many forms offers Mina access to her innermost feelings, to the deepest part of the imagination, a path to her vital life, and to healing. This is Almond's most meditative, philosophical work, different from his work such as *Skellig* that reaches into the realm of the inexplicable. Almond stays close to the perimeters of reality here and beautifully works the end into resolving some of Mina's original pain and confusion. When she visits the school for troubled children, which she rejects attending, she is, nonetheless, able to stay open, despite the way she feels it may threaten her dream of being homeschooled. She listens eagerly to the vital exercises in writing and storytelling, and, most important, she empathizes with Alicia, a student who bears the scars of cutting, and identifies with others, Wilfred in his rage and Harry in his shyness. She recognizes that there are others like her, who appreciate the dark, who do not fit in. At that point, she has a vision of her father and feels him "in her mind and heart, her body and blood, and she knew that despite everything, everything was OK" (240)—in other words, that she is okay. She feels her father's support, something she can access even though he is gone, and that she can accept her loss and go on.

At the end, in a visit to her father's grave with her mother, she asks, "Do you ever stop feeling frail and weak?" Almond expresses what I consider his ultimate message to children, to all of us, through the voice of this intelligently loving mother: Her mother answers, "There's always a little frail and tiny thing inside … like a tiny bird right at the heart of you … not really weak at all. If we forget it's there we are in deep trouble" (280). Her insistence on the strength that comes from acknowledging our human frailty provides children with an alternative idea of power, that power is being vulnerable, being human—flawed and frail. And this involves the power to be creative as well, to imagine even when imagining means feeling weak and exposed. Mina's final "extraordinary activity" is to "listen for the frail and powerful thing at your heart" (283).

Her final extraordinary action is to "be brave" enough to reach out to the new boy, Michael, in sympathy with the discomfort he will come to fully express in *Skellig*, by offering her mantra, her welcome gesture as she says, in her "brightest voice," "My name is Mina" (300).

From Almond's portrayal of the writer hero, which directly addresses the courage it takes to imagine the journey into the dark parts of the imagination, to render it central to the power of creativity, I want to look at two authors whose imaginative visions of childhood extend the landscapes of creativity in political and social ways.

## Challenging political and social institutions: *King Matt* and *Totto-chan*

Both Janusz Korczak, author of *King Matt, the First* (originally published in 1922), and Tetsuko Kuroyanagi, author of *Totto-chan, the Little Girl at the Window* (originally published serially in 1979–80, and as a book in 1982), embrace a deep and abiding respect for children. Autobiographical in tone and vision, their works reflect their progressive values. They feature earnest protagonists searching for ways of nurturing (Matt as child-king) and being nurtured by (seven-year-old Totto-chan) these values. Matt's voice is serious and urgent; Totto-chan's is mischievous, at times comical. They speak as innocents and, as such, feel intimate and authentic, offshoots of their authors. Although their stories begin from opposite positions, their lessons converge. Matt's journey is epic; as king he wields power, but as child-king he is stymied. Totto-chan is a naive, often shy but outspoken child, empowered by her respectful mother and by the school she will attend.

### King Matt, the First

In 2013 I had the good fortune as part of a committee to welcome Agnieszka Holland, the well-known Polish filmmaker and director, to our college. My classes on Children's Literature and her film, *The Secret Garden*, brought us together, and it is from her that I first heard of Janusz Korczak and his extraordinary children's novel, *King Matt, the First*. I think Agnieszka was surprised that I had never heard of the book, which had been as popular and widely read in Poland as *Peter Pan* was in England and the United States. Janusz Korczak was a well-known pediatrician, educator, and director of an orphanage for poor Jewish and Catholic children in Poland in the 1920s and 1930s. In 1942, he went with his 200 children from the orphanage to Treblinka, though he was offered safety for himself. As he walked with the children to the train bound for the death camp, he so movingly said: "You do not leave a sick child in the night, and you do not leave children at a time like this" (Lifton, 4). Those lines and that image continue to haunt me.

*King Matt, the First* is a testament to Korczak's love for and commitment to children. King Matt, child and orphaned king, wonders with the innocence of a sheltered child, about the many issues of power, and—most dear to children's hearts—of fairness and justice. E. B. White's *Charlotte's Web* comes to mind with its opening line: "Where's Papa going with that axe?," spoken by the child, Fern, as she challenges her father's intended slaughter of the runt pig. " 'It's unfair,' cried Fern. 'The pig couldn't help being born small, could it? If I had been very small at birth, would you have killed me?' " A child's sense of fairness illuminates the injustices of the larger adult society, no matter how naively voiced, or maybe even because so naively voiced. Lorrie Moore, well-known American fiction writer, claims that the voices of childhood in her edited collection of childhood stories serve as "the camera and conscience of the adult world" (xii). Of course, other child heroes—Alice, Huck, Dorothy—serve that purpose in their own ways as well, but none so heart-wrenchingly as Matt does. On his father's death bed, Matt pleads, "Daddy, Daddy . . . I don't want you to die" (8).

Korczak prepares us for his psychological exploration of this child, his feelings closely shown, as orphan and as newly crowned king: "A terrible sadness tugged at his heart, and he felt a great anger and resentment for the ministers who were laughing at him, Matt, and at his daddy's death. 'I'll pay them back when I'm the king,' thought Matt" (8). Forced to take his father's place, Matt begins his reign isolated from the ministers and other rulers by his age and inexperience of the world. Worse, Matt is also separated from other children, whom he sees playing and doing normal child things. This painful position frames much of Matt's journey. And it sets up Korczak's vision of the limits of children's power here—even as Matt is ruler and is able to give free reign to his imagination, though his vision is, again and again, thwarted.

Korczak clearly supported children's rights with what he knew deeply about children and what he fought to construct at the orphanage. It was there that he granted children their own parliament and their own newspaper, which he distributed as a weekly attachment to the daily Polish-Jewish paper. So his ideas here are not just abstractions. King Matt is a portrait of Korczak himself as a child. He uses his own childhood photo in the preface, in which he addresses children:

> When I was the little boy you see in the photograph, I wanted to do all the things that are in this book ... because it's important what I looked like when I truly wanted to be a king, and not when I was writing about King Matt. I think it's better to show pictures of what kings, travelers, and writers looked like before they grew up ... because otherwise it might seem that they knew everything from the start and were never young themselves. And then children will think they can't be statesmen, travelers, and writers, which wouldn't be true (1).

In his address to children, he speaks to their wishes and wonderings. The story contains this voice imagined as Matt's. Beyond a program about the social and political life of children, Korczak creates a hero story, mythic in its scope, with a believable and moving boy hero. True to the journey of the archetypal hero, Matt must leave his protected palace, in which, ironically, he has been unprotected and which has left him unprepared for the outside world. Believing that he needs to be with his people, his first task is to disguise himself as Tomek, an ordinary boy soldier, but with no experience of war, Matt does not even know that to set out for the battlefield, he needed to bring an overcoat and knapsack. Felek, his only friend, a child of the streets, confronts him: "You didn't bring a knapsack either? Only a chump would set out for war like that." Felek is horrified by Matt, so "pitiful" in his "patent-leather shoes" and "green cravat." Matt's fantasies about being a ruler and a soldier are brutally challenged: he imagines riding a white horse into battle with his subjects gazing on him, appreciative and attentive. Instead, the feet of Matt and the soldiers "were in such bad shape that blood was gurgling in their boots" (65). Nowhere does Korczak glorify war; it is consistently shown to be grim and devastating. Matt notes that killing and crippling were taken for granted. "The men, already used to it, did not make much of their lost friends" (66). And as Matt is forced into spying for his enemy to survive and then, just as quickly, is forced into spying on the other side—he learns that there are good, ordinary people on both sides. In other words, he learns that war is absurd and shattering. Matt concludes, "Diplomacy means lying all the time" (66). This insight into the way of the world seems like a loss of innocence here, and in a sense it is; however, Matt continues to be idealistic and fair-minded.

Korczak was a strong believer in the equality of children, and in the respect that should be afforded to all people. He reveals the cruelty of the class system that kept people separated—the poor in their desperate poverty—depicted in the portrait of Matt's secret friend Felek. Beaten and disrespected by his father, Felek grows into the violent culture of young men. Hierarchy and the structures of society prevent a real intimacy between Matt and Felek. There is no place for simultaneity as class dominates and Matt becomes more and more orphanized, even as he moves disguised among the people. Korczak also exposes the ignorance of the public, as a doll facsimile of Matt is toted around while Matt is away at war, the public unable to discern the difference between the false and the real Matt.

Korczak seems to challenge gender biases as well. Early in the novel Matt is rejected and taunted by boys as he plays with the girls, his only accessible companions and the ones with whom he is most comfortable. Later in the novel, his only consistent child support, Klu Klu, is a wonderful African girl, whom Matt grows to love. Her father, the cannibal African King Bum Drum, is the most loyal of the world rulers. King Bum Drum and Klu Klu are embarrassingly stereotyped, as Korczak had never met a black person and probably believed he was presenting a positive portrait.[9] Klu Klu is smart, witty, resourceful, and loyal and her father is one of the few rulers to protect and defend Matt.

Beginning his questioning early in the novel, Matt wonders, "What does a king do in peacetime?" (10). "Why be a king if you can't do what you want?" He notices the absurd nature of his state. When he returns from the war as ruler, Matt tries to make peace with his enemies, engage children and all people in fair and reasonable decisions. Most of all he tries to avoid being a tyrant or being thought of as a tyrant. But as he visits a variety of kingdoms, he observes how others rule, which is with sadness and with arbitrariness. This portrayal of the limitations of Matt's ability to undo what he sees as unfair, a betrayal of what he imagines to be just, runs throughout the story.

While Matt continues to try to bring freedom and agency to the children of his kingdom, noticeably in similar ways to Korczak's own successes (the children's court, the children's newspaper), in the end, he is only a child and cannot save himself from being manipulated and betrayed. Instead of returning home, with the experience and promise of renewal as befits the mythical hero, he is banished from his kingdom, isolated as in the beginning. This feels like a surrender, apparently to the futility of trying to rule with justice and equality—that a child cannot effect such changes.

However, throughout, Korczak exposes those structures that oppress children in the larger corrupt society of adults. Sad though the ending is, I believe he achieves a balance between showing the impossibility of the justice the character and the author long for, and possibly inspiring the reader with the portrait of King Matt, in his beautiful innocence and in his acquired experience. Even if he is not able to complete or sustain his vision for children's rights, children may take comfort in the expression of respect and the imaginative moral vision that dominates this book and in what Matt was actually able to accomplish.

In *The King of Children*, Betty Jean Lifton notes in her biography of Janusz Korczak, that as pediatrician Janusz could cure the sick child, but as educator, "he could be the 'sculptor of the child's soul'" (62). In the end, Korczak leaves us with the philosophy embodied in the republic he created for children in this orphanage:

Childen are not the people of tomorrow, but people today.

They are entitled to be taken seriously. They have a right to be treated by adults with tenderness and respect, as equals.... .

They should be allowed to grow into whoever they were meant to be: the "unknown person" inside each of them is the hope for the future (62).

### Totto-chan, The Little Girl at the Window

Totto-chan is a young Japanese girl, both ordinary and heroic—in her kindness and her vitality—who came to represent childness in Japan. The book was a runaway best-seller in 1981, selling 4,500,500 copies in a single year, when it was published in Japan. It was translated into English by Dorothy Britton and published in 2011 in the United States. It contains a constricted vision of education and an imaginative, liberating vision of education. Written by Tetsuko Kuroyanagi, it is her story of the progressive school and its idiosyncratic, spirited, compassionate headmaster, the school she attended after being expelled from the first grade. Her mother is told, "Your daughter disrupts my whole class. I must ask you to take her to another class" (11). Totto-chan is expelled for her fascination with the street musicians, who play daily outside the schoolroom window, and with her box-like desk she likes to open and close. She further distracts the class by talking to the nesting swallows outside the window, and enrages the teacher by drawing a yellow fringe that extends beyond the page to her desk. It becomes clear that Totto-chan's curiosity and the teacher's rigidity are at an impasse. So Totto-chan becomes a student at her new school, named Tomoe: "The ancient comma-shaped symbol for the traditional emblem consisting of two tomoe—one black and one white—united to form a perfect circle" (79). Drawn as yin-yang, inclusive of opposites, Tomoe exemplifies the school's commitment to educating all children and the whole child. The school is charming with its old railway cars for classrooms and offers children the free run of the pastoral landscape, their choices for each day's work, their trips, and swimming activities (without clothes) all designed to encourage imaginings and prevent shaming. Tetsuko Kuroyanagi credits her education as the main source of inspiration for her career as "Japan's most popular TV personality," and as a UNICEF Goodwill Ambassador.

Totto-chan begins her story as "the little girl at the window," a phrase that connotes her original treatment as an outsider, a voyeur rather than a

participant, and develops into an integral member of her class. This lovely
book is illustrated with small pencil sketches that suggest her young age and
depict various class activities. The chapters are short, each "a moral occa-
sion," what Lorrie Moore, mentioned earlier, called a moment "of intellectual
and emotional learning." About her book, Kuroyanagi states, "To children
it is a storybook" (199). For Kuroyanagi, it is her educational autobiography.
The anecdotal stories are epiphanies—each turning on a moment of change.
And without becoming overly didactic or oppressive, they demonstrate how
to create a school that is a just and inclusive community, one that encourages
imagining without criticism or insistence on conventional standards.

Some particularly illuminating moments: when Totto-chan comes for her
interview for this school, the headmaster listens to her for hours, where she
talks about whatever as a seven-year old she wishes; clearly the headmaster
is interested in her imagination and features imagining as a basic tenet of
the school. He responds, "Well, now you're a pupil of this school" (22). That
is the extent of the admission process. This school is built on the principle
that children need to develop the body and the mind equally, "and in perfect harmony" (79). Mostly children learn by independent study with teachers
available for questions. We are told that "whether you started on Japanese or
arithmetic or something else didn't matter at all. Someone who liked com-
position might be writing something, while behind you someone who liked
physics might be boiling something in a flask over an alcohol burner" (29).
We are told that this "method of teaching enabled the teachers to observe—as
the children progressed to higher grades—what they were interested in as
well as their way of thinking and their character . . . an ideal way for teachers
to really get to know their pupils" (29).

These are among the many moments of what I call imaginative thinking
and expression. When the headmaster, for example, tells the children that
they are to bring for lunch "something from the ocean and something from
the hills" (24)—he advocates imagining—what might a "nutritiously balanced
lunch" (31) consist of? He connects a daily part of their ordinary world to
the sources, the broadest ways of thinking about "lunch," imaginatively. And
there are many moments that demonstrate his deep respect for children and
their individual ways of perceiving their world. The headmaster resolves conflicts and acting out behavior not by reporting to the parents, but by listening

to the child, by trying to understand. When a child is shy and does not seem able to answer the simple question of what he did this morning, when the child finally says, "Well, uh, I got up," the headmaster encourages, "That's splendid ... You got up this morning. You've made everyone understand that. You don't have to be amusing ... to be a good speaker. The important thing is that you said [at first that] you hadn't anything to talk about and you did find something to say" (95). Rather than criticize the child, he encourages the child to be spontaneous, and to engage his imagination without fear.

Further, the curriculum includes lots of creative activities like music and dance. Eurythmics, the headmaster's favorite method for training both mind and body, effects children's consciousness of rhythm, a harmony between the spirit and the flesh, "awakening the imagination and promoting creativity ... [and] help[ing] the children's personalities to grow naturally, without being affected by too much adult interference" (79). The headmaster promotes Eurythmics "so [children] could walk in any way they felt was right" (77).

Children are taught not to be afraid or put off by difference: a student who drags his leg crippled by polio, another with very short legs from dwarfism, another who speaks very little Japanese (though is fluent in English)—they are all part of the school community and accepted as such. We are told, "You might wonder why the headmaster allowed the children to swim naked. There were no rules" (55). You could swim with or without a suit, but "he thought it wasn't right for boys and girls to be morbidly curious about the difference in their bodies, and he thought it was unnatural for people to take such pains to hide their bodies from each other" (55). Most significant to me is the headmaster's desire "to teach the children that all bodies are beautiful," including those who were handicapped—and his belief "that if they bared their bodies and played together it would rid them of feelings of shame" (55). All of this resonates with me as I believe it will with many children, and hopefully with parents and educators.

The real things to fear, the headmaster teaches, were, "Having eyes, but not seeing beauty; having ears, but not hearing music; having minds, but not perceiving truth; having hearts that are never moved and therefore never set on fire" (81). Of course, feeling and seeing deeply also include grief and loss. Totto-chan encounters death when a child in her school dies and the chicks she wanted "more than anything else in the world" (84) do not survive. Worst of all for her, her dog, Rocky, an integral part of her family and, in a sense, her sibling, also dies.

The book darkens as Totto-chan grows older; the consciousness of war enters and in 1945 the school is bombed and burns down. Standing at the side of the road the headmaster watches, but tries to assess the situation optimistically: he says, "What kind of school shall we build next?" Tomoe was never rebuilt, but Totto-chan remembers his words to her, words that became her mantra. He told her, "You're really a good girl, you know ... Some people may think you're not a good girl in many respects, but your real character is not bad. It has a great deal that is good about it, and I am well aware of that" (142). Totto-chan writes in her "Postscript" that she might have been thought of, and thought of herself as a "bad girl" if it were not for the headmaster and his belief that all children "are born with an innate good nature, which can be easily damaged by their environment and the wrong adult influences" (191).

In the "Epilogue," Totto-chan reports on those classmates we have gotten to know, how they evolved into fine human beings with different interests and diverse careers, many who attend the annual Tomoe reunions. Akira Takahashi, whose legs never grew longer, but who "has no complexes whatsoever about his dwarfism," became a technical specialist. Kunio Oe, "the boy who pulled my braids, is now Japan's foremost authority on Far Eastern orchids" (205–6) and so on. Some have "impressive" jobs and some are housewives with families. No hierarchy, no particular attention to specialness. This egalitarian perspective feels to me essential to empowering the imagination of children. Without worrying about whether you are at the top of your class, and with accepting, even privileging their frailties and limitations, children are freer to respect and imagine themselves and their world.

The epilogue further suggests the idea of hero as community. This story is structured around Totto-chan's perspective, but it is the story of the community the headmaster has created at Tomoe. Each child is part of the whole; thus, each one's story and how it has played out is included. Totto-chan remains a hero of the ordinary child and a representative of this children's community. Attention to the individual child's needs as well as creating a strong sense of belonging in community is at the heart of Tetsuko Kuroyanagi's vision.

Totto-chan's story is a testament to the value of progressive education. I have been inspired and feel vindicated by her story, as I often am horrified by what is happening to children educated around me. In the United States, education has become corporate, more competitive, unbearably test-oriented, and the cutbacks in music and art all speak to the loss of belief in the imagination. Obviously running a school of fifty students cannot compare with addressing hordes of students and overcrowded classrooms; however, the values and exempla of this book can inspire children to think differently about their communities and themselves, most significantly, to believe they are capable of and entitled to respect. If they act in unbecoming or antisocial ways, to think about why they do that, and to trust that there will be an adult to listen to and help them; to reimagine themselves as creative and thoughtful people, and to think of themselves, not above or beneath, but in community.

## Stories of community: A new heroic

In addition to *Totto-chan*, three stories stand out as I consider the concept of child heroes to include communities as heroes. Laura Atkins articulates community as interconnection, whether family or society, in which "the main impact of the story [is the] connection between people rather than on one individual's journey" (4). She builds on Ursula LeGuin's "carrier bag theory of fiction" where story is a flexible and metaphorical concept, a book as the bag that holds words—"the womb of things to be and the tomb of things that were, the unending story" (quoted by Atkins, 6).

### *Nappy Hair*

Carolivia Herron's *Nappy Hair* (1997) is an epic tale of community. It focuses on African American hair, addressing the negativity many African American girls were made to feel about having "nappy hair." Carolivia Herron grew up with thick, curly naps, aware of the painful incorporation of the dominant culture's values by the minority culture. In *Nappy Hair*, darkness and pain are transformed into a source of energy and light, a cause for celebration.

This story is an exultation of the nap. It involves an entire community, inclusive of young, old, healthy, and disabled. It is a call and response with an elder, Uncle Mordecai, as speaker, and the community of family and neighbors, as chorus. It is a song, offered to Brenda who, we are told, "sure do got some nappy hair." The choral responses begin with simple affirmatives: "Don't cha know," "yes," "That's what it is," and "Uh-huh." Interspersed are extended metaphors for the nappy curls, illustrated with free, curling lines and scenes of play:

> It's like crunching through snow…
> About a foot, two feet at least.…
> With two inches of crust on the top.…
> Y'all know how it sounds when you
> Scrunching through snow like that?…
> That's what her hair sounds like when
> She comb it out in the morning.

Feelings of shame are transformed into pride. "Brother, you ought to be ashamed" is followed by "Ashamed? I'm not ashamed. I'm proud. / She's the only one in her school knows how to talk right." Brenda becomes "a rose among a thousand thorns."

This story is mythic in scope and, like all myths, the hero reaches into the heavens as well as into the underworld. First, Uncle Mordecai claims Brenda's hair as "an act of God," and reports that the angels addressed God: "Why you gotta be so mean, why you gotta be so willful, why you gotta be so ornery, thinking about giving that nappy, nappy hair to that innocent little child … naping up her hair, five, six, seven, maybe eight complete circles per inch." God, in a hilarious affirmation, says, "'Get outta my way … this is my world, and this child … this sweet little brown baby girl chile … she's going to have the nappiest hair in the world … Ain't going to be nothing they come up with going to straighten this chile's hair.' And it was done." Brenda is shown, running from a huge comb and brush and a crowd of children and adults trying to straighten her hair.

What follows this anthropomorphizing, this humanizing of the heavenly, is the human underworld, hell—back to Africa where Brenda sits, "squenching her eyes and looking deep." What she sees are the slaves "getting ready to come to America." The horror of slavery is told at this point through African American voices and in syncopated rhythms. On one side of the page we hear fragments of the familiar blues lines: "Sold your momma for a nickel" with the choral refrain, "Yes, Lord, they did it," "And your daddy for a dime," with the repetition and incantation, "I say they sold your momma for a buffalo … And your daddy, they sold him for one thin dime." The pivotal point now comes with the liberating nap, which we are told "come riding express, coming on across the ocean from Africa, wouldn't stop for nothing." The nap, this emblem of resistance, "danced right on through all the wimp hair … Wouldn't stop, wouldn't mix, wouldn't slow down for nobody."

Brenda is "the one," who stands out among the many. She is singled out here by God, who "looked down on this cute little brown baby girl," and said, "Well done." And proclaimed, "One nap of her hair is the only perfect circle in nature," a celebration of identity. This mythic story is inclusive, an incantation of the multiplicity of voices and genres. It is an epic, a blues song, a childhood accumulative tale built incrementally on an African call and response structure that contains the high and the low, humor and tragedy, the spiritual and the earthly, a ritual for children of healing and revelry, Herron explained on her website, in order to "show the power and beauty of African American oral and epic poetry."[10] Brenda is reimagined with her community heroically providing the reversal of conventional stereotyping of African American culture, transformed into an appreciative aesthetic of African American creativity—the horror of the past retold in this story of the survival of slavery, in the music and storytelling that the culture extracted from that tragic time. There is no denial of that story; rather, it is incorporated into this heroic song that celebrates the creativity of this culture.

### The People Could Fly

In this story there is no visible hero. *The People Could Fly* is a folktale retold by Virginia Hamilton (1985), which features a community of slaves outwitting the vicious, brutal master with one word, passed around the community of slaves by an old man, until all fly away together at its command. Hamilton names him Toby, names the pregnant woman who's beaten for her slow work picking cotton in the fields, and others, but the communication between the slaves is the feature, not the named individuals. The powerful memory of "long ago in Africa," when people could fly, "like blackbirds up above with their wings shining against the blue sky," has been forgotten, but is intensely resurrected in this story of American slaves. And Julius Lester, in his tale "People Who Could Fly," from Joanna Cole's *Best-Loved Folktales of the World* (1983), does not use names. This omission further stresses the community aspect, though the son of the witch doctor who knows the word to liberate the slaves is notably heroic. The young man's legacy points to the sacred power of cultural communication. As Lester says, "This young man carried with him the secrets and powers of the generations of Africa." Lester's incantatory prose is equally powerful here:

> One day, one hot day when the sun singed the very hair
> on the head ... the highest part of the day, the very air
> seemed to be on fire (664).

And after the young witch doctor speaks the commanding word, the first "Now!," the pregnant slave "rose from the ground and, waving her arms like wings ... flew ... out of sight." Following this, the young witch doctor yells, "Now! Now! Everyone!" as the "Africans dropped their hoes, stretched out their arms, and flew away, back to their home, back to Africa." Lester concludes with urgency: "That was long ago, and no one now remembers what word it was ... that could make people fly. But who knows? Maybe one morning someone will awake with a strange word ... and, uttering it, we will all stretch out our arms and take to the air, leaving these blood-drenched fields of our misery behind" (665). The brutal history is not disavowed. But the cadences and the images are transformative: they contain the longing and the hope that can only resolve in wishful fantasy, as folktales tend to do. These two variants of that folktale affirm the power of belonging—if the individual cannot save himself and the community as its hero, perhaps its humanity and its creativity, reimagined here in community, can.

### Brothers in Hope: The Story of the Lost Boys of Sudan

*Brothers in Hope* (2005), written by Mary Williams, is based on the astonishing community of hundreds of boys who journeyed together from southern Sudan, after their farms and families were destroyed by war. They went through the jungles and deserts, 1,000 miles or so on foot to Ethiopia where they were welcomed—for a while—but had to leave as war broke out there as well. Then they arrived in Kenya at a refugee camp, where life became very hard—not enough food, much illness—and finally in 2000 the United States offered 3,800 of them a home.

Many adjusted to life in this developed country; however, many did not. There have been adult books and films about the Lost Boys.[11] But this picture book is written and illustrated for children: to inform them, to help them understand what these children went through, and to inspire them. The heroism of these orphans is extraordinary and their story portrays the strength of this community of children. Williams points to the boys' loyalty to one another and "their desire to acquire an education ... a powerful testament to the strength of the human spirit."

There is a protagonist, Galag, who leads a group of thirty-five boys and becomes attached to one five-year-old named Chuti. There is another heroic figure, an adult headmaster of the refugee camp, named Tom; however, there are many boys who are pictured as part of the heroic struggle to survive. This is an adventure story, but it is propelled and deepened by the interrelationships of the boys, particularized with Galag and Chuti. It is emotionally engaging, the voices of the boys distinct. Chuti says to Gulag: "I'm scared you will leave me like my mother and father," and, though only a child himself, Galag answers: "Chuti, your mother and father did not want to leave you . . . They lost you when the war came. Don't worry, I will take care of you ... I put Chuti down under a tree. He was so tired from crying that he fell right to sleep. As I lay down beside him, I thought of my own parents and how much I missed them."

Interestingly layered, the story is presented through the first-person point of view that establishes the readers' intimacy with Galag and his reflective perspective, after soothing the younger child, though only a child himself. The story itself ends with Galag going into the forest "to be alone and think about all the things Tom told us ... [and] I remembered my father's words: Your heart and mind are strong. There is nothing you cannot do ... My heart was strong with faith and the love of my brothers, and my mind was filled with wisdom from books ... I was no longer afraid. I would find the strength to make a new life." Many did, as part of the bonds they formed in community.

Williams addresses young adults and adults reading this book in the afterword, where she tells more of the story of the boys growing up in the United States—what, why, and how many could and could not adjust. Her final message locates how to participate in supporting the organization she founded as The Lost Boys Foundation. Her "Author's Note" that serves as a preface also prepares the reader for the story "as told to [her] by the young men who lived it." The illustrations are vibrant and feature the individual boys, Galag and Chuti, as well as the hordes of children as they form the communities in discussion, swimming across rivers, walking on their way to Ethiopia and Kenya. The last painting is of Galag, alone on a tree stump with paper in hand, thinking. However, the story is not about him as an individual hero, so much as it is about the survival of children from war-torn countries, communities formed in relationship.

I stress this aspect of heroism as an alternative to the focus on a single individual of many stories, for children and adults. It dramatizes, through an informative, emotionally engaging, and inspiring historical narrative, another way of looking at the cult of the special child that singles out one rather than a community that we should support and nurture.

# 7

# Imagine Empathy: Kate DiCamillo's *The Tale of Despereaux* and *The Miraculous Journey of Edward Tulane*

If there is one quality that can help us reach across global spaces of all kinds, it is empathy. Empathy goes beyond sympathy, even compassion. It is the strongest bond of kindness as it requires us to imagine ourselves in another's shoes, to know another, with the heart. Empathy urges us to imagine the other in her otherness—and imaginative literature provides the space for such bonding. Maria Nikolajeva notes that J. K. Rowling "linked imagination with empathy, emphasizing how it enlists our capacity to feel as well as to see." She points out that Rowling understands the transformative power of the imagination and calls it, "the fount of all invention and innovation" (197). Empathy allows us to engage emotionally with the lives of those we might never know. Frederick Buechner writes in *Secret Spaces of Childhood*, "When I was a child novels gave me the world, a chance to participate in a wider, less circumscribed world than my own" (32). He writes about "exulting in Tom and Huck's 'rebellion,' for example. This kind of imagining involves an empathy that, for me as a child, was exhilarating, enlarging the circumference of my world. It continues to be a core fundamental part of myself, as I am sure it is for many adults" (33).

It is not only realistic characters and situations we can locate in time and space that hold that power for readers. The removal from the world as we know it, a passage into fantasy, can bring the world more sharply into focus, which allows us to see with the heart as well as the mind—without established defenses that accompany our experience of the known world. Fantasy allows for us to imagine a world we do not already recognize; it allows us to connect to the odd, the unlikely, and the impossible. Leslie Jamison, in *The Empathy*

*Exams*, notes that "empathy requires inquiry as much as imagination" (5); that "empathy ısn't just something that happens to us … it's also a choice we make: to pay attention, to extend ourselves" (23).

Empathy can also be tricky—particularly for children who have been raised in what Alice Miller described in her groundbreaking book *Prisoners of Childhood or the Drama of the Gifted Child* as the child who does not get mirrored properly, who learns to carefully watch the mother or other care-taking adult to meet their needs. This child may learn to please others at the expense of the self. This child's feelings may be usurped, deeply and early, by another's needs and, therefore, the child has not developed a safe boundary between the self and other. Maria Nikolajeva asserts that "to be able to feel empathy, young readers must separate themselves from literary characters, just as they in real life must learn to abandon solipsism and start interacting with other individuals" (189).

Empathy involves the ability to hold onto the self and listen to the other, not to become the other, not to merge in overidentification. Merging and projection eclipse the space for real empathy that is natural in childhood. Children easily identify with the characters of stories—note the easy feeling for animals and the popularity of talking animal stories as a genre in children's literature. However, for the child set up emotionally to take care of the parent figure, the ability to advocate for the self can be obliterated. Here are two incidents I associate with overidentification, where my own wishes became obscured.

When I was around ten, I was shopping with my mother for shoes. In those days, when you went into a shoe store, a salesperson came over to measure your foot. There was an engagement with the salesperson—some you liked, some you did not. This particular day we had a fairly kind one who brought out several pairs of shoes, none of which I really liked. Finally, I agreed to a pair the shoe salesman particularly liked, so as not to hurt his feelings. I got lost, in other words, in what I projected to be *his* needs.

The second instance involved a series of incidents when I was in the second grade. There was a student, I will call her Mary, who was clearly unlike the other students in the class, including myself: she was poor, dirty, and hence unpopular. I felt so bad for her that I would play with her in the schoolyard during recess, even though I wanted to play with the other children. I could not say no when she invited me to her house for her birthday party. I did not want to go. I was somewhat tempted by a large tube of candy sprinkles in different colors that she offered me. However, I felt uneasy and when I got to her house it was only me and her—her huge older brothers were there, looking, to me, somewhat threatening. But I found a way to incorporate her into the class with the others that I wanted to play with. And this, for me, makes it a learning experience that I did not recognize at the time. The good part is that I, who was popular, nominated her for class president and campaigned for her, and she won. However, I could not do the kind act without drowning in my feelings for her. And who knows what the shoe salesman or Mary felt. But I, in my projections, could not get out from under the heaviness of these feelings.

Both *The Tale of Despereaux* and *The Miraculous Journey of Edward Tulane* address the concept of empathy—*Despereaux* directly, and *Edward Tulane* as an opposing example. Both belong to the fantasy tradition of talking animal and toy stories that have been embraced by both children and adults. *The Tale of Despereaux*, which won the 2004 Newbery Medal, has achieved major motion picture status, and *The Miraculous Journey of Edward Tulane* is a Horn Book Award Winner. Both books are taught regularly in many American elementary schools.

In *The Tale of Despereaux* the hero is a mouse, traditionally conceived in that readers may trust his goodness and his innocence. He is familiar to fairy tales as the unpromising hero—smallest, least expected to be the quester, and this is precisely what makes him heroic. In his lack of the questing hero's physical prowess, apparent cleverness, and strategic skill, his abilities are overlooked. Those abilities encompass a new way of seeing and feeling, most desperately needed to replenish tradition, a new way of configuring convention so that the world seems a more just place. The balance between what needs to be retained from tradition and what needs to be changed is at the heart of fairy-tale literature. Like many modern fairy tales, *Despereaux* creates a paradigm in which innocence is retained or transformed into a Blakean higher innocence, a wisdom that allows us to remain open-hearted and flexible in the face of experience. Despereaux is small, clumsy, and disinterested in ruling and rules. He is bookish and imaginative. And he can hold together in his imagination a transforming vision of a princess, a servant, and a cruel and ugly rat. As a hero, he promotes, for children and adults alike, an imaginative vision of paradox and complexity.

*The Tale of Despereaux* is a quest story with the familiar talking animals, a princess, and a king—and addresses the archetypal questions: What is evil? What is goodness? What is valuable? It is a search for the soul, for happiness and beauty, for the inner life. Unlike most fairy-tale characters, these characters are given a past, a psychology, complex feelings. They speak like "real" people. And although, as with much fantasy, the sweep is large, from the lowest to the highest, from mouse hero to king, here the king is flawed and foolish, and the mouse courageous but faint-hearted. Included are ordinary people and their ordinary failures, like parents who betray their children in horrifying but recognizable ways, damaged souls who will be redeemed and forgiven, in limited and realistic ways.

Despereaux, the mouse hero, is born with his eyes open: to the light streaming in, to the sweet sounds that he hears as music, and to the patterns of squiggly marks that form the words, "Once upon a time," words that begin the heroic romance he reads and that he adopts as his own mantra. Although Despereaux is born into and from sadness, he does not despair. Though he is the littlest mouse, rejected by his vain mother and betrayed by his father, brother, and community of mice, he embraces the uplifting and ennobling concepts of honor and love. He sees the princess, falls in love with her, and eventually saves her from the dungeon. His father warns, "Get your head out of the clouds and hunt for crumbs" (18); his sister urges him to *eat* not *read* the pages of the fairy-tale book, but Despereaux cannot resist. Nor can he meet the expectations of his conventional mouse community. We are addressed almost immediately, "Reader, you must know that an interesting fate … awaits almost everyone, mouse or man, who does not conform" (25). Despereaux is the artist-hero though his creative vision does not produce anything concrete. He is the animal whose imagination is more vibrant, more pressing than his animal instincts. He imagines differently; he sees, hears, and believes differently. He fearlessly sits at the feet of the king to hear the song he sings about stardust, a song "as sweet as light shining through stained-glass windows, as captivating as the story in a book" (29), and he refuses to deny his love for the princess. For this he is banished to the dungeon by the mouse council, which "indulge[s] in a collective shiver of disgust … That is the way of the world, our world" (43), we are told.

At this point in the story, we are asked to imagine how that might feel, to have "your own father not voting against your being sent to a dungeon full of rats? Can you imagine him not saying one word in your defense?" (44). And when his mother yells, "Farewell," as he is led into the dungeon, the narrator notes, "'Farewell' is not the word you would like to hear from your mother as you are being led to the dungeon by two oversize mice in black hoods. Words that you *would* like to hear are 'Take me instead. I will go to the dungeon in my son's place.' ... Reader, there is no comfort in the word 'farewell' ... a word that promises absolutely nothing" (65–6).

By directly addressing the reader continuously throughout the story, Kate DiCamillo significantly changes the relationship between reader and tale teller. She moves beyond the boundaries where the reader dives into the story, has in fact forgotten that the story is a fictional construction, or where the authorial presence is somewhat distant, addressing the reader occasionally—like *Jane Eyre,* when Charlotte Brontë announces, through the voice of Jane, "Reader, I married him." However, here this relationship is at the heart of the story: it develops; it becomes intimate and urgent—a new configuration, while the reader still stays close to the story.

Through this bond between reader and narrator, DiCamillo draws the reader into imagining the feelings and situations of a whole range of characters, beginning with the easiest identification, with Despereaux. We stay close to his feelings—we empathize. We laugh with him when he "marvel[s] at his own bravery" and "admire[s] his own defiance" (56). And then, when he faints, we experience his terror at facing "the sea of mice" (51) and being led to the dungeon. Courage, the narrator implies, includes fear, even fainting. Through our closeness to Despereaux, DiCamillo urges the reader to deepen empathy with reflection. We are urged to reflect on words such as *courage, honor, devotion*, and *bravery*—in the pockets of reflection where the plot is withheld.

As the relationship deepens between reader and narrator, we are asked to imagine the feelings of other characters, those to whom we are drawn as well as those by whom we are repelled. We are asked to consider how the Rat, the antagonist, must feel: "Imagine, if you will, having spent the whole of your life in a dungeon. Imagine that late one spring day, you step out of the dark and into a world of bright windows and polished floors, winking copper pots, shining suits of armor, and tapestries sewn in gold. Imagine" (103). We are asked to understand each and every character's position and decisions, and for this we need to know the story behind each life. This is a process that involves going backward into the past and lingering long enough to experience each character's history. And this process can help children understand themselves as well as others, to delve into their own past and think about how they came to be who they are.

The story is structured with the last piece, chronologically, the story of the mouse, appearing first, and the first, the story of Mig, a servant girl, appearing last. In other words, Book I begins with the birth of Despereaux, our most inspiring character, the hero with whom it is easiest to empathize. It is followed by Book II, the story of Chiaroscuro the rat, the most antithetical character, called Roscuro, who was "born into the filth and darkness of the dungeon several years before the mouse Despereaux was born upstairs in the light" (85). Fairy tales are made of such opposites—good/evil, light/dark; but here is where the complexity comes in. Roscuro contains the word "oscuro," which means "dark," though his original name, Chiaroscuro, denotes a pattern of light *and* dark. This suggests that nobody, even this destructive, disgusting character, is without the capacity for light. Once he sees the light from a match dance "before [his] eyes ... his rat soul longed inexplicably for it; he began to think that light was the only thing that gave life meaning, and he despaired that there was so little of it to be had" (88). Light encompasses love, desire, and beauty—all things the soul yearns for—and Roscuro becomes enchanted by everything he sees upstairs, including the princess. However, when he falls into the queen's soup after he's spotted hanging from the chandelier, he hears his name "rat," as "[a] curse, an insult, a word totally without light. And not until he heard it from the mouth of the princess did Roscuro realize that he did not like being a rat, that he did not want to be a rat" (109). As with her other characters, DiCamillo gives Roscuro a backstory, so that rather than an allegorical symbol of evil per se, he becomes a figure of complexity. Roscuro's story is part of DiCamillo's engagement with empathy, a significant portrayal of what's behind cruelty; in other words, by reimagining Roscuro etiologically—how he became corrupt and cruel—children are encouraged to understand him.

Here, before we can indulge in sentiment, the narrator addresses us, "Reader, in the spirit of honesty, I must utter a difficult and unsavory truth: Rats are not beautiful creatures ... particularly if one happens to appear in your bowl of soup with pieces of watercress clinging to his whiskers" (111). This comical aside, however, does not lessen the empathetic pull of the story. The narrator continues, "Did you think that rats do not have hearts? Wrong. All living things have a heart. And the heart of any living thing can be broken" (113).

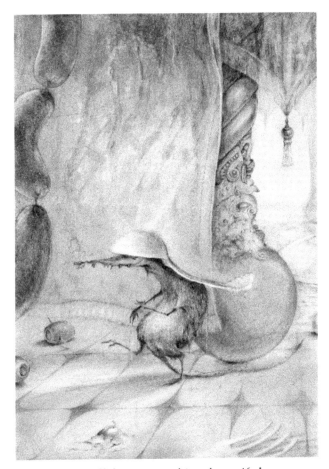

*"I will have something beautiful.
And I will have revenge."*

**Figure 5** "A difficult and unsavory truth." Text copyright © 2003 by Kate DiCamillo. Illustrations copyright © by Timothy Basil Ering. Reproduced by permission of, Candlewick Press, Somerville, MA.

The rat's heart is broken by the princess' look that says, "Go back into the darkness where you belong" (113). This is where Roscuro becomes the force of destruction, his energy reminiscent of the resentment of the child who has been excluded, who has been shamed. It offers a complex explanation, clearly and simply enough for children to understand, of how people become twisted and cruel. This story about love, which may seem ridiculous or uplifting, either way, renders the lover vulnerable. His or her heart may be broken, and Roscuro announces, in the face of his devastation, "I will have something beautiful. And I will have revenge" (116). Again, we are addressed, "There are those hearts, reader, that never mend again once they are broken. Or if they do mend, they heal themselves in a crooked and lopsided way, as if sewn together by a careless craftsman. Such was the fate of Chiaroscuro" (116).

The third story woven into these two is of Mig, a servant girl, who has been abandoned by her father, sold to a cruel and unsavory man for "a hand-ful of cigarettes, a red tablecloth, and a hen" (126). Again we are asked, "Can you imagine your father selling you for a tablecloth, a hen, and a handful of cigarettes? Close your eyes, please, and consider it for just a moment. Done? I hope that the hair on the back of your neck stood up as you thought of Mig's fate and how it would be if it were your own" (127). And if the reader wishes to read on without feeling Mig's feelings, the narrator insists: "Reader, it is your duty"—as a human being to empathize through imagining what another per-son might have to live through.

Mig is forced to call her owner "Uncle," as we are given an account of the "alarmingly frequent" abuse she suffers in realistic dialogue:

UNCLE: "I thought I told you to clean the kettle."
MIG: "I cleaned it, Uncle. I cleaned it good."
UNCLE: "Ah, it's filthy. You'll have to be punished, won't ye?"
MIG: "Gor, Uncle, I cleaned the kettle."
UNCLE: "Are ye saying that I'm a liar, girl?"
MIG: "No, Uncle."
UNCLE: "Do ye want a good clout to the ear, then?"
MIG: "No, thank you, Uncle, I don't."

"Alas, Uncle seemed," we are told, "to be as entirely unconcerned with what Mig wanted as her mother and father had been. The discussed clout to the ear was always delivered" (129).

Brutal though it is, the directness and lightness of tone help the reader to digest this information that is, interestingly, both vivid and distant. Even the effects of such treatment—for Mig, words "lost their sharp edges alto-gether and became blurry, blankety things that she had a great deal of trou-ble making any sense out of" (130)—are presented matter-of-factly. But they clearly explain how people shut down, physically and emotionally. "The less Mig heard," we are told, "the less she understood. The less she understood, the more things she did wrong; and the more things she did wrong, the more clouts to the ear she received, and the less she heard" (130). Ignorance, in other words, comes from abuse, from not feeling that anything you want matters, and this makes you lose the desire to engage or imagine—until Mig also sees light in the form of the royal family, brilliant with their crowns and jewels, and feels "as if a small candle had been lit in her interior" (134). This kindles her desire to be a princess, to wear a crown. Even Uncle's derision, when he laughs at her, calls her "an ugly dumb thing" (137), does not wipe out her vision. We are told, "hope is like love ... a ridiculous, wonderful, powerful thing" (134). At twelve Mig is discovered and since "it is against the law to own another" (141), she is taken into the castle as a servant. And having had absolutely no ability to discern what is possible, having never been consulted or her desires considered, she is seduced by the Rat who "speak[s] directly to the wish in her heart" (171) to become a princess.

The right to imagine is the most basic human right, and if you have never been asked to consider what you want, you may not have a measure to balance what is possible. Mig first wants to be the princess, as the princess represents her first real glimpse of the light; she is vulnerable to violence and cruelty because she has lost her mother, has been abused, and has never been asked, "What do *you* want?" The narrator reminds us of the balance that Mig lacks, but not without empathy for Mig: "Reader ... no one would ever, not for one blind minute, mistake Mig for the princess or the princess for Mig" (186). But we are also reminded of how desperately Mig wants to become a princess and how, "it was because of this terrible wanting that she was able to believe in Roscuro's plan with every ounce of her heart" (187)—which is to capture the princess, drag her down into the dungeon where both Mig and the Rat are sent, and to exchange the princess for Mig.

So far, we have been asked to understand the feelings of Despereaux, our hero; Roscuro, our villain; and Mig, the ordinary person whose state of deprivation renders her capable of cruelty, and who belongs to neither category. Now we are asked to imagine the princess' feelings. And we are told, "Like most hearts, it was complicated, shaded with dark and dappled with light. The dark things ... were these: a very small, very hot, burning coal of hatred for the rat who was responsible for her mother's death. And a tremendous sorrow, a deep sadness that her mother was dead and that the princess could, now, only talk to her in dreams ... Of the light," we are told, "Pea was a kind person, and perhaps more important, she was empathetic.

Do you know what it means to be empathetic?" At this point, the reader is directly asked to reflect on this most significant concept. "It means that when you are being forcibly taken to a dungeon, when you have a large knife pointed at your back, when you are trying to be brave, you are able, still, to think for a moment of the person who is holding that knife." Asking the reader to empathize with the person holding the knife borders on the absurd. The young reader might feel this request blots out her feelings—of fear and anger. However, we are already empathic toward Mig, and so, extreme as that request is, we move on. DiCamillo writes, "You are able to think: 'Oh, poor Mig, she wants to be a princess so badly ... What must it be like to want something that desperately?' And now you have a small map of the princess's heart (hatred, sorrow, kindness, empathy), the heart she carried inside her" (197–8).

What follows from empathy is forgiveness, which, we are told, is like hope and love—"a powerful, wonderful thing. And a ridiculous thing too" (202). Always, the high and the low of everything, the light and the dark, the serious and the comic—the sacredness of love and the profaneness of ridicule, the ridiculousness of love and reverence for the fool. Once you have heard another's story, once you have imagined yourself into his or her feelings, you can no longer turn away from such humanness. This is DiCamillo's sacred duty, honoring another human being, even when they are acting in dishonorable ways.

So Despereaux hears and acknowledges his father's plea for forgiveness. "Isn't it ridiculous," asks the narrator, "to think that a mouse could ever forgive anyone for such perfidy?" An explanation for "perfidy," like many difficult words and concepts here, is provided for the comprehension of young readers.

"But still ..." [he] said, "I forgive you Pa."

"And," we are told, "he said those words because he sensed that it was the only way to save his own heart, to stop it from breaking in two ... to save himself" (208). Forgiveness soothes not only the one who is forgiven, but also the pain of the one who forgives. This connection is a bond that is also at the heart of empathy.

The princess and Mig find their common ground in the loss of the mother. We are told, again and again, that "we must go backward before we go forward" (251). For Mig this means going back to her primal desire, what she really wants, what she needed in the past, what she still needs: her mother, so that for the first time, when the princess asks her what she wants, she says, "into the silent waiting world," "I want my ma!" When she is close to the light, the real light of empathy from the princess, she is able to answer the simple and bold truth, "I want my ma." That bond helps her to heal and to go beyond her desire to be a princess, something she can never be. The princess, holding out her hand to Mig, says, "I want my mother too" (254), and all that "mother" means—nurturing, comfort, safety, love.

So Mig is forgiven. Even the Rat is forgiven, though he never heals completely. DiCamillo acknowledges that there are some ruptures that cannot be restored. His is the damaged heart; he is seen moving "back and forth from the darkness of the dungeon to the light of the upstairs. But, alas," we are told, "he never really belongs in either place"(266). Although the princess remains repelled by the rat, her quest is to descend into the dungeon where our darkest feelings lie. Significant knowledge comes to her from this quest: "how fragile her heart was, how much darkness was inside it, fighting, always with the light" (264).

In the final chapter the familiar fairy-tale ending is presented as a question: "Did they live happily ever after?" And the answer comes, honestly and paradoxically, "Yes ... and no" (266). The rat effects the reunion of Mig and her father who atones for his betrayal of his daughter. Again, with forgiveness. Mig, of course, does not get to be a princess, but she does get treated by her father "like one for the rest of his days" (267). And, of course, we are reminded that "a mouse and a princess cannot marry," but they can be and are friends. *The Tale of Despereaux* deals with what you can and cannot have, and with desire. Mig and Pea cannot have their mothers back; Mig cannot become a princess; Despereaux cannot marry the princess; Roscuro will not be totally transformed from the darkness into the light, but will remain a liminal figure. Despereaux is reunited with his family, who, finally, witness him "in his place of honor, right next to the princess" (269). Most significantly, when Despereaux does get the chance to kill the rat, he wonders, "Would killing the rat really make the darkness go away?" (262). This story moves through imagining and empathizing, away from the tradition of killing off the bad and reestablishing the disinherited, to providing a new heroic paradigm, one of forgiveness. The *Coda*, the final words, stresses the power of stories "to save [oneself] from the darkness," and through empathy to inspire hope, at the heart of which is active imagining.

DiCamillo's *The Miraculous Journey of Edward Tulane* (2006) tackles the same subject, but the other way around. Edward is the toy rabbit who, locked in his own world, concerned only with his comfort, utterly lacks empathy. The quest that he resists, at times consciously and at times unconsciously, is to become a listener, someone who feels for others. The story of Edward Tulane asks where hope comes from. And love: Where does love come from? Empathy is at the core of hope and of love. To imagine what another feels, through listening and observing, suggests the hope for love and for a more humane, more expansive world. Edward's adventures thrust him into a range of experiences that force him into this kind of imagining.

It is interesting that Kate DiCamillo creates her hero, or, as he first appears, her antihero, as a toy. Toys, unlike animals, are inanimate, and in this story the toy transforms from a passive object of his owner's projection into an expressive and feeling character. In other words, DiCamillo suggests how one comes to be a feeling person, the process of this psychological quest. As a toy, Edward is a passive receptacle, a plaything. He is made of porcelain and, therefore, somewhat fragile, delicate, valuable, and refined. He cannot move on his own and relies on his owner, the little girl who loves him, for agency. It is fitting then that his journey, however he is tossed and thrown, wherever he lands, no matter how many different landscapes he experiences, is an interior one. It is emotional and his changes are internal.

Edward's miraculous journey involves learning to imagine. This learning is not just aesthetic; it is observing the feelings of others: how to witness, how to reflect on another's experience, and ultimately how to reflect on one's own. Feeling involves many skills: listening, observing, imagining, creating, and reflecting. In this story, the movement is from resistance to acceptance, and what Edward comes to accept broadens him and makes him more compassionate. He also learns the importance of play, something he dismissed as beneath him before his adventures took him to the bottom of the ocean, to the underside of a garbage heap, to an old couple's modest home, to a hobo's storytelling circle, to a child's sickroom, to a doll shop, and back, in full circle, to his original home. From the upper classes to the underclasses, from sea to farm, Edward journeys far and wide, though, as a toy, he is always at the mercy of those who find him and those who love him. There are highs and lows; he is lost and found several times as the process of learning to feel is carefully documented.

At first he spends his days inert, waiting impatiently for Abilene to come home from school, staring at his own reflection in the mirror, admiring his "elegant figure" and his own "fineness" (8). He cares nothing for Abilene, a fact that goes unnoticed, except by Abilene's grandmother, Pellegrina, who offers a cautionary tale of a princess who is turned into a warthog because she loved no one. The predictable characters—the sympathetic wise older woman, the innocent beautiful girl—are rendered less predictable by this interpolated tale that has no happy ending, because, as Pellegrina says to her granddaughter, "How can a story end happily if there is no love?" And to Edward, she whispers, "You disappoint me" (35), words that continue to haunt him.

If this feels heavy-handed, the lighter, subtler touches come with the process of learning compassion—which begins with fear. When Edward is thrown overboard and lands at the bottom of the ocean "with his head in the muck, he experienced," we are told, "his first genuine and true emotion" (49). That he is afraid, as he "hits bottom," so to speak, flung about "until the storm wore itself out," tears away at his complacency. Thus begin his changes, as he is forced into the clothes of a girl by his next owner. Stripped of his male privilege, he is at first horrified. But as he is humbled, he begins to love. He concludes that "wearing a dress won't hurt me" (68), and the stories he is told "struck him as the most important thing in the world ... he listened as if his life depended on what [Nellie, his owner] said" (69). And now his cold, distant staring at the stars shifts to "learning the names of the constellations one at a time," which demonstrates his love for "looking up at the stars" and for "the sounds of the constellation names ... [which] were sweet in his ears" (71).

Naming is a significant step in Edward's development as it is for any new language learner. But for Edward, accepting the various names he is given by his various owners expands his consciousness. To the kind old woman, he is Susanna; to the hobo and his dog, he is Malone; to the nasty old woman, he is Clyde the scarecrow; and to the two neglected and abused children, Bryce and Sarah Ruth, he is Jangles, the entertainer. As Edward's quest sends him out into the world, he encounters various classes, like the classical hero who begins as the son of nobility, and then is cast out so that he must experience what the ordinary person does, without the benefit of his name. Often the hero descends into Hades or the equivalent of the world beneath the world, the lower echelons of society, even the habitats of animals. Edward's quest, from nobility to the lower classes, is suggested in the landscapes into which he is cast. He moves from the upper-class home of Abilene to the bottom of the ocean; to a garbage heap; to the humble home of the fisherman Lawrence and his wife, Nellie; to the campfires of Bull the hobo; to the unprotected farm-lands as a scarecrow; to the poverty-stricken makeshift home of Bryce and Sarah Ruth; to the homeless state of living on the streets; to the doll-maker's shop, which is no one's home; and, finally, back to his original roots. He also has contact with the land, the sea, the stars in the skies, and the dream world, all of which indicate his large, heroic scope. This wide range of experience opens him up to imagining a larger world of difference. In order to survive, he must learn empathy, to imagine what others might feel.

The renaming of Edward many times over further signifies the range of his experience. As a passive hero, tossed from owner to owner, his name reflects class and gender. As Edward Tulane, he belongs to a formal and refined class; as Susanna, he is a girl without a last name to establish social position; then as Malone, he is defined only by his Irish, working-class last name. And as Jangles, he is a clown, a plaything—without either class or gender. His own-ers likewise reflect the range of his experiences. And as he gets to know their names and is named by them, his knowledge expands, demonstrated by the significance of naming. I recall Beowulf who withholds his name from the messenger at Hrothgar's court whom he distrusts. He will only allow the king himself to know his name. I am also reminded of the fairy tale *Rumpelstiltskin* and the liberating power of guessing the name, where the miller's daughter cannot own her own creation—her baby—until she guesses the name of her rescuer—until she, metaphorically, understands the creative power of spin-ning straw, the ordinary element, into gold. Naming implies identity and is a significant step toward empathetic imagining—as mentioned before, one needs to know who one is, to retain a sense of self while empathizing with others.

Edward's constant name changing also records his instability. In con-trast, Despereaux's name is fixed and in his journey, though also from high-est (the castle) to lowest (the dungeon), he is stable. Though he sometimes overreaches, Despereaux knows who he is, is steadfast in his vision of what is important, what needs to be done. It is the outside world—his family and community of mice, the rat community, and the royal family—that needs to understand his significance.

Still, whether from inside or outside, whether the net of the story is cast wide or narrow and deep, these stories are about agency. They emphasize empathy as an active state of love. By creating a character who essentially has no agency, DiCamillo illuminates his internal and dynamic journey. Though Edward sees all the time (in fact, he cannot even close his eyes as they are painted on), like Narcissus, he sees only himself as he gazes in the mirror. He stares at the distant stars, but only through his trials does he see their beauty. He hears everything but must learn to listen empathically to the stories and lives of those around him.

Illustrations are powerful texts in this story. First through Edward's consciousness, we see Edward holding a watch, as he waits for Abilene to come home, suggesting the way in which he views her. In the second illustration, Abilene holds Edward, but is still faceless, unseen by him; further, he looks like he's choking rather than enjoying her embrace. In the third illustration, Edward is being dragged around by the dog. This is the first illustration in color suggesting that—ah! He notices the insult. And so on. Each illustration reveals Edward's thoughts, all leading to the illustration of the house that he comes home to in a dream. After Sarah Ruth's death, after he is set loose, damaged and alone, he dreams of those who loved him and those whom he has loved. He dreams that "he was walking on his own ... without any assistance from anybody ... wearing a fine suit ... of red silk" (161). Clearly the book designer saw this scene as a turning point as it is depicted as the cover. Edward has come home in his dream, which presages the homecoming that will follow once his quest is complete.

But first, he has to struggle against desperation and despair. Ironically Despereaux himself was never plagued by despair. However, for Edward, disappointment leads to self-protective denial. His heart shuts down in the dollmaker's shop, when he has lost all his friends. "I am done with being loved ... I'm done with loving. It's too painful," he says. When the old doll asks, "Where is your courage?" he responds, "Somewhere else, I guess." She then echoes the cautionary refrain of Pellegrina, "You disappoint me ... If you have no intention of loving or being loved, then the whole journey is pointless" (189). Edward must learn patience. "Someone will come for you," she tells him. His only agency is to love and be loved—to see and to listen, to empathize and to hope.

Though both books are for young children, they embrace the complex lesson of empathy that is at the heart of difference. They tell their stories with grace and with poignancy, without losing sight of their message. It unfolds simply, without sacrificing the subtle paradoxes of the light and the dark—the light within the dark and the dark within the light. No hero is without darkness, no villain without light. In breaking down the psychological process of learning empathy and its power to reach across differences, gaps, and misunderstandings, these books stress the potential of the imagination to help children grasp and put into practice this intricate task of imagining the other—one the adult world would do well to mirror.

8

# New Ways of Imagining the Picture Book:
# States of Mind, States of Feeling

Contemporary picture books are informed by new techniques and perspectives. They incorporate methods from graphic novels, where the text and images are positioned in unconventional ways that suggest new meanings. They use digital formats to evoke technology in reshaping image and word. Postmodernism, a dominant philosophical stance of contemporary art, has opened the picture book into a new genre, what critics have identified as the Postmodern Picture Book.[1] This genre engages readers in co-authoring, inviting them to interpret beyond the usual ways that we see and read. The postmodern picture book tells stories in a nonlinear way, so that more than one perspective is represented and more than one story is told. *The Tale of Despereaux*, as we have seen, moves back and forth in time; it is told through multiple perspectives, and directly addresses the reader as a partner in meaning making.

Another popular feature of the postmodern picture book is a contrapuntal relationship between text and picture. Neither text nor picture possesses meaning without the other. Text and illustration present two different stories. We have seen how Maya Angelou's text in *Life Doesn't Frighten Me* offers the opposite feeling from Jean-Michel Basquiat's illustrations. The threatening illustrations alternate with her words, "life doesn't frighten me," contradicting the reassuring, bold statement. Life can and does frighten the child. The book presents the imagination of the child who needs to reassure herself when she is picturing frightening aspects of her life. Those two seemingly paradoxical positions depend on each other: one chants those reassuring words to combat the mind's terrifying images. Words suggest a more rational, comprehensible reality and, as child fear does not parse out into sentences, images are needed to express the chaos of fear.

## Shaun Tan

Prime examples of experimental picture books are Shaun Tan's many surrealistic works that illuminate internal states. They subtly echo the written texts, and are often surprising with their odd and intrapsychic meaning. *The Red Tree*, for example, one of the best that includes children in its audiences, depicts depression.

According to Andrea Schwenke Wyile, "*The Red Tree* is a picture book that dismantles dichotomies and hierarchies of certainty" (120–1). For example, Wyile claims that the gender of the red-headed protagonist is "not definitive" (123), though she acknowledges that Tan refers to the protagonist as a girl on his website (131), and sees the story, especially the character's take on it, as existential. Wylie stresses that it extends the depiction of depression, not as an illness, but rather as part of the human condition.

*The Red Tree* opens, before the story begins, with two extraordinary images: the first is of the little red-headed girl on a chair in a field with a megaphone from which letters tumble out. In the second, a clock is set in what looks like a hayfield; the clock extends beyond the landscape, and a red leaf marks the number 12 on the clock. All the other leaves marking the numbers on the clock are brown. Red is set apart—it becomes the symbol of hope and vitality. There are also random letters in the hayfield. This prelude, two pages of surrealistic images, suggests the themes and their accompanying images that are developed throughout the story: alienation, a feeling of not being heard, not being able to be coherent or put words together. Words take no shape and time has little meaning.

The story begins with the little girl in bed, a few brown leaves randomly strewn; the metaphoric intense gathering of leaves inside the bedroom threatening to drown the little girl portrays the heaviness of depression, often unrecognized in children as well as in adults. The story begins, without capital letters, in medias res, without order, "sometimes the day begins with nothing to look forward to." Dreamlike and out of control the leaves become a thick mass from which the girl tries to escape, as the text reads, "and things go from bad to worse." The story unfolds with bizarre landscapes—mechanistic and claustrophobic—a seascape with a large bottle in which an outerspace figure is encapsulated; a double-page spread of buildings, an airplane, even a piano, all covered in incomprehensible words with the little girl pictured on a ladder that seems to reach into a small box within a smaller box, with the written words that are quite comprehensible: first "nobody understands," followed by "the world is a deaf machine," and ending in the double-page spread that reads, "without sense or reason." Certainly, Tan captures the feeling of depression—its complexity and range. It is a snail, in different sizes, with words in different fonts that identify "waiting." It is surreal landscapes of being locked in and being locked out, followed by images and words of angst that articulate such an existential statement: "Sometimes you just don't know what you are supposed to do or who you are meant to be or where you are." The illustrations are intriguing. My favorite is a large one of the girl painting the unfinished outline of herself on a colorful wall, her shadow behind her, with birds on the floor casting tiny shadows. This depiction of the girl's incomplete attempt to draw herself whole demonstrates just how difficult it is for her to define or imagine herself. Her shadow threatens to prevent a sense of freedom, suggested by the birds—though they also cast shadows, a sign of the darkness even in the symbols of freedom.

Tan's work grabs the reader darkly, until the book ends with an image of hope. The girl in the doorway to her bedroom enters with light cast from the outside into the inside onto a small red flower, matching her red hair, as the words read, "but suddenly there it is right in front of you / bright and vivid / quietly waiting." Hope comes in the form of a tiny red leaf that persists, but is barely noticeable, on each page. It suggests the way the adult writer/ illustrator knows that the depression will lift and things will be all right. However, the child does not know this, may not perceive or know what to make of the lovely red leaf—though clearly it is identified with the girl, with her red hair, and how nature will restore her equilibrium. The final words, "just as you imagined it would be," are situated under an illustration of the girl looking at a large red tree that seems to have bloomed suddenly inside her bedroom—a huge, bright, optimistic symbol, indicative of the way despair can suddenly come on and just as suddenly leave. The drawings align with the words in a deeply felt way, so that children can relate to both the words and the images. Tan claims that he sees *The Red Tree as*

> a meditation on feelings of alienation and displacement ... representing emotion as landscapes ... inspired by the way that both children and adults can describe intangible feelings using visual metaphors: monsters, sunlight, rainbows, storm clouds, and so on. In this case, I felt that my own personal experience of depression was a perfect subject for a similar treatment. Partly I wanted to create something useful from what can seem to be a useless experience—an abject feeling of hopelessness—but more important, to simply acknowledge its reality, its strange distortions of perspective and reason, and illuminate something that is often invisible (end piece for *Lost and Found*).

Tan writes that with the first publication, the book was "both criticized as depressing and celebrated as overwhelmingly optimistic and affirmative." He found that children seemed intuitively to get it. They were "often the first to notice details such as the small red leaf that is always present." He claims, "There is an implicit recognition here that important things in life ... can't always be named, or even fully understood." Further, that some things that "are entirely imaginary—like a red tree growing suddenly in a room"—are not any less real. Particularly for children, imaginary things can seem real, palpable, and present. The reasons for states of mind are not clear, though the feelings are recognizable. Visualizing them in their complexity and distortion and identifying them in simple language can be, as Tan writes, "useful."

The idea of representing depression as part of where the imagination can go (as well as the way it can be broad and engaging) may help the young reader to allow for a larger range of feeling. *The Red Tree* demonstrates a way of normalizing depression for children who suffer from it; whether it is debilitating in its pervasiveness or just disturbing in moments, it is a component of experience that needs to be recognized and accepted as part of the world of the imagination. All of Tan's work seems to resonate with readers as highly imaginative and playful—even in its darkness.

## Brian Selznick

Illustration creates what Perry Nodelman calls "simultaneity of perception," where one sees the moment, the whole at once, and time is halted. Words, on the other hand, tend to locate narrative and move through time and space. In his trilogy, *The Invention of Hugo Cabret* (2007), *Wonderstruck* (2011), and *The Marvels* (2015), Brian Selznick offers illustration as a series of temporal moments. He tells his stories in the two modes, the visual and the temporal, equally. In *Wonderstruck*, he uses intricate full-page illustrations to tell the story of the past, and words to tell the story of the present. When the two stories come together, the two modes alternate. In *The Marvels,* the last book of the trilogy, Selznick tells the first half of the story visually and the second half in words. We do not get the full picture until the words fill us in and provide answers to the questions raised in the first part, where the illustrations are suggestive rather than definitive.

Selznick also incorporates different artistic modes. In the first book, *The Invention of Hugo Cabret*, he uniquely transforms cinematic presentation into book format. Selznick was always fascinated by and connected to cinema. His grandfather's first cousin, David O. Selznick, made the original *King Kong* and *Gone with the Wind*. As Selznick says, "Though they both died before I was born, my grandmother's house was filled with books about David O. Selznick that I loved to read" (*The Hugo Movie Companion*, 12). From the first few pages of *Hugo*, Selznick establishes the slow filmic zooming in with his elaborate pencil sketches: first of the moon, then of Paris, a train station in Paris, a crowd in the train station in which a boy is subtly illuminated, and then a double-page close-up of the boy's face in profile looking out at us. John Schwartz, in his *New York Times* book review, describes this novel as "a silent film on paper" (March 11, 2007). And in an article about readers in a digital age, Eliza T. Dresang and Bowie Kotria note, "Each sequence of drawings can itself become a miniature silent movie if the reader employs a flipbook technique." They point to Selznick's creation of a "highly interactive reading experience with vivid visual appeal, intertextuality, and multiple layers of meaning ... a dramatic departure from the typical picture-book tradition."

Selznick's intention is clear. He engages the reader in imagining. In his "Brief Introduction," he uses a fictional author to address the reader: "Before you turn the page, I want you to picture yourself sitting in the darkness, like the beginning of a movie." In *Hugo* a series of full-page illustrations tell one part of the story, interspersed with verbal texts that provide a counterpoint, like the way a movie uses visual and verbal techniques. In *Wonderstruck* and *The Marvels*, the artistic venues include museum dioramas and theater sets.

Selznick wrote the three novels as a trilogy, linked not by character or plot, though there are similarities; rather the novels are connected through their formats, their unique intricate pencil-like images of past and present, in braided experimental mixtures of fact and fiction. They are also connected by theme: they all feature fictionalized child heroes in search of their history, and all are oddly biographical in their use of extensive details from real people's lives. In an interview in 2015, Selznick affirms his idea of the trilogy as a way of telling stories. He talked about his love of theater, his interest in the history of cinema, his process of translating cinematic storytelling and theatrical storytelling into visual and verbal book telling; how to represent panning and zooming, the tools of cinema, like "that momentous moment [of] the turning of the page" or the curtain opening in a theater on a scene, with the immediacy of wonder and awe (quoted from Dan Hurlin, in Selznick's Caldecott Medal Acceptance Speech).

The first story, *Hugo*, features an orphan who lives behind the clock in the train station in Paris and steals for his survival. He is set up as an observer: "From his perch behind the clock," we are told, "Hugo could see everything" (46). The fact that maybe half of these books is visual raises the following questions: What do the characters see (and what do they not see)? Through whose gaze does each story unfold? (There are at least two stories in each novel.) What part of each story can be told through words (or only in words) and what part can be told only in images? Each novel features the sense of sight.

With Hugo's story the cinematic approach, slowly zeroing in from the farthest outside force (the moon) to close-ups of Hugo's eye, suggests the symbolic connection of the moon with the imagination and the *künstlerroman*, the story of the young artist like James Joyce's *Portrait of the Artist as a Young Man*. However, Joyce's *Portrait* begins with the infant self and moves outward as Stephen Daedalus begins to name his surroundings. Here Hugo is the young artist who needs to recover his past—so it is fitting that his journey moves backward toward memory, to the interior of the self.

Hugo's quest, like that of Selznick's other principal boy characters, involves a search for his past. He has discovered an automaton in the ashes of a museum that burned down where his deceased father worked. His desire to connect with his father involves deciphering the notebook his father left behind. He believes that the notebook will enable him to fix the mechanical

**Figure 6** The moon and the rocket. From *The Invention of Hugo Cabret* by Brian Selznick. Scholastic Inc./Scholastic Press. Copyright © 2007 by Brian Selznick. Used by permission.

man that is poised to write something, and that it will reveal a message from his father. The mechanical man, "built entirely out of clockworks and fine machinery" (114), is Hugo's legacy. It becomes Hugo's creative task to decipher what the mechanical man will tell him.

Over several pages, we follow Hugo into the grate in the station behind a clock, from which he looks out at an old man and a shop. As we get closer, we come to a double-page spread of the man's face with a sideways glance similar to Hugo's, followed by a close-up of the old man's eye, then to the clock at the train station, then the number 5 behind which the boy's eye looks out. The old man turns out to be Georges Méliès, the early cinematographer and magician, and the position of the glance and the eyes establishes the connection between him and Hugo. All this is revealed without words. Much of the subtlety of Selznick's story is revealed visually.

The drawings in the notebook turn out to be by Méliès, the most prominent of which is the rocket going into the eye of the man in the moon—an image from one of Méliès's films. As a real historical character, Méliès provides the complicated backstory that also connects Hugo with Isabelle, Méliès's granddaughter, and through Isabelle, Hugo becomes attached to this family. His complex feelings are read in his eyes. Selznick's close-ups of eyes and the connection of the eyes with the recurring image of the moon suggest the emotions and the imagination as primary sources of experience. He balances the uncanny and the realistic, the fictional and the biographical, in his desire to explore the connection between dreams and the imagination. He writes that for Méliès, "film had the power to capture dreams [rather than] reflect real life" (355), and that is what Selznick is after in his trilogy. Here the mysterious recurring image of the rocket in the eye of the man in the moon establishes the importance of the visual imagination and the cinema as places of magic and dreams.

Selznick also reimagines the concept of family in this trilogy. In each novel, the child has been born into the wrong family—a chance formation that does not work, either because in Hugo's case his parents are dead and his uncle cruel and deserting, or because the child does not fit into his family. Hugo is transformed from an alienated outsider as he joins Isabelle in the cinema and becomes part of the Méliès family. Hugo and Méliès connect as artists—Méliès himself is finding his own path back to his imaginative life.

Selznick is interested in the journey to find the family that is "right" for the child, the quest to find "your people." In *Wonderstruck* the bond is between a boy and his grandmother—whom he never knew, and in *The Marvels*, the boy finds a new family with his uncle—someone he did not know but went in search of—and, as in the other two novels, he discovers the "right family."

In *Wonderstruck*, the two stories unfold separately, one in the present and one in the past, one story told visually and the other verbally, and they come together in the present time with the meeting between the boy Ben and his grandmother Rose. Again the story is a complicated search for a father, whom Ben has never met or heard anything about. His grandmother's past is recounted: she was a deaf child, imprisoned in her room by a family that supposedly feared for a deaf girl to be out in the streets of the city. The mystery unfolds with clues—a bookmark, a letter, a book, a museum trip—all occurring after Ben too becomes deaf when he is hit by lightning. He leaves the home of his aunt and cousins to go to New York where he winds up in the Museum of Natural History, and where he meets Rose, his grandmother, for the first time.

That both Ben and his grandmother are deaf intensifies Selznick's use of the sense of sight. Katherine Eastland, in "Deaf Meets *Wonderstruck*," describes the ways in which Selznick researched the culture of deafness. Eastland writes that in his desire to tell two stories, one in words and the other entirely through images, he looked for a story that made sense "being told just in pictures." He had seen the film *Through Deaf Eyes*, and "remembered a line 'about how the deaf ... are the people of the eye and that sign language is a language you must see in order to understand.'" Selznick thought it might work to "echo the way [the deaf] live." Rose was born deaf, and during the 1920s, Eastland points out, the cinema changed from silent film to talking movies. So it is particularly fitting that her story be told almost entirely visually. As Ben has become deaf, they share an experience that Selznick explores throughout the trilogy: the experience of "being part of a culture outside of the one you're born into." They also both had parents who were not able to empathize with them—Rose's parents were strict and distant; Ben's loving mother has died and his aunt and uncle do not share his values or understand his sensibility.

Rose's story goes backward in memory to 1927 while Ben's story begins in 1977 and goes forward; the narratives alternate. As Rose sneaks out of her house into the world, her narrative is interspersed with Ben's story in 1977, when he also sneaks out in search of his father. Until Ben and Rose meet in the present where Rose is an old but vibrant woman and Ben is her grandson in the Museum of Natural History, Rose's story is told entirely visually; Ben's is in words. As the cinema and the clock in *Hugo* are the locations of artistry, in *Wonderstruck* the museum is the site of creativity. While a museum typically houses the rarest things, Selznick's narrator points out that a museum is also "a collection of acorns and leaves on a back porch" (97), all things that tell some kind of magnificent story. Objects and images, as well as words, contain stories in Selznick's world and need to be regarded as contributions to the imagination.

Place is also intensely evocative in this trilogy. In addition to the richness of the museum as a site of imagining, in *Wonderstruck* there are two childhood locations: Ben's childhood home is Gunflint Lake, Minnesota, a rural and harsh landscape where wolves inhabited the forest areas around the lake, where his bond with his mother before she died was close and exclusive. They shared an odd sensibility—both loved research and objects, from stones to stars; they were collectors. Artists in Selznick's trilogy are not necessarily painters or writers or actors, or even cinematographers. They are magicians, builders, clockmakers; they are artisans; and they are imaginative and creative people, children and adults, who share a sensibility.

In all three books, Selznick uses a recurring image or line as a leitmotif to build incrementally the intensity of the theme of the artist and his quest. The recurring image in *Hugo* of the moon, first seen flat against the page, where it builds to the Méliès cinematic image, connects Hugo to the artist, so that Hugo is able to "fix" the automaton—that is his creative act—and to find his new, compatible family, as artist with artist.

In *Wonderstruck*, there are two recurring lines. One is from the David Bowie song, "This is Major Tom to ground control," a song about "sitting in a tin can far above the world" (68–9)—which represents experience as ethereal as well as grounded; it captures Ben's desire. Ben discovers the second recurring line in a wood box left to him by his mother, which says, "We are all in the gutter, but some of us are looking at the stars" (22). These words are mysterious to Ben; however, as they recur, his understanding of them deepens. They link the high with the low, the stones and the stars and, like the David Bowie line, they connect the idea of being grounded, deep in the underbelly of things, with the stars and the spirituality of the heavens. It is the artist who connects the gutter with the stars, the ordinary with the extraordinary, often in the same object. The artist in these books is linked to hard times, darkness, despair, and beauty. The recurring quote from his mother establishes the quest for the imagination as an internal and external exploration, from pastoral to urban, the largeness of the imagination that connects opposites in time and place—the unifying factor that goes deep enough to find meanings and connections between seemingly incoherent things.

This search comes to rest in the Museum of Natural History, where, Selznick tells us, "Great and glorious works of art resided … side by side with the wonders of nature" (108). In a direct address to his readers, he says: "If you've ever stood beneath the skeleton of a dinosaur, or gazed at a giant diamond, a glowing red flower perhaps, growing alone from a cracked sidewalk, you know this feeling of wonder" (109). The most uncanny and powerful discovery occurs in the museum when Ben comes across the diorama of two wolves running, just as he saw them chasing him in his dreams in the opening of the novel. Selznick writes, "It was as if someone had cut out the dream from his brain and put it behind glass" (359). The uncanny works in recurring images of the wolves as well as the recurring words, "We are all in the gutter." From the gutter to the stars, the quest is to embrace that wide arc, to reach

**Figure 7** Dream image: Two wolves running. From *Wonderstruck: A Novel in Words and Pictures* by Brian Selznick. Scholastic Inc./Scholastic Press. Copyright © 2011 by Brian Selznick. Used by permission.

back into the past to 1927 and ahead fifty years to 1977, and to look toward the future, with boy and grandmother united in present, without losing the past—which now can include the story of his father. The wolves diorama was made by his father, and Ben comes to realize that "he'd been dreaming of his father's wolves" (577). Though he does not remember, nor does he remember his early visit to the museum with his mother to see the diorama, here Selznick suggests that we are sometimes haunted by what we do not remember, by that which resides somewhere in the unconscious. Ben comes to the conclusion that "all this time the wolves hadn't been chasing him, they'd been guiding him, leading him onward, through the snow, to his father" (577–8).

The other diorama that his father built is of a miniature city, "with its skyscrapers and bridges, green rolling parks and twisting black roads, marshes, graveyards, and power plants" (565). While his mother could not leave Gunflint Lake, and his father could no more leave the city, Ben has experienced and will integrate both. We also see him and his grandmother with the city imagined from various perspectives: her large feet stepping over the tiny bridge, or the two of them, small against the city itself, suggesting that perspective is subjective or at least flexible. In these creations, Selznick notes how the artist "curates" his or her own life; he asks about "what it meant to curate your own life ... to pick and choose the objects and stories that would go into your own cabinet? How would Ben curate *his* own life?" (574). This fascinating question proclaims the uniqueness of each person's history, legacy, and sensibility. Selznick leaves us with Ben, "thinking about all the connections that led him here ... how everything could be traced (619). From bits and pieces of conversation, from objects in the museum, from stories about family, from the notebooks, Ben discovers that "he belonged here ... [with] his grandmother, and the millions of other people waiting in the dark for the lights to come back on," sitting on the roof of the museum "looking at the stars" (617).

The third novel, *The Marvels*, extends the idea of visually telling a story— the first 390 pages is all visual images—a narrative in dream images that is only pieced together fully when the entire story is told verbally. The pictures contain letters, posters, and other occasional texts that have words, but they are created artfully, as part of an image. Otherwise, most of the book and the many images of the first three-quarters of the book function subliminally, as dreams persist in fragments in our waking hours. They tell a story about storytelling, visual and verbal narratives about art, truth, time, and the past, about the theater and literature (William Butler Yeats, William Shakespeare, and Hans Christian Andersen are mentioned), and love. We get the story three times—each time is a radical departure from the preceding one. First the story is situated in 1766, a visual narrative that tells of a shipwreck, survivors, and a theatrical family—several of whom thrive in the theater. However, the two who do not survive portray the dysfunctional aspect and legacy of the family: Alexander goes mad and lives under the theater hidden away in the basement, and Leo rejects a theater life. The theater goes up in flames and we do not know what happens to Leo, whose story is left hanging.

The second story begins in 1990, a narrative told in words, in which Joseph, the main child in this story, runs away from his wealthy and neglectful family in search of the uncle about whom he knows nothing except for his address in London. His imagination informed by books such as Robert Louis

Stevenson's *Kidnapped,* Charles Dickens's *Great Expectations,* Madeleine L'Engle's *A Wrinkle in Time,* and C. S. Lewis's *Prince Caspian,* Joseph travels to London. There he finds his uncle who has made his home into a museum of his past, replete with images of angels, ships, beautiful tiles, even the dining room set with leftovers from some meal—all lit by candles. Many kinds of art are exhibited here, as Joseph discovers the "real" story beneath the story—the third story, where he learns that his uncle made up the first two stories. At this point Selznick raises the issue of truth—the truth of fiction. If Joseph felt like Leo, "born into the wrong family," and tells Leo's story as his own, is the story then true? In the epigraph by Wim Wenders that ends the novel, the question is raised: "Is this a true story?" Wenders answers, "I said it, so 'It is now'" (from *The Art of Seeing*). Even as Joseph insists, "Stories aren't the same as facts," his uncle Albert answers, "No, but they can both be true" (534).

So the third story unfolds, about Marcus, a child thief from an unhappy home, who was taken in by Albert and raised by the family that made him feel safe and understood. Marcus, who had dropped out of high school, was transformed into a renovator, as he worked and lived with Albert to create his museum/home. Albert also tells Joseph, rather matter-of-factly, that his "beloved" was a man: "He showed me how he painted intricate blue glaze onto trays of tiles as if it was still the eighteenth century. What could I do? I fell in love with him. I wish you could have met him" (542). This new family configuration of Albert, Billy (Albert's lover), and Marcus was restorative, founded as it was on similar views and interests. Billy moved in and brought old furniture "from plays he'd designed ... he started to fill our cupboards and armoires with old costumes from the theatre. Stories had begun to form in my mind," [Albert tells Joseph], "related to objects in the house" (543). Marcus worked on a golden ship, reframing it "using actual techniques for building boats" (545). The newfound family did "mudlarking" together, "collecting little things that wash in from the water, bits and pieces of London's history that have fallen into the river over the centuries" (545). The imaginations of the characters thrive on actual, factual things, transforming them into art each with his own unique creative process. Several tragedies are also intertwined in these stories: Billy died of AIDS as will Albert. Marcus was hit by a car. We are told, "That's what life is, Joseph realized, miracles and sadness, side by side" (602). The sadness mixes with the miraculous: along with the stories Joseph inherits the museum/house. "The story beneath the story made itself clear to Joseph, like an X-ray" (602)—the story as a gift. At this point the reader is returned to the images—we follow Joseph through the house as the site of creativity and spirituality, the house functioning almost as a main character in this story. We do not see Joseph here. We *become* Joseph. In the images that follow, and from a letter, Joseph, now a grown man, is raising a baby he has named Albert, with another man. It is now 2007; seventeen years have passed. And so the new family here is, again, comprised of two men and a child they are raising. It is wonderful that the presentation of gay couples and newly formed families is represented without it being pointed or self-conscious.

We find out, in an afterword, that this book about storytelling is based on the lives of Dennis Severs and David Milne. The house at 18 Folgate Street, Spitalfields, on the edge of London's East End, the location of the fictional house here, was their home. We are told that it became "a famous time-machine ... those prepared to enter his empathetic historical imagination and to suspend disbelief ... could find themselves transported into a dream which illuminated the complicated and poignant social history of that ancient part of London" (660). Selznick's vision of history, like that of Dennis Severs, was to "bring [the house] to life ... with a candle, a chamber pot and a bedroll ... And to illuminate these atmospheres ... Severs invented a family called Jervis who had lived there over the century and whose members had apparently just left each of the rooms entered" (663). He wanted to "emotionally" understand the past. "His vision was holistic and therapeutic, almost spiritual.... to summon up past eras not through history books, but through empathy with objects and places, to tell a fictional true story 'aimed at those who want to make sense of the whole picture of being alive'" (664).

Sight and insight dominate *The Marvels*, as they do the entire trilogy. "You either see it or you don't" (451) is the recurring line here. As the words begin to sound "like a threat," Joseph worries, "What was he not seeing?" (453). He comes to hear those words as "an invitation," rather than a warning. The drawings in this book seem to Joseph, "as if he was looking at the pictures of his own dreams, sprung to life" (529). Here again is the uncanny that connects unconscious and consciousness. Again we find the protagonist feeling severed from birth family, feeling like he was "born into the wrong family" (510). Joseph also creates a family of choice—a combination of blood family, his uncle, with a friend and her mother, a group of like sensibilities. Though most everything is resolved, Joseph's friend, named Blink, who had gone missing, is never found. His name, another sight metaphor, suggests that eyes that open and shut quickly are not able to see fully. Further the world is not perfect, the search goes on, but with new life, "the whole picture of being alive" (664). The book ends with a close-up of a baby, with eyes open to the new life he sees.

Selznick's enormously inventive trilogy encourages new ways of seeing, of connecting images, and of using metaphor for intensifying his stories about art and creativity—art beyond works of art. The imagination of his characters is expansive, so that his books become an exploration of reimagining family, and connecting artists and those of artistic sensibility, as well as exploring connections between music, theater, visual art, and language. As Joseph says, "the whole picture of being alive."

## Peter Sis

Peter Sis's work also rests between the world of words and the world of images. Although he uses the page in some ways like comics, in that text is not limited to lines that move from left to right or even up and down, his work is different from comics and graphic novels, books without consistent positions for speech. There are words used as frames, words within pictures, pictures incorporated into texts, complex images used as "visual prologues," and print types used to distinguish parts of the stories. His picture books confront memory and history with sophistication, so that beyond the double audience of many of the best children's picture books, his books invite, even make necessary, multiple readings for children and adults. They reach across genres: they are autobiography, biography, history, adventure, fiction, and nonfiction—and hybrids, mixtures of genres. His narrative sweep is large as he connects the individual with the larger world outside, and illuminates both as multilayered and complex. His picture books join the ordinary and the extraordinary, the fantastic, the mythic, and the realistic with the power of story.

Sis tells many stories at once. On a single page, there may appear script in circles, straight left to right print, images that stretch across, in and out, and loop around text, to suggest memory as layered. As much of his work attempts to imagine or recapture the past, the suspension or reconfiguring of time is crucial to creating internal as well as external landscapes. Time acts psychologically as well as chronologically with the juxtaposition of the individual and his society, the personal and the collective, the many aspects of a particular childhood. In *The Tree of Life* and in *Starry Messenger*, his books about Charles Darwin and Galileo Galilei, for example, they are both viable realistic boys, ordinary in some ways, extraordinary in others, growing up in times in which they adhere to certain traditions and challenge and refute others. In *Madlenka*, *Madlenka's Dog*, and *Madlenka Socca Star*, Madlenka is an ordinary little girl with a vibrant imagination. In *Madlenka*, her story, which centers around a loose tooth, is so wondrous for her that she must share it with her diverse neighbors, who, in turn, serve to introduce her to many points of the globe. Sis begins that story with the globe and zooms in closer and closer to the one child with her ordinary little experience of human development.

Stories are an integral part of Sis's search for the richness of life. *A Small Tall Tale from the Far Far North* begins with the declaration of Jan Welzl, the explorer who travels to Alaska: "There must be a better life than this. I'm going to find it," he declares. And whether Sis imagines or reimagines travels and discoveries, like Darwin's and Galileo's, his stories take us all over the world through his use of intricate icons, maps of all kinds, and image-filled, overlaid texts. His reach is beyond single or even double narratives. His work contains multiple narratives: multilayered temporally and spatially as they portray daily life, dream, memory, and the presentness of the past. As Sis says, "The essential part of adventures that impressed me as a child ... [embodied my] curiosity about life, courage, decency." In Galileo's story, the world is a large starry sky below which a tiny figure with a telescope is illuminated in a small tower—the one small boy against the many stars—as Galileo wonders, "What if things are not the way everybody believes them to be?" Wonder, in all of Sis's work, is reflected in fragments of unfinished stories, pockets of reflection, alternative narratives told through many perspectives, and placed, through illustrations, in their largest contexts. Even when these pictorial and textual narratives contradict each other, Sis holds them in a single connection to suggest the complexity of imagining, for child and for adult.

In his autobiographical picture books, Peter Sis looks toward another aspect of experimentation. These books present stories that suggest the limits of human agency: its spectacular reaches as well as its limitations. Particularly in *Tibet through the Red Box*, Sis recognizes the contradictions implicit in memories, particularly childhood memory, and in his attempt to present his childhood memories he uses images in extraordinary ways. In *Tibet*, he uses multiple lenses to tell his story—which is, itself, his story of his father's story, and the intersection that is, at times, confusing. To portray his confusion so that it is comprehensible, Sis presents this story dialogically, so that his adult voice and his child voice, along with his father's diaries and the letters, represent different voices in the present tense. The stories are told here through the point of view of Peter as a child remembered by Peter as an adult, as well as by Peter's father's diaries, letters, and objects in the red box. Of course, time is one thing for Peter the child and another for Peter the adult, hence the need to contextualize and concretize the stories by locating them in time and space. The variety of texts derived from the red box are in the present, but all evoke the past. They suggest and depict the complexity of childhood memory and imagining.

Postmodern critics read subjectivity as a self-conscious understanding of the instability of the self and of the text(s). Traditional autobiography has been described as "the ability to construct a socially-based selfhood [and] the ability to step back from the immediacy of a situation and reflect upon past events ... [as well as] the ability to distinguish one's own experience from other people's experiences " (Kümmerling-Meibauer, 205–6).

But the postmodern stance challenges the stability of life story. With his vital images of the memory, Sis portrays the way in which the past functions in and dominates the present, beyond words—and perhaps that is the essential role of the images.

His two autobiographical stories, *Tibet through the Red Box* and *The Wall*, each unique in form and content, are representative of his experimental and artistic brilliance. In *Tibet through the Red Box* (1998), Sis attempts to make sense of the gaps in his memory from his childhood in the 1950s when his father journeyed into Tibet. In her psychoanalytic reading of *Tibet*, Aparna Gollapudi notes that Sis brings "a special poignancy to the peculiar combination of angst and adoration" of the father-son relationship. She writes of the "unusual depth … [of] this tale of love and healing" (10). She observes that in "reworking his father's Tibetan diary and the stories he told upon his return, Sis creates a layered picture-book narrative that captures the psychological processes underlying loss … in complex text-image relations" (11).

*Tibet through the Red Box* begins with longing—"father is calling me home" (n. p.). His task is to unlock the stories of his father's journey to Tibet through the memorabilia left to him in a red box. He reads the stories from the fragments of his father's diary, letters, buttons, pieces of stones, and butterfly wings—the "texts" of his father's trip so many years ago—through illustrations that tell the story from one perspective and verbal images that tell it from another. Gollapudi invokes Kristeva's idea of "the dialectic between the semiotic [nonverbal signifying systems] … [and] the text [that] is representative of the symbolic" (12–13). What fascinated me with this reading is the concept of early memory represented as preverbal images and later development as verbal representations intertwined, almost simultaneously. Images are layered, superimposed over other images and verbal stories are wrapped around images and other verbal texts. Thus, time is represented as multi-chronological—unconscious, subconscious, and conscious time, each with the fitting chronology—moments emerging through the various stories Peter uncovers in the red box. The basic story is centered under each image. Another story is written around it in the margins, which serves as frame. The interpolated tales—those his father told him when he returned—are hybrids: some feel like a mixture of fairy tale and realism; there are creation myths from the Tibetan cultures he encountered; there are interior maps of the rooms Peter enters in memory, colored in red, blue, green, and black. It is hard to distinguish which part belongs to which stage of his life, as they are remembered by Peter as a child, when the stories took shape and solidified. There are also mandalas constructed with the symbols from the journey and maps of Tibet imagined. Through all these representations of memory, we come to trace a double consciousness inherent in nostalgia: that of past longing and present desire.

However, the path of nostalgia is winding, fractured, rummaging. It demonstrates, he tells us, "why [my father] could never clearly write or tell about what he went through in Tibet." And, why neither Peter's words nor his images could fully capture what he comes to understand about his father's absence.

He tells us early in the story that as a child he became his father's listener to "his magical stories of Tibet," as friends and peers could not understand a world "outside their own country, and they probably wouldn't have believed him anyway ... I would try to draw the things he talked about, things I could hardly imagine." While suggesting that telling these stories helped his father, he also notes how much they helped heal his own serious childhood illness. He describes how he "couldn't move his arms or legs." He tells us that listening to "a story about a jingle-bell boy ... I could feel my hands ... another story about some gentle giants ... and I could feel my feet ... [A] third story about a magic lake, [and] ... I could see colors again." Thus, he hopes that through recovering these stories he can fill the longing created by his father's absence, that stories and recapturing memories can bring him closer, as he describes it, to "the magic garden of our house, what was enclosed by a high, safe wall." In trying to recapture the past, he most profoundly asks, "But what did I know then?" followed by "But what do I know now?" And he comes to understand that his longing for the "Tibet" he has looked for all his life can never be fully satisfied. He asks about his father, "Did he ever completely return?"

Even as his journey begins Sis represents the simultaneity of the past and the present. Two images flank the first page: on the left is a small boy, Peter, running on the cobblestone street up to the house we assume is his childhood home; on the right, a man, Peter, also on cobblestones, is about to climb the stairs to his father's study where the red box awaits, colored a striking red, among the pale blue houses and stones. The boy and the man, this first illustration asserts, also have clearly delineated shadows that prepare us for this study of the past—the past of Peter, as a young child, and the father's past captured through the eyes of Peter, the adult, as he deconstructs the texts within the red box.

Searching through the layers of memory generates many perspectives. He writes, "The red box is on the table, waiting like an ancient anthill or a grave of memories buried in the sweet smell of honey, rosin, and sandalwood." The red box itself has a story, told by the man Peter about the boy Peter remembering times he and his father spent together, narrated in the past tense, a cohesive chronology that begins, "When I was little, my father spent a lot of time with me" and ends with, "It was not until I myself had gone far ... that I became interested in the red box again." The images, which appear as small medallions of distilled memory, capture the spots of time that depict a special moment: father helping son to ride a bike, father and son canoeing, father with son on a horse, and so on. At the end of this page of verbal and visual memories, he writes, "I begin to read my father's dairy."

The diary is, of course, in first person, in the present tense, accompanied by various mandalas facing the words; they are Peter's images of the stories he was told—of the jingle bell boy, the fish with a human face, the yeti—the characters of his father's unfolding narratives expressed in several genres. There are the creation tales, mythic stories of giants and fish "with distinctly European features," epistolary fragments, and gorgeous full-page mandalas that accompany each story. In the center of several of the stories is a family picture of Peter with his mother, sometimes with his sister, and always with

**Figure 8** From *Tibet Through the Red Box* by Peter Sís. Reprinted by permission of Farrar, Straus, and Giroux, a division of Macmillan Children's Publishing Group. All Rights Reserved.

an empty white outline of his father—missing a family picnic; missing in a picture of the boy dressed for school; missing his birthday; and, before a fully decorated Christmas tree, missing, a clear and poignant way of portraying the presence of absence.

There are double-page spreads that capture the effects on Peter of reading his father's diary. In the room that becomes red as he reads, Peter's memory of his childhood is conflated with stories his father told him, and the diary narrative as images are superimposed on other images, which he frames in the margins with his associations with the color red. Framing the double-page illustration, are his words, "Red is the color of fire. Red was the sunset in the valley as well as the evening light in my father's room. How many times, throughout my life, had I sat in this room asking or answering questions about my school, my behavior, my future, always red in the face? Red was the color of my youth—red flags, red stars, red tulips, blood." The picture of the red room is of the boy sitting in his father's chair, reaching out to a huge, gentle Tibetan yak. Boy and animal look directly and happily at each other, with superimposed images of Tibetan mountains, a sun god, butterflies with faces—complex dream images. His youth, he suggests, was captured by Communist Prague (which we will learn more about in *The Wall*) and by his childhood shame; however, in the illustration, the child sitting in his father's chair is happy in his connection with the animal of his imagined Tibet.

In the next room the color darkens to green (but in a transitional stage of yellow), for which Peter writes, "Green represents the earth. The walls of my father's room were green. The peaceful green of meadows and trees." But there, as in the red room, these cheerful associations darken. He writes, "Yet as a child I had a recurrent dream of a vast green lawn which horrified me."

Sis's images and words suggest the ambiguity of memory. It is rarely tapped without conflict, suggesting that the process of imagining and recapturing the past requires courage. As we enter each of the rooms we continue to be confronted with his ambivalence. Each color is associated with a basic element: red is fire and green is earth; the blue room, darkening further, is framed by these lines: "Blue is the colors of water, oceans, and sky, the color of freedom and flying. It was a rare color in the landlocked country of my childhood, surrounded by an iron curtain. A color I could only imagine." Blue is his deprivation, associated with longing. And the images of the blue room are faces of older unsmiling men and of frightening animals.

At last we come to Potala, the palace where the Dalai Lama sits; the story, he writes, "as I remember it from the white bed, is hazy. The jingle-bell boy with his little spear gets confused in my mind with the Boy-King, the fourteenth Dalai Lama, sitting under the peacock umbrella on a golden throne." In this part of the story it is clear that his father met the child Dalai Lama, and warned him about "what he thought he understood," about what was coming to Tibet, "about the outside world pouring in and invading this untouched place." But the palace is remembered, as Peter writes, through his father's hints and realization that "beneath the color and splendor of its rooms ... his state of mind was somehow being reflected. It was all here, recorded on these walls, the past and the present." The presence of the past, the confusion and conflation of past and present, suggest the impossibility of separating the dreamer from the dream, or the viewer from the view. The book then returns to the rooms in the colors red, green, and blue—each with its associations—spatially reconstructed as rooms of the palace his father visited—each with a clear statement placed squarely beneath it. Red is "sunrise and sunset, heart of time." Green is "square and circular, ear of the earth." And the blue room is "frozen in light and dark, eye of the soul." However, the frame of each poetic representation portends invasion: red trucks, green tanks, and blue planes are repeated framing images. "And at last [his father comes to] a deep dark room." In this black room where the Dalai Lama is tiny but clear, bordered by Tibetan mountains, Sis portrays the emptiness of peace—free of the war icons and threats of the Western world. Sis writes, "Black is the color of night, of magic and shadows, of the unknown. You can project all your dreams—or nightmares—onto black." It is here, in this "perfect backdrop for the stars and for hope," that he hears his father's voice—"Why are you sitting here in the dark?"—which brings us back to the present, where Peter is reunited with him. They close the red box and Peter remarks, we "walk through the streets of the city where I grew up, happy to be together again."

His quest for Tibet ends with the red box. He reminds us, "Time is measured quite differently by the very young," and this is true of the spatial boundaries as well. His narrative ends as he wonders, "Did he ever completely return? Is he still happy and young somewhere in Tibet?" Thus, Tibet becomes a

**Figure 9** From *Tibet Through the Red Box* by Peter Sís. Reprinted by permission of Farrar, Straus, and Giroux, a division of Macmillan Children's Publishing Group. All Rights Reserved.

medallion of the past, where we continue to exist with our youth and dreams, and Peter, in recognizing Tibet as a place "that never really existed," acknowledges that his quest is, finally, to let go of his father's past, and to relinquish his own. The last image of the book returns us to the simplicity of the first image of the two figures, here boy and father, and their shadows. Here they are two men, holding hands, as are their shadows, one of a man, and the other of the boy—the past always present and in shadow. As imagining or reimagining in memory, always the past is present and ultimately suggestive, but unstable and unknowable.

Sis leaves us with a quote from Nabokov's "The Gift," a gorgeous assertion of the past depicted as " 'the whisper of spirits calling you aside' and the queer flicker of the air, an endless progression of whirlwinds … coming to meet you … thousands of spectral faces in their incorporeal way pressing upon you, through you, and suddenly dispersing … not … even a half of what he had in fact seen." Philosophical and adult-oriented, this epigraph captures the density of Sis's exploration.

In considering the complexity of *Tibet through the Red Box* and its supposed double audience, I think about what propels adults to write children's books; I suspect that the image of the double audience—the adult reading over the shoulder of the child, or the adult reading to the child—is part of what the author of children's literature counts on; that the adult reader will engage in memories of childhood as the author does. The images presented here suggest a reimagined past as it might have been offered through family stories and photographs and through those memories that have been stored away in the conscious or unconscious imagination. Often this retrospective gaze at childhood is a search for a desired or an imagined self. It can both obscure and highlight the pain of the past; it can also generate a liberation, a unification of remembered child and creative adult. For children, who have little if any retrospective sense, the present can be basically an undifferentiated consciousness. But in the literature of childhood, the adult and child can come together with their separate agenda—the child to imagine and the adult to reimagine.

In the other of Sis's overtly autobiographical work, *The Wall: Growing Up Behind the Iron Curtain* (2007), he uses some of the same techniques and formats as with *Tibet*. There are the frames of words around pictures and other verbal tags in the margins. There are the double-page illustrations with images within larger images, including a double-page map with the Berlin wall running across the page separating east and west. Embedded and spread out across the west are the words representing the ideals Sis yearned for during his youth growing up behind the Iron Curtain: "hope," "justice," "inspiration," "truth," "integrity," "dreams," "joy," "freedom," "liberty," "respect," "dignity," "wisdom," "love," "morality," "happiness," "benevolence," "virtue," "equality," "spirit," "honor," "pride," "art," "trust," and "knowledge." These words are opposed to those of his youth in the east—"stupidity," "terror," "suspicion," "fear," "injustice," "envy," "lies," and "corruption."

Sis's plan for *The Wall* is unambiguous and clearly executed. In a direct address to the reader he writes, "The Soviet Union and the Western nations managed their territories in very different ways. The Western Bloc countries were all independent democracies, while the Eastern Bloc was tightly controlled by the Soviet Union ... This period was called the Cold War. It lasted until the Berlin Wall fell and the Soviet Empire collapsed." This story of his growing up behind the Iron Curtain positions the Berlin Wall as bifurcating not only the city, but also the clear opposed values of each side. Framed around the first illustration of a baby with pencil and paper in hand are definitions of "Iron Curtain," "Cold War," and "Communism," under which Sis asserts his individuality and talent: "As long as he could remember, he had loved to draw."

*The Wall*, then, is a history, personal and political, of how Peter first "drew shapes" and "people," drew "what he wanted to at home," but soon after, the Soviet Union invaded Czechoslovakia in 1948, and took control of the schools. Indoctrination, then, characterized all activity, including "children [being] ... encouraged to report on their families and fellow students." It was in that atmosphere that he learned to draw "tanks," "wars," "not to question what he was being told," [until] "he found out there were things he wasn't told." These pages are in black, white, and red.

From his journals, dating from 1954, the margins begin to have color and include the young Peter's illustrations and photographs of the years of his questioning. He joins a rock group and "painted music." His rebellion prepares for the Prague Spring of 1968, and the double-page spread of this time is with all kinds of color and images—no borders, no boundaries. Featured prominently are two large colorful figures: one looks like a flower child rocker; the other maybe a punk rocker. The illustrations of rock musicians and other heroes like Allen Ginsberg, "poet of liberation," signaled to Peter the end of Soviet control. He reports in his journals, "Censorship is lifted! We can have long hair and wear jeans!" He travels to England, and paints his dreams and his nightmares in this time of transition, but he notes that his drawings could be used against him. Phones continued to be bugged, mail opened, and he writes that "Western-style art is banned again." Images of his paintings and of the wall painted over and over again follow. Dissidents like Vaclav Havel are jailed and, as he writes, "Things got worse," he still asserts freedom in his "wild dreams." He continues to dream with hope imagined in the figure of a boy on a bicycle with colors of paintings clutched in his arm—sometimes the figure is small, sometimes frozen in a large spotlight. However, the book ends with frames of facts about the ending of the Cold War, the wall coming down, the tiny image of the boy on the bicycle now with wings, and the words, "Sometimes dreams come true. On November 9, 1989, the Wall fell."

The baby reappears now as an old man, with pencil and paper on which is written a large question mark, with the words that assert the absolute conflation of freedom and memory: He writes, "As long as he can remember, he will continue to draw." Facing this page, in the afterword, he quotes his children questioning—"Are you a settler, Dad? ... How did you decide to settle here in America?" Peter answers, clearly and modestly, "It was all because of drawing." He says he does not know if he was born to be an artist. He does not position himself as special. He simply affirms his story of the story—that of the Wall, that of walls, of suppression and censorship in opposition to the freedom he does not take for granted but relishes, even in the face of fear of not being able to see his family again when he was called back to Prague in 1984 by the Soviets. His resistance, a tough decision, centered around his refusal to be brainwashed. He had to think, and he had to draw.

Like his children who find it hard to imagine colorful Prague as "a dark place full of fear, suspicion, and lies," children reading this book may have a similar response; however, he brings his readers close to his experience with the power of his drawings and experimental use of text. The last image of the baby boy with an old face lined with his artistic vision suggests and brings us close to the child in the man.

# Epilogue: Surviving Childhood

No matter how happy a time we would like to imagine childhood to be, we know that it is often riddled with cruelty and shame. Without diminishing the joys or the spontaneity of childhood, it is important to consider the challenges ranging from difficult to horrific that many children live with, and acknowledge what it takes to survive childhood. And for so many writers and illustrators of childhood, reading and imagining stories provided ways of preserving the imagination and the incandescence of their memories.

Valerie Krips writes, "Fiction written for children has a special place in memory ... it offers itself as a site of memory, both for the child reader ... and for the adult, for whom books of childhood are a symbol of the past" (15). She goes on to say that "children's books provoke memory in adults" that function as a kind of "interior rejuvenation" (15), providing moments of pleasure, strength, and courage that can fortify us as we grow older. These "sites of memory" are "removed from history and returned to what remains of memory no longer quite alive but not yet entirely dead ... whose temporal reference is both to the past and the present" (17). Thus, these books, these "sites of memory" are liminal; they serve to help adults feel whole, integrated. They are like Jung's dream house of memory—the many rooms of his metaphoric house, which held memories reconfigured in his dreams, from the attic where he stored his conscious, intellectual experience, to the basement of his unconscious. Childhood stories align the imagination with memory so that all parts of the self, past and present, feel connected and coherent.

These stories can help children imagine things that they may not otherwise be able to. They can tell the story that provides courage, offers inspiration, inspires hope, and provides an escape from moments of pain and sorrow, when boredom and frustration threaten to take over. They can provide a safe place to imagine, as the writers in Elizabeth Goodenough's *Secret Spaces* attest.

After her book, *Brown Girl Dreaming*, won the 2014 National Book Award for Young People's Literature, Jacqueline Woodson said, about her decision to write this sort of epic poem:

> It's a book of memories. And it's how memory comes to us. It comes in these small moments with all of this white space around it, and I think that that's what you get in reading it. You get that small moment, and that moment, I'm hoping, is very, very clear on the page. And then the moments are, of course, linked together to tell the story.[1]

*Brown Girl Dreaming* is a memoir that begins:

> I am born on a Tuesday at University Hospital
> Columbus, Ohio,
> USA—
> a country caught
> between Black and White.
> I am born not long from the time
> or far from the place
> where my great-great-grandparents
> worked the deep rich land
> unfree
> dawn till dusk
> unpaid
> drank cool water from scooped-out gourds
> looked up and followed
> the sky's mirrored constellation
> to freedom.
> I am born as the South explodes,
> too many people too many years
> enslaved, then emancipated
> but not free, the people
> who look like me
> keep fighting
> and marching
> and getting killed
> so that today—

February 12, 1963
and every day from this moment on,
brown children like me can grow up
free. Can grow up
learning and voting and walking and riding
wherever *we* want.
I am born in Ohio but
the stories of South Carolina already run
like rivers
through my veins. (2)

Even the title, *Brown Girl Dreaming*, is a testament to the courage to imagine. In another interview, Woodson said, "In writing this book, I was trying to answer the question 'How did I become a writer?' I know that artists don't just 'happen', that we're years and generations in the making. I wanted to understand more about how I came to this place of so many books, of thinking very deeply about the world across lines of race, gender, economic class and sexuality." Tapping into her memory to trace her evolution as a writer, she creates a narrative full of powerful images, bright and dark, that demonstrate the courage to imagine. Woodson asserts that there needs to be space to think, feel, and reflect; to capture and place childhood experiences; and to make clear to children that there is hope in this process. And always, books provide privacy for children, the sacred space for reading by oneself, to oneself, and for oneself. For those of us for whom books and the characters were vital throughout our childhood, these stories are there for us—private, within our purview to recall when desired.

# Notes

## Introduction

1 https://en.wikiversity.org/wiki/Talk:Albert_Einstein_quote.
2 He also includes the intellect, but sees it as informing the sciences rather than the arts.
3 Although Clémentine Beauvais and Maria Nikolajeva contest the issue of the child's powerlessness, I assert that literally children are relatively powerless to affect their world, as they are under the control of family and other institutions.

## Chapter 1

1 See my discussion of the dark pastoral in *The Poetics of Childhood*.
2 David Almond, "The Necessary Wilderness," *The Lion and the Unicorn* 35, no. 2 (2011): 115.
3 Not every scholar sees the father as good. See James B. Hoyme, "The Abandoning Impulse in Human Parents." *The Lion and the Unicorn* 12, no. 2 (1988): 32–46.
4 See Zipes, *Trials and Tribulations*.
5 Quoted in Singer and Singer, "Memories of Childhood Play," *The House of Make-Believe: Children's Play and the Developing Imagination*, Cambridge: Harvard University Press, 1990, p. 13.

## Chapter 4

1 See Landsberg, *Prosthetic Memory*.

## Chapter 5

1 See, among the many psychologists who address trauma study and creativity, Meredith Edgar-Bailey and Victoria E. Kress, "Resolving Child and Adolescent Traumatic Grief: Creative Techniques and Interventions," *Journal of Creativity in Mental Health* 5, no. 2 (2010): 158–76. See also Cathy Malchiordi, ed., *Creative*

*Interventions with Traumatized Children*. New York: Guilford Press, 2nd ed., 2008, rpt. 2014.

2 From talk "Green Man/Wild Man and Children's Culture" Conference, Trinity College, Dublin, July 20–21, 2012.

## Chapter 6

1 "Thanks and Acknowledgments," *The Birchbark House*.

2 Conversation with Heid Erdrich, August 2008.

3 Several critics have expressed discomfort with Wilder's attitude toward Indians in the *Little House* books. The most detailed and inclusive is Philip Heldrich's "'Going to Indian Territory': Attitudes toward Native Americans in *Little House on the Prairie*," *Great Plains Quarterly* 20 (Spring 2000): 99–109.

4 From Theodore Reik's most famous book, *Listening with the Third Ear*.

5 From a personal email dated December 31, 2007, and from conversations.

6 M. Sedgwick, "My Name Is Mina by David Almond." *The Guardian* 4 (2010).

7 *Publishers Weekly*, August 15, 2011.

8 Eve Tandoi (2014) notes that the different fonts and formats create both an intimacy and a distance in emphasizing the "materiality of the spoken and written word rather than its meaning." I think that the visual use of fonts and formats highlights the word in all its capacity for meaning.

9 Esmé Raji Codell, in the introduction to *King Matt the First*, claims, "It's clear that King Matt is, in fact, partial to the Africans and that they are more trustworthy and adept than their white counterparts" (ix).

10 Carolivia Herron's website: http://carolivia.com/.

11 Dave Eggers's *What Is the What*, New York: Vintage, 2007, is probably the best-known fictionalized version of the story of the boys as adults.

## Chapter 8

1 See critics such as Bette P. Goldstone, "The Postmodern Picture Book: A New Subgenre," *Language Arts* 81, no. 3 (2004): 196–204; Michele Anstey, "'It's Not All Black and White': Postmodern Picture Books and New Literacies," *Journal of Adolescent and Adult Literacy* 45, no. 6 (2002): 444–57; and Eliza T. Dresang, *Radical Change: Books for Youth in a Digital Age*, New York: H. W. Wilson, 1999, 59–60.

## Epilogue

1 Interview by Terry Gross on NPR's "Fresh Air," December 10, 2014.

# References

Abate, Michelle Ann, and Kenneth Kidd, eds. *Over the Rainbow: Queer Children's and Young Adult Literature*. Ann Arbor: University of Michigan Press, 2011.

Ackerman, Diane. "In the Memory Mines," in Goodenough, *Secret Spaces of Childhood*, 271–83.

Alcott, Louisa May. *Little Women*. New York: Dover, 2000, Originally printed in 1868, 1869.

Alexie, Sherman, and Ellen Forney. *The Absolutely True Diary of a Part-Time Indian*. New York: Little, Brown, 2007.

Almond, David. "The Necessary Wilderness." *The Lion and the Unicorn* 35, no. 2 (2011): 107–17.

Almond, David. *Skellig*. New York: Delacorte Press, 1999.

Almond, David, and David McDougall. *My Name Is Mina*. New York: Delacorte Books for Young Readers, 2011.

Anderson, Laurie Halse. *Speak*. New York: Farrar, Straus & Giroux, 1999.

Angelou, Maya, Jean-Michel Basquiat, Sara Jane Boyers, and Paul Zakris. *Life Doesn't Frighten Me*. New York: Stewart, Tabori & Chang, 1993.

Anstey, Michèle. " 'It's Not All Black and White': Postmodern Picture Books and New Literacies." *Journal of Adolescent & Adult Literacy* 45, no. 6 (2002): 444–57.

Ariès, Philippe, and Robert Baldick. *Centuries of Childhood: A Social History of Family Life*. New York: Vintage Books, 1965.

Ashley, Kathleen M., Leigh Gilmore, and Gerald Peters. *Autobiography and Postmodernism*. Amherst: University of Massachusetts Press, 1994.

Atkins, Laura. "Gathering Seeds in a Bag of Stars: The Interconnected Narrative as an Alternative to the Hero's Journey." MFA thesis, Vermont College, 2016.

Baum, Frank L. *The Wizard of Oz*. New York: Oxford University Press, 2000, Originally printed in 1900.

Beauvais, Clémentine. "Child Giftedness as Class Weaponry: The Case of Roald Dahl's *Matilda*." *Children's Literature Association Quarterly* 40, no. 3 (2015): 277–93.

Beauvais, Clémentine. "The Problem of 'Power': Metacritical Implications of Aetonormativity for Children's Literature Research." *Children's Literature in Education* 44, no. 1 (2013): 74–86.

Bechdel, Alison. *Fun Home*. New York: Houghton Mifflin, 2006.

Bellorin, Brenda, and Cecilia Silva-Diaz. "Surprised Readers: Twist Endings in Narrative Picturebooks," in *New Directions in Picturebook Research*. Edited by Teresa Colomer, Bettina Kümmerling-Meibauer, and Cecilia Silva-Diaz. New York and Abingdon: Routledge, 2010, 113–28.

Bernstein, Robin. "The Queerness of Harriet the Spy," in Abate and Kidd, *Over the Rainbow*, 111–20.

Bradford, Clare. *Unsettling Narratives: Postcolonial Readings of Children's Literature*. Waterloo, ON: Wilfrid Laurier University Press, 2007.

Buechner, Frederick, "A Symposium of Secret Spaces," in Goodenough, *Secret Spaces of Childhood*, 28–29.

Buelens, Gert, Samuel Durrant, and Robert Eaglestone, eds. *The Future of Trauma Theory: Contemporary Literary and Cultural Criticism*. New York: Routledge, 2013.

Butler, Francelia. "Death in Children's Literature." *Children's Literature* 1, no. 1 (1972): 104–24.

Campbell, Joseph. *The Hero with a Thousand Faces*. Princeton, NJ: Princeton University Press, 1972, Originally printed in 1949.

Cohen, David, and Stephen A. MacKeith. *The Development of Imagination: The Private Worlds of Childhood*. London: Routledge, 1991.

Cole, Brock. *The Goats*. New York: Farrar, Straus & Giroux, 1987.

Colomer, Teresa. "Picturebooks and Changing Values at the Turn of the Century," in *New Directions in Picturebook Research*. Edited by Teresa Colomer, Bettina Kümmerling-Meibauer, and Cecilia Silva-Diaz. New York and Abingdon: Routledge, 2010, 41–54.

Craps, Stef. "Beyond Eurocentrism," in Buelens et al., *The Future of Trauma Theory*, 45–62.

Dahl, Roald. *Matilda*. New York: Viking Penguin, 1988.

DiCamillo, Kate. *The Miraculous Journey of Edward Tulane*. Cambridge, MA: Candlewick Press, 2006.

DiCamillo, Kate. *The Tale of Despereaux*. Cambridge, MA: Candlewick Press, 2004.

Dresang, Eliza T., and Bowie Kotrla. "Radical Change Theory and Synergistic Reading for Digital Age Youth." *The Journal of Aesthetic Education* 43, no. 2 (2009): 92–107.

Edkins, Jenny. "Time, Personhood, Politics," in Buelens et al., *The Future of Trauma Theory*, 127–40.

Egan, Susanna. *Mirror Talk: Genres of Crisis in Contemporary Autobiography*. Chapel Hill: University of North Carolina, 1999.

Elliot, Andrea, and Ruth Fremson. "Invisible Child Girl in the Shadows: Dasani's Homeless Life." *New York Times*, December 9, 2013.

Elliott, Zetta. "Decolonizing the Imagination." *Horn Book Magazine*, March–April 2010.

Elliott, Zetta. *The Door at the Crossroads: A Novel*. CreateSpace Independent Publishing Platform, 2016.

Elliott, Zetta. "The Trouble with Magic: Conjuring the Past in New York City Parks." *Jeunesse Jeunesse: Young People, Texts, Cultures* 5, no. 2 (2013): 17–39.

Elliott, Zetta. *A Wish after Midnight*. Las Vegas, NV: AmazonEncore, 2010.

Erdrich, Louise. *The Birchbark House*. New York: Hyperion Books for Children, 1999.

Erdrich, Louise. *Books and Islands in Ojibwe Country: Traveling through the Land of My Ancestors*. New York: Harper Collins, 2014, Originally printed 2003.

Erdrich, Louise. *The Game of Silence*. New York: Harper Collins, 2005.

Erdrich, Louise. *The Porcupine Year*. New York: Harper Collins, 2008.

Ettin, Andrew V. *Literature and the Pastoral*. New Haven, CT: Yale University Press, 1984.

Fisher, Michael M. J. "Ethnicity and the Arts of Memory," in *Writiing Culture: The Poetics and Politics of Ethnography*. Edited by James Clifford and George E. Marcus. Berkeley: University of California Press, 1986, 194–233.

Fitzhugh, Louise. *Harriet the Spy*. New York: Harper Collins, 1968.

Gaiman, Neil. *The Graveyard Book*. New York: Harper Collins, 2008.

Gaiman, Neil, and Dave McKean. *The Wolves in the Walls*. New York: Harper Collins, 2003.

Gallagher, Stephen. "Foreword: The Rat's Whiskers." *The Tale of One Bad Rat*. Milwaukee, OR: Dark Horse Books, 1995.

Gardner, Howard. *Multiple Intelligences: New Horizons*. New York: Basic Books, 2006.

Gardner, Martin. *The Annotated Alice*. New York: Random House, 1990, Originally printed in 1960.

Gargano, Elizabeth. "Oral Narrative and Ojibwa Story Cycles in Louise Erdrich's *The Birchbark House* and *The Game of Silence*." *Children's Literature Association Quarterly* 31, no. 1 (2006): 27–39.

Garza, Carmen Lomas. *In My Family/En Mi Familia*. San Francisco, CA: Children's Book Press/Libros Para Niños, 1996.

Goldstone, Bette P., and Linda D. Labbo. "The Postmodern Picture Book: A New Subgenre." *Language Arts* 81, no. 3 (2004): 196–204.

Goleman, Daniel. *Emotional Intelligence*. New York: Bantam Books, 1995.

Goodenough, Elizabeth, ed. *Secret Spaces of Childhood*. Ann Arbor: University of Michigan Press, 2003.

Green, Hannah, and Joanne Greenberg. *I Never Promised You a Rose Garden*. New York: Henry Holt, 1964.

Griswold, Jerome. *Audacious Kids: Coming of Age in America's Classic Children's Books*. Oxford and New York: Oxford University Press, 1992.

Grollman, Earl A. "Explaining Death to Children." *The Searchlight, Journal for Spiritual and Consciousness Studies* (July 2014): 143.

Hamilton, Virginia. *The People Could Fly: American Black Folktales*. New York: Knopf Books for Young Readers, 1985.

Harris, Mark Jonathan. "A Symposium of Secret Spaces," in Goodenough, *Secret Spaces of Childhood*, 32–6.

Hatkoff, Isabella, Craig Hatkoff, P. Kahumbu, and Peter Greste. *Owen & Mzee: The True Story of a Remarkable Friendship*. New York: Scholastic, 2006.

Hatkoff, Isabella, Craig Hatkoff, P. Kahumbu, and Peter Greste. *Owen & Mzee: The Language of Friendship*. New York: Scholastic, 2007.

Herman, Judith Lewis. *Trauma and Recovery*. New York: Basic Books, 1992.

Herron, Carolivia, and Joe Cepeda. *Nappy Hair*. New York: Knopf, 1997.

Heuscher, Julius E. *A Psychiatric Study of Fairy Tales: Their Origin, Meaning and Usefulness*. Springfield, IL: Thomas, 1963.

Hourihan, Margery. *Deconstructing the Hero: Literary Theory and Children's Literature*. London and New York: Routledge, 1997.

Hoyme, James B. "The 'Abandoning Impulse' in Human Parents." *The Lion and the Unicorn* 12, no. 2 (1988): 32–46.

Huggan, Isabel. *The Elizabeth Stories*. Ottawa: Oberon Press, 1984.

Igus, Toyomi, and Daryl Wells. *Two Mrs. Gibsons*. New York: Children's Book Press, 1996.

Jamison, Leslie. *The Empathy Exams*. Minneapolis, MN: Graywolf Press, 2014.

Jung, C. G. (with Aniela Jaffé). *Memories, Dreams, Reflections*. Translated by Richard and Clara Winston. New York: Vintage Books, 1989, Originally printed in 1961.

Keats, John. "Keats's Epistle to John Hamilton Reynolds." http://www.john-keats.com/

Kidd, Kenneth B. *Freud in Oz: At the Intersections of Psychoanalysis and Children's Literature*. Minneapolis and St. Paul: University of Minnesota Press, 2011.

Kingston, Maxine Hong. *The Woman Warrior: Memoirs of a Girlhood among Ghosts*. New York: Alfred A. Knopf, 1976.

Korczak, Janusz. *King Matt the First*. Translated by Richard Lourie. New York: Farrar, Straus & Giroux, 1922/1986.

Krips, Valerie. *The Presence of the Past: Memory, Heritage, and Childhood in Postwar Britain*. New York and London: Garland, 2000.

Kümmerling-Meibauer, Bettina. "Remembering the Past in Words and Pictures: How Autobiographical Stories Become Picturebooks," in

*New Directions in Picturebook Research.* Edited by Teresa Colomer, Bettina Kümmerling-Meibauer, and Cecilia Silva-Diaz. New York and Abingdon: Routledge, 2010, 205–16.

Kuroyanagi, Tetsuko, and Chihiro Iwasaki. *Totto-chan, the Little Girl at the Window.* Translated by Dorothy Britton. Tokyo: Kodansha, 1981/2012.

Kuznets, Lois R. "The Fresh-Air Kids, or Some Contemporary Versions of Pastoral." *Children's Literature* 22 (1983): 156–68.

Lagerlöf, Selma, and Lars Klinting. *The Wonderful Adventures of Nils.* New York: Harper Collins, 1907.

Landsberg, Alison. *Prosthetic Memory: The Transformation of American Remembrance in the Age of Mass Culture.* New York: Columbia University Press, 2004.

Lane, Margaret. *The Tale of Beatrix Potter.* London: Frederick Warne, 2001.

Lear, Linda. *Beatrix Potter: A Life in Nature.* New York: Macmillan, 2008.

Lester, Julius. "People Who Could Fly," in *Best-Loved Folktales of the World.* Edited by Joanna Cole. New York: Anchor Doubleday, 1983.

Lester, Julius. *When Dad Killed Mom.* New York: Houghton Mifflin, 2001.

Levy, Andrew. *Huck Finn's America.* New York: Simon & Schuster, 2015.

Lifton, Betty Jean. *The King of Children: The Life and Death of Janusz Korczak.* New York: Macmillan, 1997.

Lindgren, Astrid. *Pippi Longstocking.* New York: Viking Press, 1950.

Masson, Sophie. "Death in Children's Books." *Orana* 30, no. 4 (1994): 274.

Medina, Tony, and R. Gregory Christie. *DeShawn Days.* New York: Lee & Low Books, 2001.

Miller, Alice. *The Drama of the Gifted Child: The Search for the True Self.* Translated by Ruth Neils Ward. New York: Basic Books, 1997.

Miller, John E. *Laura Ingalls Wilder's Little Town.* Lawrence: University Press of Kansas, 1994.

Moss, Anita. "The Spear and the Piccolo: Heroic and Pastoral Dimensions of William Steig's Dominic and Abel's Island." *Children's Literature* 10, no. 1 (1982): 124–40.

Myers, Walter Dean. *Monster.* New York: Harper Collins, 1999.

Nafisi, Azar. *The Republic of Imagination: America in Three Books.* New York: Viking Penguin, 2014.

Natov, Roni. *The Poetics of Childhood.* New York: Routledge, 2003.

Ness, Patrick, and Jim Kay. *A Monster Calls.* Somerville, MA: Candlewick Press, 2011.

Ngozi, Adimamanda. "The Danger of the Single Story." Proceedings of TED Lecture, Oxford University, Oxford, UK, July 2009.

Nikolajeva, Maria. "The Identification Fallacy: Perspective and Subjectivity in
   Children's Literature." *Telling Children's Stories: Narrative Theory and Children's
   Literature.* Edited by Mike Cadden. Lincoln and London: University of Nebraska
   Press, 2010, 187–208.

Nikolajeva, Maria. *Power, Voice and Subjectivity in Literature for Young Readers.*
   New York and London: Routledge, 2010.

O'Donoghue, Odhran. "A Monster Calls." *The Lancet Oncology* 13, no. 5 (2012): 458.

Ogata, Amy F. *Designing the Creative Child: Playthings and Places in Mid-century
   America.* Minneapolis: University of Minnesota Press, 2013.

Olafson, Erna. "Child Sexual Abuse: Demography, Impact, and Interventions."
   *Journal of Child & Adolescent Trauma* 4, no. 1 (2011): 8–21.

Potvin, Liza. "The Elizabeth Stories and Women's Autobiographical Strategies."
   *Studies in Canadian Literature/Études en Littérature Canadienne* 14, no. 2 (1989).

Rabinowitz, Rebecca. "Messy New Freedoms: Queer Theory and Children's
   Literature," in *New Voices in Childrens Literature Criticism.* Edited by Sebastien
   Chapleau. Staffordshire: Pied Piper, 2004, 19–28.

Reik, Theodore. *Listening with the Third Ear: The Inner Experience of a Psychoanalyst.*
   New York: Farrar, Straus & Giroux, 1983, Originally printed in 1948.

Rothberg, Michael. "Preface," in Buelens et al., *The Future of Trauma Theory.*

Santiago, Chiori, and Judith Lowry. *Home to Medicine Mountain.* San Francisco,
   CA: Children's Book Press, 1998.

Schneider, Dean. "The Novel as Screenplay: *Monster* and *Riot* by Walter Dean
   Myers." *Book Links*, January 2010. www.booklistonline.ckom/booklinks, 20–24.

Schwarcz, Joseph H. *Ways of the Illustrator: Visual Communication in Children's
   Literature.* Chicago, IL: American Library Association, 1982.

Selznick, Brian. *The Hugo Movie Companion: A behind the Scenes Look at How a
   Beloved Book Became a Major Motion Picture.* New York: Scholastic, 2011.

Selznick, Brian. *The Invention of Hugo Cabret.* New York: Scholastic, 2007.

Selznick, Brian. *The Marvels.* New York: Scholastic, 2015.

Selznick, Brian. *Wonderstruck.* New York: Scholastic, 2011.

Silko, Leslie Marmon. "Language and Literature from a Pueblo Indian Perspective,"
   in *Critical Fictions: The Politics of Imaginative Writing.* Edited by Philomena
   Mariani. Seattle, WA: Bay Press, 1991, 83–93.

Singer, Dorothy G., and Jerome L. Singer. *The House of Make-Believe: Children's Play
   and the Developing Imagination.* Cambridge, MA: Harvard University Press, 1990.

Sipe, Lawrence R. "How Picture Books Work: A Semiotically Framed Theory of Text-
   Picture Relationships." *Children's Literature in Education* 29, no. 2 (1998): 97–108.

Sís, Peter. *Madlenka.* New York: Frances Foster Books, 2000.

Sís, Peter. *Starry Messenger: Galileo Galilei.* New York: Square Fish, 2000.

Sís, Peter. *Tibet: Through the Red Box*. New York: Farrar, Straus & Giroux, 1998.

Sís, Peter. *The Tree of Life: A Book Depicting the Life of Charles Darwin—Naturalist, Geologist & Thinker*. New York: Farrar, Straus & Giroux, 2003.

Sís, Peter. *The Wall: Growing Up behind the Iron Curtain*. New York: Farrar, Straus and Giroux, 2007.

Spitz, Ellen Handler. "Ethos in Steig's and Sendak's Picture Books: The Connected and the Lonely Child." *The Journal of Aesthetic Education* 43, no. 2 (2009): 64–76.

Steig, William. *Abel's Island*. New York: Farrar, Straus & Giroux, 1976.

Steig, William. *The Amazing Bone*. New York: Farrar, Straus & Giroux, 1976.

Steig, William. *Dominic*. New York: Farrar, Straus & Giroux, 1972.

Steig, William. *Sylvester and the Magic Pebble*. New York: Windmill Books, 1969.

Steig, William. *The Zabajaba Jungle*. New York: Farrar, Straus & Giroux, 1987.

Stevenson, Robert Louis. *Treasure Island*. Oxford and New York: Oxford World Classics, 1993, Originally printed in 1883.

Stewart, Susan. "Shifting Worlds: Constructing the Subject, Narrative, and History in Historical Time Shifts," in *Telling Children's Stories: Narrative Theory and Children's Literature*. Edited by Mike Cadden. Lincoln: University of Nebraska Press, 2010.

Stokey, Lorena L. *Louise Erdrich: A Critical Companion*. Westport, CT: Greenwood Press, 1999.

Tan, Shaun. "Author's Notes." *Lost and Found*. New York: Scholastic, 2011.

Tan, Shaun. *The Red Tree*. Sydney, Australia: Thomas C. Lothian, 2001.

Tandoi, Eve. "Unruly Girls and Unruly Language: Typography and Play in David Almond's *My Name is Mina*." *Barnboken* 37 (2014).

Talbot, Bryan. *The Tale of One Bad Rat*. Milwaukee, OR: Dark Horse Books, 1995.

Tolmie, Jane. "Modernism, Memory and Desire: Queer Cultural Production in Alison Bechdel's *Fun Home*." *TOPIA: Canadian Journal of Cultural Studies* 22 (2011): 77–93.

Trites, Roberta Seelinger. "Manifold Narratives: Metafiction and Ideology in Picture Books." *Children's Literature in Education* 25, no. 4 (1994): 225–42.

Trites, Roberta Seelinger. "'Queer Performances': Lesbian Politics in Little Women," in *Little Women and the Feminist Imagination: Criticism, Controversy, Personal Essays*. Edited by Janice M. Alberghene and Beverly Lyon Clark. New York: Garland, 1999.

Trites, Roberta Seelinger. *Waking Sleeping Beauty*. Iowa City: University of Iowa Press, 1997.

Updike, John. "Introduction." *The World of William Steig*. New York: Artisan, 1998.

Viorst, Judith. *The Tenth Good Thing about Barney*. New York: Simon & Schuster, 1971.

Wilder, Laura Ingalls. *The Little House on the Prairie*. New York: HarperTrophy, 2007, Originally printed in 1935.

Williams, Mary, and R. Gregory Christie. *Brothers in Hope: The Story of the Lost Boys of Sudan*. New York: Lee & Low Books, 2005.

Wilner, Arlene. "'Unlocked by Love': William Steig's Tales of Transformation and Magic." *Children's Literature* 18 (1990): 31–41.

Winnicott, D. W. *Playing and Reality*. London: Routledge, 2005.

Wong, Hertha Dawn. *Sending My Heart Back across the Years: Tradition and Innovation in Native American Autobiography*. New York and Oxford: Oxford University Press, 1992.

Woodson, Jacqueline. *Brown Girl Dreaming*. New York: Penguin, 2014.

Wyile, Andrea Schwenke. "Perceiving *The Red Tree:* Narrative Repair, Writerly Metaphor, and Sensible Anarchy." In *Telling Children's Stories: Narrative Theory and Children's Literature*. Edited by Michael Cadden. Lincoln: University of Nebraska Press, 2010, 120–39.

Yang, Gene Luen, and Lark Pien. *American Born Chinese*. New York: First Second, 2006.

Zipes, Jack. "Introduction: Recalling Scheherazade." in *Outfoxing Fear: Folktales from around the World*. Edited by Kathleen Ragan. New York: W. W. Norton, 2006, xix–xiii. .

Zipes, Jack. *The Trials and Tribulations of Little Red Riding Hood: Versions of the Tale in Sociocultural Context*. South Hadley, MA: Bergin & Garvey, 1983.

# Index